AI SEO

by Nathan Gotch

for dummies®
A Wiley Brand

AI SEO For Dummies®

Published by: **John Wiley & Sons, Inc.,** 111 River Street, Hoboken, NJ 07030-5774, www.wiley.com

For general information on our other products and services, please contact our Customer Care Department within the U.S. at 877-762-2974, outside the U.S. at 317-572-3993, or fax 317-572-4002. For technical support, please visit https://hub.wiley.com/community/support/dummies.

Wiley publishes in a variety of print and electronic formats and by print-on-demand. Some material included with standard print versions of this book may not be included in e-books or in print-on-demand. If this book refers to media that is not included in the version you purchased, you may download this material at http://booksupport.wiley.com. For more information about Wiley products, visit www.wiley.com.

Library of Congress Control Number: 2026946737

ISBN 978-1-394-41898-5 (pbk); ISBN 978-1-394-41900-5 (ebk); ISBN 978-1-394-41899-2 (ebk)

SKY10164172_073026

Table of Contents

INTRODUCTION 1
About This Book. 1
Foolish Assumptions. 3
Icons Used in This Book 4
Beyond the Book. 4
Where to Go from Here 5

PART 1: AI SEO, IN PLAIN ENGLISH 7

CHAPTER 1: **Introducing AI SEO**. 9
Exploring What AI SEO Is and Who It's For. 10
Seeing how AI SEO fits with traditional SEO 10
Determining what AI systems need 11
Knowing who benefits from AI SEO 11
Noting How the Evolution of Search Works for You. 12
Moving beyond rankings 13
Seeing how AI answers are assembled 13
Recognizing why your website isn't the whole game. 14
Keeping the goal simple 15
Creating Your Quick-Start Plan Today 15
Establish your baseline. 15
Fix your source of truth 16
Make your best pages easier to retrieve 17
Build off-site consensus 17
Track, test, and adjust. 18
Avoiding Pitfalls 18
Treating AI SEO like a magic trick 19
Declaring traditional SEO dead 19
Measuring only traffic. 19
Ignoring accuracy and consistency. 19
Publishing faster than you can govern. 20

CHAPTER 2: **Understanding How Search Works Now** 21
Examining How Traditional Search Works. 22
Crawling: How search engines find your pages 22
Indexing: How search engines organize information. 22
Ranking: How search engines choose the best results 23
Reranking: How personalization and context reshape results. 24
Identifying AI Models and Platforms 24
What a model does 25

What an AI platform does 25
Where SEO has influence 25
Revealing How Answers Are Assembled and Cited 26
Step 1: Retrieve 26
Step 2: Read 27
Step 3: Synthesize 27
Step 4: Cite 28
What this process means for you 28
Discovering Levers You Actually Control 29
Onsite levers 29
Offsite levers 31
Evidence discipline 33
Avoiding false levers 33

CHAPTER 3: **Undertaking Your First 30 Days with AI SEO** 35
Week 1: Determining Baseline and Benchmarks 36
Capture your Day 0 baseline 36
Verify and strengthen your entity 37
Select a few practical benchmarks 38
Deliverables for Week 1 38
Week 2: Setting Up Tracking 39
Create your evidence library 39
Automate your tracking routine 41
Deliverables for Week 2 41
Week 3: Taking Quick Wins to Ship 41
Focus on facts that machines can verify 42
Refresh passages that answer questions directly 42
Strengthen offsite proof 43
Publish one new bottom of funnel asset 43
Deliverables for Week 3 44
Week 4: Building a 90-Day Road Map 45
Compare your starting point to now 45
Choose your 90-day themes 45
Map work to metrics 46
Create a weekly schedule 46
Deliverables for Week 4 47

CHAPTER 4: **Talk Like an AI SEO Pro** 49
Sifting through AI Visibility Terms 50
Measuring share of voice 50
Entities: The building blocks of AI SEO 52
Looking at the roles of indexes and knowledge graphs 54
Allowing SoV, entities, knowledge graphs, and indexes to work together 55

Looking at LLMs and AI Platforms. 55
How retrieval and LLMs work together 56
How the AI platform controls what users see. 56
How to optimize AI answers 57
Working with Pages and Passages 58
Writing brand-friendly passages 58
Knowing why both levels matter. 59
Getting Up to Speed on Signals of Credibility .59
Striving for backlinks. 60
Garnering citations and mentions 60
Building a fact hub. 61
Earning consensus across the web. 61
Measuring signal impact 62
Integrating Structured Data and Schema 62
Identifying schema types 63
Keeping data focused with checks and balances 66

PART 2: MEASURING AI SEO. 67

CHAPTER 5: **Tracking the Metrics That Matter** 69
Looking at Prompt Protocols. 70
Working with prompts and intent. 70
Developing helpful prompts for tracking. 70
Building an AI SEO prompt database 71
Measuring Metrics: Coverage, Position, and Share of Voice. 75
Coverage. 75
Position 76
Share of voice. 77
Noting Citation Growth and Traditional Rankings 78
How citations influence AI answers 78
How citations send referral traffic 79
How to track citations. 79
Spotting Patterns via Self-Reported Wins and Soft Signals. 81
Understanding journey compression. 82
Watching branded search with context 82
Factoring in the recency effect 83
Looking for category legitimacy 83

CHAPTER 6: **Setting Up Your AI SEO Dashboard** 85
Tracking AI Traffic with Google Analytics 86
Log in to the right Google account 86
Create an AI channel group in GA4. 86
Understand what this AI channel captures .87
Give the AI channel time to fill in. 88

Building an Evidence Library 88
Create a simple folder and sheet 88
Capture answers on a regular cadence 89
Use logs when you ship changes 90
Getting Looker Studio Started 91
Copy the AI SEO Tracking template 92
Connect GA4 on Page 1 92
Add an AI platform field 93
Review AI landing pages on Page 2 93
Connect the Search Console and create prompt buckets 94
Connect your evidence library and calculate the citation rate 95
Run a simple weekly cadence 96
Monitoring Change Logs and Sanity Checks 96
Keep a simple change log 96
Run sanity checks before you report results 97
Use your dashboard to guide, not to obsess 97

CHAPTER 7: **Using Competitive Intelligence for AI SEO** 99
Seeing Why AI Winners Aren't Always Google Winners 100
Benchmarking competitors with share of voice 100
Turning AI answers into a competitor score 102
Citation Gap Analysis: Finding the Evidence That AI Systems Trust 103
Collect recurring citation sources 104
Group sources by type 104
Build a simple who's-featured-where matrix 105
Turn gaps into a target list 105
Seeing Why AI Picks Certain Sources 106
Find AI-ready passages 106
Check entity clarity 106
Compare reputation footprints 107
Tracking Market Share across AI Platforms 107

CHAPTER 8: **Conducting Experiments That Don't Fool You** 109
Why AI SEO Experiments Can Fool People 110
Putting Experiments to the Test 110
Design the test 110
Run the test 114
Reading Results without Getting Fooled 115
Evaluate using the core metrics stack 115
Look for patterns, not single wins 116
Compare test movement to control movement 116
Drawing Conclusions and Taking Action 117
Keep outcome labels simple 117
Turn wins into playbooks 117

PART 3: BUILDING AN AI-FRIENDLY WEBSITE 119

CHAPTER 9: Building Your Topic Game Plan 121
Sorting Out Customer Awareness Stages 122
Unaware 122
Problem Aware 123
Solution Aware....................................123
Product Aware 124
Most Aware.......................................125
Creating Your Topic Plan 125
Creating a keyword research template 126
Developing a knowledge base...............................127
Using a client knowledge base 128
Finding Topics 130
Probing for prompts 130
Examining visibility and opportunity signals.................132
Identifying competitor keyword gaps.........................133
Looking at user-generated content 134
Generating keywords from scratch 135
Expanding topic coverage with query fan-out and People Also Ask 136
Qualifying and Prioritizing Topics...........................138
Qualifying with primary filters..............................139
Prioritizing topics based on current rankings.................142
Setting up a simple scoring system 143
Enhancing Your Work with Clusters and a Roadmap.............144
Creating clusters using ChatGPT............................144
Building and judging your cluster...........................145
Focusing on one critical cluster at a time.....................146
Producing a pillar asset 146
Launching a simple cluster roadmap.........................148

CHAPTER 10: Conducting an AI-Readiness Checkup 151
Crawling Your Site and Reading the Findings 152
Start with the right crawl scope (so that you don't drown)......152
Set up your crawl lenses.................................153
Launch a whole-site crawl 154
How to read crawl output without becoming overwhelmed......155
High-impact issues and how to interpret them 157
Deciding What to Fix First.................................161
Group findings into issue clusters..........................161
Score each issue with the 4-factor triage model...............162
Use AI eligibility blockers as automatic escalators............163
Create your Top 10 Fixes page 164
Build your prioritized fix list...............................164

Tag every item to a fix-it bucket 165
Pick the first sprint 165
Producing a Minimum AI-Ready Checklist 166
Setting up the checklist 166
Tagging your results 168

CHAPTER 11: **Establishing Foundations That Bots (and Models) Love** 169
Focusing On Which Issues to Fix First 170
Pick your top three issues 170
Create a build ticket 171
Creating Clean, AI-Friendly HTML 172
Core build guidelines 172
How pages load 173
Good and bad HTML structure 174
Retrieval-friendly passage pattern 175
Build-validation checklist (HTML) 175
Working with Smart Architecture and Internal Links 176
Setting up a good architecture 176
Making internal links work for you 177
Differentiating good and bad internal links 177
Using a hub-and-spoke pattern 178
Build-validation checklist (architecture and links) 178
Structuring with Schemas, FAQs, and Fact Hubs 179
Knowing which schema to use 179
Using FAQ blocks 180
Setting up fact hubs 181
Build-validation checklist: Schema, FAQ, fact hub 182

CHAPTER 12: **Creating Bottom of Funnel Pages That Win Answers** 183
Controlling the Narrative 184
Building Your Answer Set 184
Pricing 185
Policies and FAQs 185
News and Roadmap 190
Quick wins 193
Creating Comparison and Review Content 194
Start with a category listicle 194
Build satellite pages from fan-out queries 195
Make each page answer-ready 195
Handling competitor concerns 196
Building Depth with Commercial Clusters 196
Build one cluster until it is exhausted 196
Make internal links do the work 197

Use a simple cluster architecture 197
Check the cluster before moving on 198
Bringing It All Together 198

CHAPTER 13: **Earning Topical Authority** 199
Expanding Coverage: Gap Analysis and Depth Planning 200
Mapping your topic universe 201
Running a gap analysis and adding depth 201
Aligning Your Entities 203
Knowing why entities decide who gets recommended 204
Building your entity home and linking everything back to it 204
Applying an entity alignment checklist across your site 205
Examining the use of sameAs signals (and what they're for) 206
Creating an entity alignment sheet 207
Keeping It Fresh and Consolidated 207
Why freshness is an authority signal 207
How to keep it fresh 208
Where consolidation matters 209
When authority needs an update log 210

CHAPTER 14: **Fixing Underperformers** 211
Diagnosing Pages before Making Changes 212
Choosing pages worth fixing 212
Clarifying the job of the page 212
Evaluating intent and page type 213
Tightening the On-Page Basics 214
Placing the primary keyword in the right spots 214
Making headings pull their weight 214
Improving scannability 215
Comparing Your Page to True Competitors 215
Pulling competitors from Google and AI answers 215
Looking for recurring patterns in top-ranked pages 216
Turning competitor coverage into a better outline 217
Looking at Additional Places Pages Break Down 217
Burying the answer too deep 218
Sending weak trust signals 218
Lacking support from the rest of the site 218
Failing after the click 219
Fixing the Page and Measuring the Fix 219
Turning diagnosis into fixes 219
Logging the change 220
Tracking the proper metrics 220
Giving the change sufficient time 221
Avoiding change overload 221
Wrapping up the fix 222

CHAPTER 15: **Making Images, Video, and Data Work for You** 223
Using Words to Explain Visual Content 224
Creating helpful captions 224
Unlocking video value with transcripts 225
Writing alt text to add meaning 228
Running a quick media check 229
Sizing Up Media Schemas 229
Starting with the page itself 230
Choosing the proper schema 230
Marking up media cleanly 230
Avoiding common schema mistakes 231
Using Public Datasets and Reusable FAQs 231
Publishing a clear dataset 232
Writing strong FAQs 233

PART 4: BUILDING CREDIBILITY ACROSS THE WEB 235

CHAPTER 16: **Identifying Signals That Move AI Systems** 237
Examining AI Signals in Depth 238
Tightening Up Brand Accuracy and Consistency 239
Clarifying your core brand facts 239
Aligning your positioning 240
Fixing outdated and conflicting information 241
Building Better Review, Sentiment, and Mention Signals 242
Earning reviews that strengthen your signal 242
Managing sentiment, not just star ratings 245
Turning mentions into stronger signals 246
Understanding Links, Mentions, and Citations 247
Differentiating links, citations, and mentions 247
Replacing old-school prospecting with retrieval-driven prospecting 248
Going after citation opportunities, not just link opportunities 249
Focusing on presence over link purity 249
Avoiding outdated link habits 250

CHAPTER 17: **Looking Good Wherever You're Found** 251
Auditing the Profiles That Shape Your Entity 252
Looking at entity and profile pages 252
Seeing how profile pages support your entity 253
Running a practical profile audit 254
Focusing on the details that matter most 255
Spotting the usual problems 255
Using a simple scoring system 256

Prioritizing Your Pages 256
Fixing high-impact pages 256
Matching priorities to your business type 257
Building a quick priority framework 259
Executing the Fixes 260
Rewriting weak descriptions 260
Updating for consistency, not sameness 260
Cleaning up duplicate pages 261
Correcting review profile weaknesses 261
Connecting profiles back to your website 262
Building a practical workflow 263
Creating a lightweight maintenance routine 263

CHAPTER 18: **Owning the Topic** 265
Exploring the True Meaning of Topic Ownership 266
Blanketing Answer Surfaces and SERPs 267
Covering the main query types 267
Creating more than one result type 268
Building a SERP blanket 269
Avoiding content cannibalization while blanketing 270
Controlling the Narrative with Owned Assets 270
Turning your site into a topic hub 271
Repurposing without becoming repetitive 271
Keeping owned assets aligned 272
Benefiting from Other People's Audiences 273
Choosing the right OPAs 273
Supplying useful content 274
Turning one appearance into many signals 274
Building Trust in Communities 275
Showing up like a human, not a billboard 275
Listening for the issues people are talking about 276
Contributing to build durable trust 277
Building Topic Ownership via Consistent Signals 277
Determining what you want to own 277
Repeating the right content 278
Measuring Your Ownership of the Topic 279
Avoiding the Most Common Topic Ownership Mistakes 280
Creating a Practical Topic Ownership Plan 280

CHAPTER 19: **Garnering Reviews That Count** 283
Picking the Right Platforms 283
Knowing why platform choice matters 284
Matching platforms to your business type 284
Auditing your current review footprint 285
Creating your priority list 286

Building a Steady Review System 286
Moving from random requests to a repeatable process.....286
Asking at the right time.....287
Creating a simple workflow 287
Writing better review requests 288
Prompting for specifics without scripting 288
Building review requests into operations 289
Managing Reviews for Long-Term Trust 289
Responding to positive reviews.....290
Handling negative reviews professionally 290
Dealing with fake or misleading reviews 291
Improving review quality over time 291
Using reviews as feedback.....291
Avoiding Common Review Mistakes.....292

CHAPTER 20: **Earning Links, Mentions, and Citations**.....293
Targeting Decision-Making Pages.....294
Finding the right opportunities 294
Prioritizing pages that matter 295
Making your brand easy to include 295
Tracking your target pages.....296
Using Expertise to Drive Digital PR.....296
Using what you already know 297
Creating better pitch angles.....298
Building a simple PR kit 299
Creating Link-Worthy Assets 299
Choosing the right asset type 300
Making the asset easy to cite.....301
Promoting the asset 301
Avoiding the Wrong Kinds of Links, Mentions, and Citations 302
Building a Simple Weekly System 303

CHAPTER 21: **Playing It Safe: Governance, Risk, and Compliance**.....305
Avoiding Privacy, Consent, and Defamation Mistakes.....306
Keeping private information off public pages.....306
Acquiring permission for personal and company content 307
Avoiding defamatory opinions 308
Separating fact, opinion, and allegation.....309
Creating a simple review trigger 309
Your next move 310
Raising Standards for YMYL, Accessibility, and Bias.....310
Introducing YMYL.....311
Using accessibility to make content easier to use 313

Reviewing content for bias 313
Reviewing AI-assisted drafts with a human brain 314
Your next move 314
Sending Clear Signals to Crawlers and AI Systems 315
Providing provenance without overthinking it 315
Using robots.txt the right way 316
Creating a crawler policy 316
Matching your signals to your true intentions 317
Your next move 317
Checking Your Content Rights 318
Knowing what you own 318
Being careful with third-party content 319
Setting internal rules for AI-assisted work 320
Reviewing your site terms 321
Keeping a simple permissions log 321
Your next move 322

PART 5: THE PART OF TENS 323

CHAPTER 22: **Ten Common AI SEO Myths** 325
Google Is Dead 326
Traditional SEO Is Dead 326
AI SEO Is Just SEO 327
Blocking AI Crawlers Is a Good Idea 328
You Can Rank in ChatGPT 328
Long Content Is Good for AI 329
AI Content Gets Penalized 330
Your Website Is the Only Asset That Matters 331
Backlinks Don't Matter 331
One Universal AI SEO Strategy Works on All Platforms 332

CHAPTER 23: **Ten Creative AI SEO Techniques** 335
Creating Citation-Worthy Assets 336
Building a Fact Hub 337
Utilizing Consensus Kits 338
Refreshing Assets Faster 339
Building Public Datasets 340
Sprinkling FAQs Everywhere 341
Maintaining a Public Change Log 342
Using MCPs to Automate with Better Context 343
Creating a Trust Network 344
Tapping into Subject Matter Expertise 345

INDEX 347

Introduction

Search has changed quickly. People still use Google, but they also ask ChatGPT, Copilot, Gemini, Perplexity, and other AI-powered tools for direct answers, product recommendations, local suggestions, and buying advice. That means search engine optimization (SEO) is no longer only about ranking pages. It's also about helping search engines and artificial intelligence (AI) systems understand your brand, trust your information, and recommend you accurately whenever someone asks a question that matters to your business.

AI SEO For Dummies gives you a practical way to respond to that shift. You don't need to become an AI engineer, rebuild your entire website, or chase every new AI platform. You need a repeatable process: Understand how search works now, measure where you stand, make your website easier for AI systems to retrieve and quote, strengthen your credibility across the web, and keep improving based on evidence rather than on assumptions.

This book shows you how to do that step by step: Assess where you stand, improve how your content is discovered and used, strengthen your authority, and measure what works.

About This Book

This book is a practical guide to improving your visibility in classic search results and AI-generated answers. You'll see how AI SEO works, which signals affect your brand's visibility, how to track progress, and how to build pages and profiles that both people and machines can understand.

You won't find hype, magic tricks, or promises that your content will suddenly appear in every AI-generated answer overnight. Instead, you get a repeatable approach that helps you:

- Audit where your brand appears in AI answers today
- Track coverage, position, share of voice, citations, and traditional SEO metrics
- Create pages that answer buyer questions clearly and accurately

- Fix technical and content issues that make your site harder to retrieve
- Strengthen brand consistency, reviews, mentions, links, and profiles across the web
- Use AI SEO responsibly, without creating accuracy, privacy, or compliance problems

Throughout this book, here's what *AI SEO* means:

> The work you do to help search engines and AI systems understand, retrieve, cite, and recommend your brand accurately.

Traditional SEO still matters. In fact, it's the foundation. AI SEO extends that framework into the answer-driven search experiences your customers increasingly use.

An *AI platform* is the user-facing product people interact with, such as ChatGPT, Perplexity, Gemini, Claude, Copilot, or Google AI Mode. An *AI system* is the larger combination of models, retrieval processes, search indexes, knowledge sources, and interfaces that produce an answer. Throughout this book, I use AI platform when referring to the product a person uses and AI system when referring to the underlying process that generates the response.

This book uses these standard conventions:

- **Bold** text means that you're meant to type the text just as it appears in the book. The exception is when you're working through a step list: Because each step is bold, the text to type isn't bold.
- Web addresses and programming code appear in `monofont`. If you're reading a digital version of this book on a device connected to the Internet, you can click the web address to visit that website, like this: `www.dummies.com`.
- This book uses the command arrow (⇨) for command sequences. For an AI SEO example, you might choose GA4 ⇨ Admin ⇨ Data settings ⇨ Channel groups to start grouping known AI chatbot referrals.

To make the content easily accessible, this book is divided into six parts:

- Part 1 gets you grounded. You learn what AI SEO is, how search works now, how to start your first 30 days, and the core vocabulary used throughout this book.

- Part 2 gives you measurement. You'll see how to track prompts, coverage, position, share of voice, dashboards, competitors, citations, and AI SEO experiments.
- Part 3 builds your onsite foundation. You plan topics, check to see that your content is AI-ready, improve HTML and architecture, create bottom of funnel pages, earn topical authority, fix underperformers, and make media and data more useful.
- Part 4 strengthens your offsite footprint. You improve brand signals, profiles, topic ownership, reviews, links, mentions, communities, and borrowed audiences.
- Part 5 helps you publish responsibly and pick the proper strategy. You reduce risk, set governance guardrails, and choose the playbook for local, e-commerce, B2B (business-to-business), SaaS (Software as a Service), or publisher models.
- Part 6 gives you quick reference and creative ideas. I bust common myths and explore techniques to make your content easier to use and more retrievable for AI systems.

Foolish Assumptions

Every *For Dummies* book makes a few assumptions about you, and this one is no different. I assume that at least some of the following statements are true:

- You own, market, or help improve a website for a business, an organization, a client, or a brand.
- You've heard of SEO, even if you don't consider yourself an advanced SEO professional.
- You're familiar with common search and AI tools such as Google Search, ChatGPT, Gemini, Copilot, or Perplexity, or you're willing to try them as you follow along.
- You want practical steps more than technical theory.
- You care about visibility, leads, sales, brand trust, or accurate representation in AI answers.
- You may use AI tools already, but you want a clear strategy for how they fit into search.
- You want to avoid wasting time chasing rumors, hacks, or tactics that cannot be measured.

You do *not* need to know how to code, train a language model, or understand every ranking system in detail. Whenever a technical topic matters, I explain the concept in plain English and show you what to do with it.

Icons Used in This Book

Throughout this book, icons in the margins highlight certain types of valuable information that call out for your attention. Here are the icons used in this book:

TIP

The Tip icon points to a shortcut, a practical tactic, or an easier way to apply the idea.

REMEMBER

This icon highlights a core concept you should keep in mind as you work.

TECHNICAL STUFF

Technical Stuff information gives you extra detail about how something works. You can skip these sections if you want the quickest path, but they're useful when you need more context.

WARNING

Warning paragraphs call out mistakes that can waste time, create risk, or make your AI SEO work less trustworthy.

Beyond the Book

You can find extra AI SEO resources online, including the Cheat Sheet for this book. Just go to `www.dummies.com` and search for **AI SEO For Dummies Cheat Sheet.** There you'll find quick-reference material you can use while planning, auditing, tracking, and improving your visibility. The Cheat Sheet includes a quick-start checklist, handy terms to know, measurement reminders, and practical site and brand checks.

You can also find downloadable templates that support the workflows in this book, including prompt-tracking sheets, evidence logs, share of voice trackers, weekly reporting templates, and related checklists. These tools help you turn the ideas in the book into a repeatable process rather than a one-time project.

There are also sample codes to assist in your content creation along with a playbook to match your business type. Simply go to `www.dummies.com/go/aiseofd` to gain access to these materials.

Where to Go from Here

You don't have to read the chapters in this book in order. If AI SEO is brand-new to you, start with Chapter 1. It gives you an overview of traditional and AI SEO and offers a quick-start plan to get you up and running.

If you already understand the basics and want to measure your current visibility, go to Part 2. If you want to improve your website, start with Part 3. If your brand information, reviews, mentions, or profiles are messy across the web, go to Part 4. If you need to think about risk, governance, and the right playbook for your business model, see Part 5. And when you need quick reminders, jump to the Part of Tens or the Cheat Sheet.

The best place to begin is simple: Go to wherever your interests or needs lie. Jump in and enjoy the ride!

1

AI SEO, in Plain English

IN THIS PART . . .

Get a grasp on the fundamentals of AI SEO.

Discover how traditional search and AI answers work together.

Set a baseline and build a 30-day action plan to put your visibility goals in motion.

Get acquainted with AI SEO vocabulary. Terms like share of voice, entities, and schema are explained so that you can navigate AI SEO without getting lost in the jargon.

IN THIS CHAPTER

- » Understanding what AI SEO means and why it matters
- » Seeing how search now blends traditional results and AI answers
- » Starting a practical quick-start plan you can use today
- » Avoiding common mistakes and choosing the right path through this book

Chapter 1 Introducing AI SEO

Search engine optimization (SEO) is no longer only about ranking. Traditional search still matters, but artificial intelligence (AI) platforms such as ChatGPT, Claude, Copilot, Gemini, Google AI Mode, and Perplexity now answer questions, summarize options, and cite brands directly inside the experience.

The change from traditional SEO to AI SEO creates a new visibility problem: Your website may rank, but your brand may still be missing when someone asks an AI platform what to buy, whom to hire, what to trust, or which source to cite.

Note: In this book, *AI platform* refers to the product people use, such as ChatGPT, Google AI Mode, Gemini, Perplexity, Claude, or Copilot. *AI system* refers to the underlying process that retrieves information, uses models, and generates or displays answers. I use AI platform when discussing where people interact with AI and AI system when explaining how AI-generated answers work.

In this chapter, you get the plain-English overview of AI SEO: what it is, who needs it, what changed in search, and what to do first. You also get a simple quick-start plan that points into the rest of the book so that you can begin with a few practical moves rather than try to master everything all at once.

Exploring What AI SEO Is and Who It's For

AI SEO is the process of making your brand easier for AI-powered search systems to discover, understand, trust, cite, and include in relevant answers. It builds on traditional SEO, but it expands the goal. You're not only trying to rank pages, you're also trying to earn accurate brand mentions, citations, shortlist visibility inside AI answers.

REMEMBER

A simple way to think about AI SEO is this: Traditional SEO helps your pages show up; AI SEO helps your brand become part of the answer.

Seeing how AI SEO fits with traditional SEO

AI SEO doesn't replace traditional SEO. It builds on it. AI systems can use only the information they can find and trust. If your pages are difficult to access *(crawl)*, poorly structured, lacking useful information (thin), slow to load, or missing signs of credibility and expertise *(authority signals)*, AI systems have less reliable material to understand, cite, and include in their answers.

Traditional SEO provides the foundation for both search visibility and AI visibility. That foundation includes these features:

- Technical SEO means making your site easy for search engines and AI systems to access, understand, and use (see Chapter 2)
- Creating content that explains what you know, what you offer, and how you solve problems
- Building trust via links, reviews, mentions, citations, and other authority signals

AI SEO adds several layers on top of the traditional SEO foundation, including these:

- **Retrieval readiness:** Your most important pages and passages need to be easy for AI systems to find, interpret *(parse)*, and cite.
- **Entity clarity:** Information about your brand, products, people, locations, and categories need to be consistent across your site and the wider web.
- **Answer visibility:** You need to track whether AI systems mention, cite, compare, include on shortlists, or ignore you when answering search questions *(prompts)*.
- **Off-site consensus:** Information about your business on other websites, such as reviews, profiles, roundups, communities, podcasts, directories, and press mentions, need to reinforce the same story that's given on your website.

» **Responsible publishing:** Verify your claims, get permission when needed, use screenshots and reviews responsibly, and review AI-generated content before publishing. Doing so helps maintain trust with your audience.

Determining what AI systems need

Traditional SEO helps search engines find and rank your content. AI SEO focuses on helping AI systems decide whether your content should be used when generating an answer. AI systems don't need hype. They need clear, consistent, and trustworthy information. When a user asks a question that might influence a purchase (a *commercial* question) or an important life decision (a *high-stakes* question), an AI system has to decide which sources and brands deserve attention. Your job is to make that decision easier for AI systems to make.

Most AI SEO work supports these five simple signals for AI systems to include your brand or business in answers:

» **Discoverability:** Can systems find your important pages, profiles, reviews, and proof assets?

» **Clarity:** Can systems understand who you are, what you offer, who you serve, and what makes you different?

» **Consistency:** Do your website, third-party profiles, reviews, and mentions repeat the same core facts?

REMEMBER

Core facts are the basic details about your business that should always match everywhere online.

» **Credibility:** Do trusted sources, customers, experts, and data support your claims?

» **Freshness:** Are your pricing, product details, screenshots, policies, examples, and stats current?

When those signals line up, your brand becomes easier to retrieve, easier to cite, and easier to include in relevant answers.

Knowing who benefits from AI SEO

AI SEO matters for any business, organization, or content publisher that depends on being found, trusted, cited, or chosen online. The exact playbook changes by business model, but the essential idea stays the same: Make yourself the clearest good answer for the right prompts. This list describes some AI needs by business type:

- **Local businesses** need AI systems to name them for nearby service, emergency situations, and best-in-city prompts.
- **E-commerce stores** (websites or online platforms where people can buy and sell products or services over the Internet) need products, categories, reviews, shipping details, and buying guides that help shoppers compare and choose.
- **B2B companies** (business-to-business companies, where one business sells a product or service that another business uses to run or operate) need proof, industry pages, case studies, and expert signals that help buyers build a shortlist of businesses to purchase from.
- **SaaS companies** (Software as a Service companies), which let you use software online without installing it, and you typically pay monthly or yearly to access it, need pricing, feature, comparison, alternative, security, integration, and onboarding pages that reduce buying friction.
- **Content publishers and media brands** (any organizations that regularly create and distribute content for an audience) need trustworthy, well-structured content that earns citations and turns visibility into audience ownership.

  TECHNICAL STUFF

  Audience ownership happens when people choose to directly follow, subscribe to, or regularly visit your content, so that you can reach them again and again without relying on third-party platforms like Google, social media feeds, or AI-generated answers.

You don't need the same strategy as every other business. Check out `www.dummies.com/go/aiseofd` for a playbook that matches how your business gets chosen.

Noting How the Evolution of Search Works for You

Search did not flip from old to new overnight. It has built up layers over time. Traditional search results are still there, but they now sit alongside other search *surfaces*, different places where information is displayed to users.

For example, *snippets* are short answers that appear at the top of search results, pulled directly from a web page to quickly answer a question. *Knowledge panels* are information boxes that show key facts about a person, company, or topic (see Chapter 3), usually pulled from trusted sources like databases and reference sites.

Along with these, you'll see maps, video results, and shopping results. On top of all these surfaces, AI-generated answers are now being added into the mix.

That's why this book doesn't tell you to abandon SEO. It shows you how to expand SEO for a world where search engines, AI assistants, and chat-based answers increasingly overlap.

Moving beyond rankings

Traditional search asked, "Which page should rank first?" AI SEO often asks a different question: "Which answer, brand, source, or option should I present to the user?"

That shift changes what *visibility* means:

- In traditional search, a win often looks like a higher ranking, more clicks, and more unpaid search traffic.
- In AI SEO, a win may look like a brand mention, a citation, a shortlist inclusion, or a more accurate answer.
- In both worlds, a win depends on clarity, usefulness, trust, and relevance.

A *win* is a successful outcome or positive result from your SEO efforts.

REMEMBER

In SEO, the individual pieces of content that help with visibility, such as pages, articles, product descriptions, videos, FAQs, and data resources, are often referred to as *assets*. These are the materials that search engines and AI systems evaluate, rank, or reuse when forming answers.

You still want rankings and traffic. But you also want to know whether your brand appears when AI systems pull evidence from the web, compare options, and help people make decisions. For more on tracking brand appearance, see Chapter 5.

Seeing how AI answers are assembled

AI answers can feel like they appear out of nowhere, but most answer experiences follow a practical pattern. AI systems retrieve information, read or process that information, *synthesize* an answer (take information from multiple sources, combine it, and then produce a single coherent response), and sometimes cite visible sources.

REMEMBER

In Chapter 2, I help you explore the mechanics of how search works. For now, here's a simple version of the search process:

- **Retrieval** finds possible sources of information, such as passages, key facts, reviews, profiles, and other evidence that may help answer a question.
- **Reading and synthesis** means that the system reviews the information, pulls together what matters, and turns it into a clear, useful answer.
- **Citations, links, or mentions** may show some of the sources behind the answer, depending on the platform.
- The **platform**, such as ChatGPT, Google AI Mode, Gemini, or Perplexity, decides how the answer appears to the user.

Your website, profiles, reviews, citations, community presence, media coverage, and original data all contribute to what can be thought of as an *evidence layer*, the combined information that AI systems and search engines use to evaluate and describe you.

Recognizing why your website isn't the whole game

Your website is your home base. It should be the best source of truth about your brand, products, services, pricing, policies, proof, and expertise. But AI SEO doesn't stop there.

AI systems and buyers often look across the broader web. They may encounter your Google Business Profile, LinkedIn page, review profiles, directory listings, podcasts, roundups, videos, Reddit threads, press mentions, author bios, and comparison articles.

If those sources repeat the same story, your brand becomes easier to trust. If they conflict, your brand becomes harder to summarize accurately.

TIP

Search your brand and your category in traditional search and AI tools. Look at what appears alongside your own site. These results create a baseline for how you're being described online and how both people and AI systems are likely to understand you.

For a deeper audit of the profiles and third-party pages that shape your brand, see Chapter 17.

Keeping the goal simple

The goal of AI SEO is not to chase every platform or obsess over every answer variation. The goal is to make your brand easier to discover, easier to verify, and easier to include for the prompts that matter.

That means your efforts should aim to improve at least one of these outcomes:

- » Your brand appears more often for commercial prompts.
- » AI systems describe your brand accurately.
- » Your website or trusted third-party sources get cited more often.
- » Your strongest pages are easy to retrieve and cite.
- » Your off-site footprint makes your positioning look more credible.

REMEMBER

If you improve these areas, you're not just increasing visibility; you're shaping how AI systems understand, trust, and represent your brand accurately. AI SEO adds new search surfaces, but it doesn't erase the old foundation. Crawlable pages, clear content, topical authority, reviews, links, and trustworthy proof still matter.

Creating Your Quick-Start Plan Today

You don't need to implement this entire book this week. Start with a small plan you can actually complete. The goal is to create a baseline so that you can fix the most obvious gaps and build momentum.

The next five sections show the basic steps to improve your presence. I cover each step in more detail throughout the rest of this book.

Establish your baseline

To start, you want to know where your brand appears right now. In Chapter 3, you choose 10 to 20 prompts that match how your customers make decisions. These should include "best," "top," "near me," "alternatives," "versus," "pricing," "review," and "for [audience]" prompts when relevant.

For each prompt, you record this information:

- The platform you tested
- The exact prompt
- The date
- Whether your brand appeared in the answer
- Where your brand appeared in the answer
- Whether your website or a third-party source was cited
- Whether the answer was accurate, positive, neutral, or wrong

This strategy gives you the Day 0 view. Chapter 3 also helps you turn that snapshot into your first 30-day action plan, and Chapters 5 through 8 show you how to measure, report, compare competitors, and run experiments.

Fix your source of truth

Your own site must clearly explain the facts that AI systems and buyers need most. Look to make improvements with your source-of-truth pages, which include your home page, About page, Contact page, pricing or cost page, product or service pages, FAQs, policies, proof pages, and any page that answers a decision-stage question.

Your source-of-truth pages should answer these questions:

- Who are you?
- What do you offer?
- Who is it for?
- Where do you operate?
- How much does it cost, or how does pricing work?
- What proof supports your claims?
- What happens next after someone buys, books, signs up, or contacts you?

You build this out in Part 3, where you plan topics, audit technical readiness, fix site foundations, create bottom of funnel, or BoF, pages (pages designed for people who are ready to take action or make a decision; see Chapter 12), earn topical authority, improve weak pages, and make media, data, FAQs, captions, and transcripts work more effectively across search and AI systems.

Make your best pages easier to retrieve

After your source of truth is clear, make the pages easier for both people and machines to use. That doesn't mean adding unnecessary content; it means adding structure.

Improve important pages by adding these elements:

- A direct answer near the top
- Clear headings that match actual questions
- Short passages that can stand on their own
- Comparison tables where choices matter
- FAQs where objections naturally appear
- Specific proof, examples, screenshots, data, or reviews
- Internal links to related pages that explain the next question

This is where traditional SEO, content strategy, and AI retrieval meet. The clearer your pages are, the easier they are to rank, cite, summarize, and include in answers.

For retrieval mechanics, see Chapter 2; for technical readiness and implementation patterns, see Chapters 10 and 11.

Build off-site consensus

AI systems don't evaluate your site in isolation. They also see what the rest of the web says about you. That's why off-site credibility gets its own part of the book.

Part 4 shows you how to improve brand accuracy, profiles, reviews, mentions, citations, links, topic ownership, communities, and third-party visibility without turning your brand into a spam machine.

I show you how to clean and strengthen the places that already shape your reputation, such as:

- Google Business Profile and local directories, if you're local
- LinkedIn, Crunchbase, social profiles, and founder bios
- Review platforms such as Capterra, Clutch, G2, Trustpilot, Yelp, and other niche directories

- Roundups, *listicles* (an article or blog post structured in the form of a list), alternatives pages, podcasts, press mentions, and partner pages
- Communities where your buyers ask questions and compare options

Track, test, and adjust

AI visibility changes over time. Platforms update. Citations move. Competitors publish. Reviews age. Your own pages change. That's why measurement matters.

In Chapter 5, I show you how to measure the metrics that matter, including these:

- **Coverage:** Does your brand appear for the prompts that matter?
- **Prominence:** When your brand appears, how prominent is it?
- **Share of voice:** How much of the answer space do you occupy compared to competitors?
- **Citation quality:** Which sources are used to support the answer?
- **Accuracy and sentiment:** Is the answer correct and favorable?

After you measure the metrics that matter to you, you can adjust based on the evidence you find. If your site is cited but your brand isn't named or included, your proof or positioning may need work. If competitors appear because review sites mention them and not you, you have a third-party evidence gap. If your brand appears on one platform but not another, you may need platform-specific testing.

The detailed measurement workflow lives in Chapters 5 through 8; this chapter only points you toward the habit of using evidence before changing direction.

Avoiding Pitfalls

AI SEO is new enough that bad advice spreads quickly. Some people overreact and abandon SEO fundamentals. Others underreact and treat AI SEO like a passing trend. The better path is practical: Keep what works, add what's new, and measure what matters. The next five sections help you avoid common pitfalls.

For more detail, see Chapters 10 and 11 for technical foundations, Chapters 5 through 8 for measurement and testing, and Chapter 21 for governance.

Treating AI SEO like a magic trick

AI SEO is not a trick. It's not a secret prompt, a hidden schema property, or a one-click tool. Tools can help you measure visibility, but they cannot manufacture trust by themselves.

Spend your energy on the assets and signals that make your brand easier to understand and verify: clear pages, consistent profiles, constructive reviews, trustworthy proof, useful media, strong citations, and true expertise.

REMEMBER

Tools track visibility. They don't create the reputation, clarity, or proof that make a brand worth citing or including.

Declaring traditional SEO dead

Traditional SEO isn't dead. Lazy SEO is. AI systems still need pages to retrieve, sources to cite, entities to understand, and authority signals to trust.

If you skip technical SEO, content quality, internal links, topical coverage, accessibility, speed, and credible mentions, you weaken the same foundation that AI SEO often depends on.

Measuring only traffic

Traffic matters, but it's no longer the only signal. AI answers can influence decisions before a click happens. A buyer may see your brand in an AI shortlist, search your name later, visit by way of direct traffic, or convert after comparing you across several sources.

That's why this book focuses on coverage, position, share of voice, citations, accuracy, sentiment, and business outcomes alongside rankings and traffic.

Ignoring accuracy and consistency

AI systems compare information across many sources. If your pricing page says one thing, a review site says another, a podcast bio uses an old description, and your LinkedIn page points to a different category, you make the system guess what's accurate.

Don't make machines guess your brand story. Create clear official pages and then update the profiles and third-party sources that matter most.

Publishing faster than you can govern

AI SEO rewards visibility, but visibility increases risk. A sloppy comparison claim, an unauthorized customer testimonial, an outdated pricing screenshot, or an unsupported health or financial statement can travel further than you expect.

Chapter 21 helps you build practical guardrails for privacy, consent, defamation, Your Money Your Life (YMYL) topics, accessibility, bias, crawler guidance, licensing, and content rights.

WARNING

Don't treat governance as red tape. Treat it as trust protection. The more visible your content becomes, the more your facts, permissions, and claims matter.

IN THIS CHAPTER

» Seeing how traditional search and AI answers work together

» Learning the difference between models and AI platforms

» Creating content that gets included

» Discovering the key levers you control to improve brand visibility

Chapter 2

Understanding How Search Works Now

Search engines, such as Google and Bing, have long crawled the web, indexed pages, and used ranking systems to decide which pages should appear for a query. Traditional search hasn't gone anywhere, but AI has added a new layer. AI platforms such as Google Gemini, ChatGPT, and similar platforms can take huge amounts of information and condense it into a single answer.

To help your brand thrive in this new AI age, you need to understand how traditional SEO and AI answers work together. Search engine optimization (SEO) helps your pages get discovered and trusted in traditional search, which gives AI systems better sources to retrieve, cite, and use when recommending brands.

In this chapter, you learn how traditional search engines work and why they still form the foundation for many AI systems. You also see how AI systems retrieve information, assemble answers, and cite sources, plus where traditional SEO work supports AI visibility.

By the end, you'll know what the current search landscape looks like and where to focus your efforts so your brand can show up wherever customers are searching.

Examining How Traditional Search Works

The key to driving brand visibility in AI answers begins with understanding how traditional search engines work. You don't need to understand every technical detail, but knowing the core process of crawling, indexing, ranking, and reranking is fundamental.

Crawling: How search engines find your pages

Search engines use a massive network of crawlers, or bots, to scour the web for new and updated pages. These bots move from page to page, following links, reading XML site maps (a file that lists a website's essential URLs, acting as a roadmap for search engines like Google), and sometimes using user submissions or API (application programming interface) notifications, which is a way for software systems to exchange information or report updates.

REMEMBER

One of your most important SEO jobs is to make your website crawler-friendly. You can influence how bots interact with your site through your robots.txt file. A *robots.txt file* is a simple text file stored on your website that tells search engine crawlers which pages or sections they're allowed to access and which ones to avoid. Most major search engines respect robots.txt, but not every bot or AI system follows the rules. Even so, it's the best place to start when optimizing crawling.

Many other variables also affect crawlability, including your site navigation, internal linking, and loading speed. Clear navigation and strong internal links help crawlers find deeper pages, and fast pages make it easier for bots to cover more of your site. You learn how to diagnose these issues in Chapter 10 and how to fix them in Chapter 11.

Indexing: How search engines organize information

Not every page that gets crawled is added to the index in Google, Bing, or other search engines. After crawling, search systems extract text, links, metadata, structured data, and other signals to determine whether a page should be stored in the index and how it should be categorized.

Think of a search index as a massive library. If your page isn't indexed, it's effectively not on the shelf, which means it can't appear in search results. Indexation has always been critical for SEO, but it's even more important now because of how

AI systems use retrieval. *Retrieval* means the system looks up outside information, such as web pages or databases, before it answers a question.

When an AI system can't answer confidently from its training data alone, it may look for fresh information from web pages, databases, or other search tools. That process is called *grounding*. Grounding helps the system check its answer against sources people can verify. It also lowers the chance of hallucination, which is when an AI system gives an answer that sounds confident but is wrong or unsupported. The main point is simple: If your important pages can be crawled and indexed, AI systems have a better chance of finding and using them.

Ranking: How search engines choose the best results

Your website reaches its first two SEO milestones when it's easily crawlable and its pages are indexed. At that point, you're in the game, but there's no guarantee your pages will rank well. Not all brands, websites, pages, or pieces of content are created equal, and that's where the ranking process comes into play.

When someone searches on Google or another search engine, the search engine retrieves relevant pages from its index and then uses many different factors to determine the order of results. The results page is called the search engine results page, or SERP. The position of each result is influenced by many ranking factors, also called signals, and algorithms, not by a single score.

Here are some powerful signals that can help a page rank:

- How well the page matches the query
- The quality and usefulness of the content
- The freshness of the information
- The authority of the website and page

This is where SEO becomes critical. Getting a site crawled and indexed is only the first step. It takes strategy and consistent SEO work to achieve and maintain strong rankings.

REMEMBER

Ranking is a byproduct of many factors working together. To win in traditional search, you need to focus on the signals that matter most rather than chase a single magic metric.

Reranking: How personalization and context reshape results

There is an initial ranking stage and then additional reranking steps that adjust results based on context. Signals such as location, device type, a user's past search behavior, and the recency of information can all influence what someone sees.

For example, if you search for *pizza,* you usually see Google's local pack with nearby businesses at the top. A *local pack* is the map-style group of nearby businesses that appears for local searches. The systems behind modern search engines infer intent from the query and the context. For *pizza,* the dominant intent is usually local and commercial, so the results highlight nearby restaurants instead of general information.

Some AI systems gather outside information before answering a question. When they use retrieval, they often rely on traditional search engines and other sources to find relevant information. They then reorder or filter that information based on relevance, freshness, authority, and internal confidence before generating an answer. In many cases, these systems lean on traditional search rankings as a quality gate because web search has spent decades determining how to separate stronger sources from weaker ones.

That connection between traditional search and AI retrieval is why traditional SEO work still matters for AI. The same factors that make your pages easy to crawl, index, and rank in traditional search also make them more likely to be discovered, trusted, and cited by AI systems.

Identifying AI Models and Platforms

Once you see how traditional search works, the next step is noting where AI fits into the user experience. To understand how AI SEO builds on traditional search, you need to know how AI models generate answers and how AI platforms present those answers to users. People often use the terms *AI model* and *AI platform* as if they mean the same thing, but they don't. The distinction matters because you can influence the sources a system retrieves, but you usually can't directly change what a model learned during training.

An *AI model* is the engine that generates text, images, code, and sometimes audio or video. The *AI platform* is the interface you see and use, such as ChatGPT, Google AI Mode, Claude, or Perplexity. Think of the model as the engine under the hood and the AI platform as the dashboard that lets people type questions, read answers, click citations, and ask follow-up questions.

What a model does

AI models, such as GPT and Gemini, are trained on massive amounts of text so that they can predict the next word in a sequence. When you ask a question, the model doesn't truly "know" the answer. Instead, it predicts the most likely answer based on patterns it learned during training.

Modern AI systems often use retrieval-augmented generation (RAG). In simple terms, RAG means the system looks up outside information before generating an answer. The system retrieves information from sources such as web pages, then passes that information to the model so the response can be more current and grounded. RAG can improve freshness and accuracy, but it doesn't guarantee a perfect answer.

For SEO professionals, RAG matters because your website can become part of what the system retrieves, reads, and synthesizes. Many AI platforms lean on traditional search engines and their own crawlers to decide which pages to fetch. That means traditional SEO still has enormous value because it helps your brand appear in the pool of sources that AI systems can draw from.

What an AI platform does

The AI platform is what you see and use. It might be ChatGPT, Google AI Mode, Claude, or Perplexity. Each platform has its own layout, features, and citation style. Some platforms show multiple clickable links to sources, and others summarize and paraphrase with fewer visible URLs.

The platform decides how the model's output is displayed, which citations are shown, and how users can follow up. It also shapes the tone of the interaction. For example, ChatGPT often feels more like an ongoing conversation, whereas Google AI Mode is tightly integrated into search results and task completion.

Where SEO has influence

Most AI models are trained on snapshots of data taken at specific points in time. Once that training snapshot is locked in, you can't change what the model learned from it. Future versions may use newer snapshots, but each release has a fixed training set.

Your ongoing work still matters for two important reasons:

- **Brand visibility:** Strong brand visibility on the open web increases the chances that future training snapshots will contain high-quality information about you.

» **Retrieval systems:** More importantly for day-to-day SEO, retrieval systems decide which sources to pull in when an AI system needs fresh or grounded information.

In practice, influencing AI answers for commercial queries depends heavily on how well you show up in the retrieval layer between the model and the web. In an ideal world, your brand is well represented in the model's training data and frequently selected as a high-quality source during retrieval.

Your job is to build a brand that search engines trust, create content that retrieval systems can find and understand, and make it easy for AI platforms to cite and recommend you when users ask commercial questions.

Revealing How Answers Are Assembled and Cited

AI-generated answers can feel like they appear out of thin air, but there's an actual process behind every response. When you understand how AI systems build and cite answers, you can create content that has a better chance of being included.

You can think of this process in four main steps: retrieve, read, synthesize, and cite.

Step 1: Retrieve

The first step is retrieval. When a user asks a question, the system looks for relevant information across several sources. These sources can include web pages, specialized databases, knowledge graphs (see Chapter 4), and sometimes specialized data feeds or APIs. In many systems, the retrieved information is then combined with what the model already learned during training.

In many AI systems, a real-time search happens when you ask a question. The AI system often simplifies or reshapes your query so that it can search more effectively. This process is sometimes called *query fan-out*.

Query fan-out is how an AI "searches for you." For example, it might take this query:

> "I'm looking for the best AI SEO software right now for agencies; we don't have a huge budget, and we have only a couple of clients."

and transform it into a core search like this:

"best AI SEO tools for agencies"

From there, the AI system might explore related queries, such as "AI SEO tools for small agencies" or even brand comparisons like "Rankability versus Clearscope" to collect more detailed evidence.

The key takeaway is that your content needs to be discoverable, clear, and aligned with the kinds of queries people actually use, because those same queries often drive retrieval in AI systems.

Step 2: Read

Once the system finds relevant information, the AI reads it. Saying AI "reads it," doesn't mean human-level understanding. Instead, the model breaks the text into *tokens*, which are words, word pieces, or small chunks of text, and processes those tokens to find patterns that seem most relevant to the user's question.

REMEMBER

During this stage, clarity matters more than cleverness. Complex metaphors, buried facts, or messy formatting can make your content harder for the system to interpret correctly.

Good content structure helps significantly. The same elements that have always mattered for SEO also help AI retrieval: clean HTML, clear title tags, useful meta descriptions, logical heading tags, and FAQ sections that answer questions directly. Pages composed of these fundamental building blocks are easier for search engines and AI systems to scan, understand, and reuse. You learn how to build this structure in Chapters 10 and 11.

Think of this step as writing for two audiences at a time: the human reader and the machine reader. Both need to understand what your content means, even if they "read" it in very different ways.

Step 3: Synthesize

After gathering and reading the evidence, the model combines it into a coherent response. This step is called *synthesis*.

During synthesis, the model looks for strong patterns and areas of agreement between sources and then summarizes the key points. It may downplay or ignore information that looks contradictory or low confidence. The resulting answer is then presented through the AI platform, which determines how it is displayed to users.

For example, imagine several trusted sites describe the same software tool. One says it helps agencies optimize SEO content. Another says it includes content scoring and topic recommendations. A third says it works best for teams managing multiple client campaigns. The AI may synthesize those sources into a statement like this: "This tool helps agencies improve SEO content by scoring pages, suggesting topics, and supporting client campaign workflows."

Step 4: Cite

Finally, the AI platform presents citations or links, which are selected from the sources used during retrieval. Not every AI platform handles citations in the same way.

Some tools, such as Perplexity, display multiple clickable sources alongside the answer. Others, such as ChatGPT with Search, use compact footnotes or links that expand to reveal sources. Google's AI features often list a small set of sources beneath the answer card.

Receiving a citation means your content was used as evidence somewhere in the process. It doesn't mean you ranked first the way you might think about a normal Google result. The goal isn't to win a single position. It's to be included, trusted, and referenced as part of the answer.

REMEMBER

Visibility in AI answers depends on relevance, clarity, and authority. The more often your content gets selected and cited as evidence, the more exposure and credibility your brand can gain over time.

What this process means for you

Focus on being the best source of truth on your topic. When your content is factually accurate, well structured, and easy to interpret, it becomes a natural candidate for retrieval and citation in AI-generated answers.

TIP

Consistency is also key. Use the same terminology, entities, and schema across your site so AI systems can connect the dots more easily. You learn more about entities in Chapter 4 and more about structuring content for AI readability in Chapter 11.

Discovering Levers You Actually Control

You can easily feel overwhelmed when you think about all the moving parts of AI SEO. The good news is that you don't need to understand every technical detail to get results. You need to know which *levers*, or controllable actions that influence your visibility, actually move the needle – make a measurable impact.

TIP

If you invest most of your time and effort into the high-impact actions in this section, you'll start to see visibility gains for almost any brand in AI.

Onsite levers

Onsite levers are the changes you can make on your own website. Your website is critical for driving visibility in both traditional search and AI answers because it gives search engines and AI systems official information to crawl, retrieve, and cite. The following sections introduce the core onsite levers you'll explore in much more detail later in this book.

Content

Content matters because it gives search engines and AI systems something clear to retrieve, understand, and quote. Your site needs a few different types of content, each with a different job.

Brand and fact hubs

Create pages that let you control the narrative about your brand. If you don't clearly explain who you are, what you do, and who you serve, AI systems will lean on third-party sources to answer questions about you.

Later in this book, I show how to build fact hubs, which answer common questions about your brand directly on your website so AI systems can treat your site as the primary source of truth.

Commercial pages

Your site also needs pages that target commercial intent. *Commercial intent* means the searcher is comparing options, checking prices, evaluating providers, or getting close to a buying decision. The exact page format depends on your business type:

- **For local businesses, use service and location pages:** Service pages explain what you do, and location pages connect those services to the cities or areas you serve.

- **For e-commerce, use category and product pages:** Category pages help shoppers compare groups of products, and product pages answer the final questions before someone buys.
- **For Software as a Service (SaaS), use product, feature and comparison pages:** Product pages, feature pages, and comparison pages help buyers understand what the tool does, who it's for, and how it compares with alternatives.

These pages help you show up when users are close to buying, which is where AI recommendations matter most.

Anti-AI content

The days of pumping out generic informational blog posts are over. AI can already write generic content. To win, you need content that AI can't easily fake.

That includes content that relies on firsthand experience, proprietary data, case studies, unique frameworks, and real stories from your work. This kind of content makes your brand stand out and gives AI systems something distinctive to cite.

Technical

Technical SEO means improving the parts of your website that help search engines crawl, index, understand, and display your pages. It's also critical for visibility inside AI answers because many systems rely on the same crawl, render, and index foundations that feed traditional search.

Keep a few key principles in mind:

- **Use HTML that's easy to interpret.** Make sure your important content lives in clean HTML. JavaScript frameworks can be used, but they should still output "crawlable," server-rendered content. Some crawlers and retrieval systems don't execute complex JavaScript reliably, so HTML-first content is the safest option.
- **Prioritize speed and mobile-friendliness.** Fast, mobile-friendly pages help both users and crawlers. Search engines and AI systems can process more of your site when it loads quickly and responds well on phones.
- **Make your site easy to crawl and index.** Good site architecture is essential. Aim to keep important pages within a few clicks of the home page and use consistent internal links to point to your site's core pages. Clear navigation and internal linking help search engines and retrieval systems discover more of your content.

I dive deeper into technical diagnosis in Chapter 10 and implementation in Chapter 11, but the principle is simple: Make your site easy for both humans and machines to move through.

Offsite levers

Offsite levers are signals outside your website that shape your visibility and trust. These signals matter because AI systems often look beyond your site when deciding which brands to mention, recommend, and cite. The following categories show where to build that outside proof.

SERP domination

Your website is important, but it's not the only asset that matters. SERP domination means getting your brand to appear in several relevant results for the same important query, not just on your own website.

Start by making your own primary page the best answer for the query. For example, if you want to win "best AI SEO software for agencies," your site needs a strong page that targets that topic clearly. Then review the rest of Page 1 of the results page to see which other assets already rank, such as videos, review sites, directories, Reddit threads, or industry articles.

You often see platforms, such as YouTube, Reddit, Quora, industry blogs, publications, directories, and review sites on Page 1 for commercial queries.

TIP

Where it makes sense, build a presence on those platforms too. That might mean publishing YouTube videos, answering questions on Quora, contributing to industry blogs, or building strong profiles on key directories.

If your brand appears in multiple places on the first page for a commercial query, you increase your odds of being chosen as a retrieval source in AI systems. The goal isn't just to rank your website. It's to rank many different assets that all point back to your brand.

Reviews and reputation

In almost every industry, reviews are critical for driving brand visibility in AI SEO.

The exact platforms depend on your niche; here are some examples:

- **Local businesses:** Google Business Profile, Bing Places for Business, or niche directories, such as Avvo or FindLaw for lawyers and Angi, Yelp, or Thumbtack for home services
- **E-commerce:** Onsite product reviews plus marketplaces, such as Amazon or niche retail platforms
- **SaaS:** Review sites like G2, Capterra, and Trustpilot

REMEMBER

AI systems often treat reviews and ratings as signals of trust and relevance, especially when they pull data from directories and review platforms. Getting real, recent reviews is hard work, but it's one of the highest-leverage activities you can invest in. You learn more about reviews and reputation signals in Chapter 16.

Mentions, citations, and links

You want your brand to appear on the important sites that AI systems and search engines use when building answers. Those appearances can take several forms:

- **Mentions** are references to your brand, product, or company, even when there is no link.
- **Citations** are sources that AI systems reference or quote when generating answers.
- **Links** are clickable references that point users back to your website.

The sites that matter most often include industry blogs, media publications, expert roundups, review platforms, community discussions, and authoritative directories. The more frequently your brand appears across trusted sources in your niche, the more likely it is to become part of the evidence and consensus that AI systems use when answering related questions.

TIP

One simple way to identify these sources is to look at AI answers in your space and collect the citations they reference. If the same websites repeatedly appear in answers, add them to your target list. Those sites are already influencing retrieval and answer generation for your category. Your goal is to earn legitimate mentions, citations, and links from those sources, so your brand becomes part of the common evidence set that AI systems rely on.

Profile hygiene

You need to make sure that your brand entity is consistent across platforms.

TIP

Create a standard description that clearly explains what your brand does and which topics, locations, and services are associated with it. Then reuse that description everywhere it matters: your website, Google Business Profile, LinkedIn, directories, and social profiles. You can adjust wording slightly for each platform, but the core facts should stay the same.

For example, rather than say, "We're a law firm in Chesterfield," you might say, "We're a personal injury law firm in Chesterfield, Missouri, that focuses on medical malpractice, car accidents, and slip and fall cases."

AI systems use natural language processing (NLP) to extract entities and relationships from sentences like that. When you're consistent and explicit, it's easier for these systems to understand who you are and what you do. You learn more about entities in Chapter 4.

Evidence discipline

Evidence discipline is an important lever to consider because it helps you connect the work you publish (or *ship*, in SEO-speak) to the visibility changes you see later. Keep records of the assets you publish, when you update those assets, and how those assets perform. Save screenshots of AI answers that mention your brand and log the prompts that triggered them.

These records create evidence of impact and help you see whether your changes are improving visibility. They also give you proof if someone copies your work or if a platform misrepresents your content.

TIP

Build an internal AI SEO evidence tracker by recording the prompt, platform, date, whether your brand appeared, which sources were cited, and a link to the screenshot. I show how to build this tracker in Chapters 5 and 6.

Avoiding false levers

WARNING

As in traditional SEO, don't rely on spammy tactics to manipulate AI answers. Flooding the web with misleading claims or fake mentions can backfire and create legal or ethical problems.

When working with brands and clients, you need a long-term strategy that builds durable visibility, not shortcuts that can backfire or create legal or ethical problems.

You have two clean ways to influence AI over time:

- **Static training data:** Make your brand visible across high-quality sites on the open web. Strong coverage increases the chance that future model training snapshots will include accurate, helpful information about you.
- **Retrieval and search:** Show up in traditional search wherever your customers are looking. Web search is still a primary retrieval source for many AI systems. If you're visible and trusted in search, you're more likely to be pulled into AI answers.

IN THIS CHAPTER

» Establishing your AI SEO baseline and simple benchmarks

» Setting up tracking systems you can maintain

» Shipping early wins to build momentum

» Creating a focused 90-day road map you can execute

Chapter 3
Undertaking Your First 30 Days with AI SEO

Search optimization becomes much easier when you start with clarity and quick wins. In Chapter 2, I explain how traditional search and AI answers work together. This chapter gives you a 30-day plan to turn that knowledge into action for your brand.

To start, you capture where you stand today in both classic search results and AI-generated answers. Then you set up simple tracking, ship (or publish), and complete, a few early improvements, and use what you learn to plan your next moves with confidence.

This chapter gives you baseline metrics, simple dashboards that show movement, and a short-term plan you can actually follow. No guesswork, no overload, just steady progress built week by week.

Week 1: Determining Baseline and Benchmarks

The first step in any AI SEO effort is understanding where you stand right now. Before you change anything, make sure your online information is accurate and consistent. Then create a clear Day 0 baseline, which is a snapshot of your visibility in traditional search results and AI-generated answers before you begin making improvements.

Capture your Day 0 baseline

Start by gathering your current performance data from both classic and AI SEO sources. The next three sections show you how.

Traditional search

Export your top queries and pages from Google Search Console. Focus on the keywords and URLs that already attract impressions or clicks. These are your current foot-in-the-door opportunities and will serve as your baseline for future comparison.

TIP

To export this data in Google Search Console, open Performance, choose Search results, set the date range you want to use, and click Export. Save the file in your Day 0 Baseline folder so you can compare future results against it.

AI SEO

Check your brand or content visibility in AI platforms such as ChatGPT, Perplexity, Microsoft Copilot, Google AI Mode, and Google AI Overviews. Google AI Mode is a conversational search mode, while AI Overviews are summaries that can appear in standard Google Search results. Run 10 to 20 of your most relevant prompts and note whether your brand is:

- Cited as a source
- Mentioned by name
- Completely absent

You're not trying to test every possible query. You just want a realistic sample of how often your brand shows up when customers ask the kinds of questions that matter for your business.

For example, a local plumber might test prompts such as "best emergency plumber near Chesterfield" or "Who should I call for a leaking water heater?" A software company might test "best AI SEO tools for agencies" or "Rankability alternatives."

Documentation

Take screenshots and record the exact prompt, date, and any model or version information for each AI platform. Store everything in a single folder on your desktop or in a cloud drive labeled Day 0 Baseline so you can quickly compare future results to where you started.

Verify and strengthen your entity

AI systems rely on facts they can confirm about your business or brand. If your *entity data*, the key facts that identify your business or brand across the web, is incomplete or inconsistent, it's harder for any system that builds on web data to recognize you and use you as a trusted source.

To verify and strengthen your entity, follow these steps:

1. **Start with the information on your own website.**

   Review your About page, Contact page, and any Organization or Person schema (see Chapter 4) you already use to make sure your name, description, logo, and key URLs are accurate and up to date. If you use multiple domains or subbrands, add a short explanation on the relevant About, Contact, or product pages so readers and crawlers understand how those brands or sites relate to one another.

2. **Look beyond your site to verify your profile across the web.**

   Check to ensure that your brand or personal name, role, and website URL appear consistently across major profiles such as Google Business Profile, LinkedIn, Crunchbase, and any other important industry directories. Fix typos, outdated descriptions, and old links so that readers and search engines see the same story everywhere.

3. **Connect profiles using structured data.**

   If you use *structured data,* which is machine-readable code that helps search engines understand the meaning of a page, you can link profiles here. Add `Schema.org`'s sameAs property in your Organization or Person schema and point it to the verified profiles you reviewed in Step 2.

REMEMBER

This step helps search engines recognize that your website and profiles on different platforms all refer to the same business, person, or brand. When your website clearly links to your official profiles, search engines can more confidently connect those sources into a single entity. Those connections may contribute to a *knowledge graph,* which is the behind-the-scenes system search engines use to organize information about people, organizations, products, and other entities.

Select a few practical benchmarks

Don't try to track everything at one time. Choose a small set of baseline measurements that matter most to your AI SEO efforts and record your current numbers. These starting measurements will serve as benchmarks you can use to evaluate your progress over time.

Start with the following three categories of baseline measurements:

- **AI visibility:** Record how often your brand appears in AI answers, how often it appears first in lists of multiple brands, and how many citations your test prompts generate. These figures show whether AI platforms are starting to recognize and reference your brand more often.
- **Traditional visibility:** Record clicks and impressions for your key pages and branded searches. These figures show whether traditional search visibility is improving alongside your AI visibility work.
- **Operational progress:** Track how many improvements and fixes you ship. These figures show whether your plan is turning into real work instead of staying stuck in planning mode.

Create a simple spreadsheet or dashboard and record your starting numbers. As you make changes, compare new results against these benchmarks to see whether your visibility, traffic, and implementation efforts are moving in the right direction.

Deliverables for Week 1

By the end of Week 1, you should have these items:

- A Day 0 baseline folder with screenshots and a prompt list
- Updated entity information and, where you use it, cleaner schema
- A benchmark spreadsheet showing your starting AI and traditional visibility numbers

When you finish this first week, you'll know exactly where you stand and what matters most to track. Next, you'll put simple systems in place to measure every improvement you make.

Week 2: Setting Up Tracking

With your baseline in place, you're ready to install tracking that helps you see progress without drowning in data. Good tracking isn't about building complex dashboards, it's about setting up a simple, repeatable system you can use every week to monitor your visibility and connect results back to your work.

If you want a deeper dive into metrics, dashboards, and experiments, you can jump ahead to Part 2, where I expand this foundation into a full measurement stack.

TECHNICAL STUFF

A *measurement stack* is the group of tools you use together to track performance, such as Google Search Console, Google Analytics, Looker Studio, and your AI SEO tracking sheet.

Create your evidence library

Your evidence library sits at the center of your AI SEO tracking system. It expands the Day 0 Baseline folder you created in Week 1 into an ongoing archive of screenshots, prompt logs, tracking sheets, and results over time so you can show before-and-after improvements.

To create your evidence library, follow these guidelines:

- Create one main folder named AI SEO Tracking (or similar) and add subfolders by date or week.
- Inside each subfolder, store screenshots, prompt lists, and notes for each platform you test (ChatGPT, Google AI Mode, Perplexity, Microsoft Copilot, and any others you use).
- Use consistent filenames, such as `2025-11-10_GoogleAIMode_[PromptTopic].png`.
- Keep your Day 0 Baseline folder and benchmark spreadsheet in the main AI SEO Tracking folder. Treat the Day 0 files as your starting point and use the weekly subfolders to store new screenshots and notes as your evidence grows.

Over time, this becomes your visual audit trail. It shows what changed, when it changed, and which platforms were involved.

Build a simple tracking sheet

For inclusion in your evidence library, create a master spreadsheet to log each test you run. Include columns such as these examples:

- Date
- Platform
- Prompt
- Brand coverage (Yes/No)
- Position (First/Second/None)
- Citations or links shown
- Notes

TIP

Retest the same prompts every week so that you can see trends in coverage over time. Use color coding to highlight improvements in coverage, new citations, or better placement in multibrand answers.

This master tracking sheet doesn't replace your analytics tools, such as Google Search Console or Google Analytics. It complements them by measuring how well AI platforms recognize and cite your brand from week to week. Keep the benchmark spreadsheet as your starting snapshot and use the master tracking sheet for ongoing weekly checks. In Part 2, I show how to build on this idea when you formalize coverage, position, and share of voice (SoV) as core AI visibility metrics.

Connect analytics for traditional search

To complete your tracking setup for traditional search, follow these steps:

1. **Connect Google Search Console (GSC).** Use it to track impressions and clicks for your top pages and key queries.
2. **Connect Google Analytics 4 (GA4).** Use it to monitor traffic and engagement on the pages you optimize.
3. **Connect Looker Studio.** Use it to combine GSC and GA4 into a simple dashboard that shows organic trends at a glance.

Even if AI SEO visibility is your main focus, traditional SEO data still shows where search demand exists and where people still click through to your site. That context helps you prioritize which pages and keywords to improve first.

Automate your tracking routine

Set a recurring 20-minute calendar event each week called AI SEO Check, for example. During that time, you should:

- Retest your prompt list across your chosen AI platforms.
- Log the results in your master tracking sheet.
- Save new screenshots to your evidence library.
- Note any meaningful changes in coverage, citations, or brand mentions.

Keep a separate change log for onsite edits and new publications. When you ship a change, write down the date, page or URL, and a short description of what you did. That way, you can connect your edits to shifts in AI and search visibility later.

Deliverables for Week 2

By the end of Week 2, you should have:

- An organized AI SEO Tracking folder
- A master tracking spreadsheet for weekly AI answer checks
- A simple Looker Studio dashboard for web analytics
- A weekly AI SEO Check reminder in your calendar

Once these pieces are in place, you'll have a reliable tracking system that shows whether your optimizations are moving the needle. In Week 3, you'll start shipping quick wins so that those dashboards and logs begin to show true, visible progress.

Week 3: Taking Quick Wins to Ship

Once you have your tracking running smoothly (see the previous section), it's time to make visible progress. The goal this week is to ship, or publish and complete, small, strategic changes that help search engines and AI features that depend on web data recognize your brand more quickly. Quick wins build momentum and prove that your process works in practice, not just on paper.

To do that, this section shows you how to make your brand facts clearer, refresh passages that answer questions directly, strengthen offsite validation, and publish one bottom of funnel asset.

Focus on facts that machines can verify

AI systems that use web data depend on clear, consistent facts. When your site and profiles use different names, descriptions, or claims, it creates confusion that can hurt visibility in both traditional search and AI answers. In Week 1 (see the earlier section "Verify and strengthen your entity"), you focus on the broader job of helping search engines recognize your entity. Here, you focus on specific facts that you can improve quickly.

To make sure search engines can verify key information, follow these guidelines:

- **Review your About, Contact, and Product or Service pages for factual clarity.** Make sure your company name, offer, location, and contact details match across all of your pages.
- **Add a short Facts section near the top of your main pages.** It should include your company name, a description of what you do and where you operate, and your key differentiators.
- **If you already use structured data, you can apply schema types.** Examples are Organization, LocalBusiness, Product, and FAQ. `Schema.org` writes some type names as one word, so keep those names exactly as shown when you use them in code.

The main benefit of this work is for search engines and other systems that index the web. Clear, consistent facts and, where appropriate, schema help crawlers build a more accurate picture of your brand. Many AI features retrieve information from these indexes and knowledge graphs, so you're improving the information they often rely on to generate answers, even though schema isn't something AI answers reward on its own.

Refresh passages that answer questions directly

In AI SEO results, a single passage can matter more than the rest of the page. Each core page should include a short paragraph that clearly answers the main question or intent behind the topic.

Follow these guidelines for your top pages:

- **Start with your most important topics.** Then write a clear two- or three-sentence summary that gives a complete answer to the main question behind the page.

  For example, a service page for a plumbing company might say: "Emergency plumbing services fix urgent leaks, backups, and burst pipes that can't wait for a normal appointment. ABC Plumbing serves Chesterfield and nearby areas with 24/7 emergency calls, licensed technicians, and upfront diagnostic fees."
- **Use natural language and simple phrasing.** Avoid keyword stuffing or awkward repetition.
- **Place this passage near the top of the page.** Then users, crawlers, and any retrieval systems are likely to see it.

REMEMBER

Think of these short passages as AI-ready content blocks. They should stand on their own inside an AI answer while still helping human readers understand your offer quickly.

Strengthen offsite proof

External validation is a major trust factor for both traditional search engines and many AI systems that lean on web data. Week 3 is a good week to tighten your offsite presence. Follow these guidelines:

- Update your company profiles on high-authority sites, meaning trusted sites that already rank, get cited, or influence buyers in your niche, such as LinkedIn, Crunchbase, and key review platforms.
- Submit your brand to credible industry directories or comparison sites that accept listings for your type of business.
- Make sure your descriptions, claims, and links match the onsite facts you updated earlier in the section "Focus on facts that machines can verify."

When multiple trusted sources confirm the same entity data, search engines and other retrieval systems are more likely to treat those details as reliable and reuse them in AI features and answers.

Publish one new bottom of funnel asset

Quick wins aren't just technical. They also include fresh content that targets people who are close to taking action. A bottom of funnel asset is a page for buyers who are comparing options, checking fit, or getting ready to contact you or buy (see Chapter 12). These pages help people make a decision and give AI systems clearer sources to reference for commercial prompts.

This week, create and publish at least one bottom of funnel (BoF) asset, such as:

- **A Best for [Use Case] page** that explains when your solution is the right fit
- **An Alternatives to [Competitor] page** that clearly positions your offer and helps buyers compare options

When you publish the asset, follow these guidelines:

- Use structured data where it naturally applies, but remember that its primary role is to clarify content for search engines, not to "force" AI visibility.
- Include simple comparisons and reference third-party reviews if you're allowed to do so.
- Link this page internally from your home page, product pages, and relevant blog posts so that visitors and crawlers can find it easily.

Even a single, well-written BoF asset like this one can start appearing in both traditional search and AI-influenced results in a relatively short time, especially for more specific queries.

Deliverables for Week 3

By the end of Week 3, aim to have these elements:

- Three to five updated or newly optimized pages
- One new BoF content asset published
- Updated offsite profiles and directory submissions
- Before-and-after screenshots saved in your tracking folder
- All changes logged in your change log

At this point, you may start to see measurable movement, including new mentions, citations, or ranking improvements. Those early results will help you decide what to prioritize and scale in your 90-day road map in Week 4.

Week 4: Building a 90-Day Road Map

Week 4 is about turning your early progress into a repeatable plan. It's time to analyze what worked, choose clear priorities, and create a road map that keeps your AI SEO momentum humming for the next three months.

Compare your starting point to now

Contrast your current visibility to your Day 0 baseline. Record these notes in your master tracking spreadsheet and summarize the highlights in your change log. Follow these parameters:

- **AI SEO**
  - Look at your coverage rate across prompts.
  - Note how often you're cited and any new brand mentions.
  - Look for patterns in which prompts or topics perform best.
- **Traditional search**
  - Review changes in clicks, impressions, and keyword positions for your target pages.
  - Note which pages moved, even if it's just a small shift in the right direction.
- **Operational progress**
  - Scan your change log to see how many optimizations you shipped and which ones were most substantial.
  - Match visible gains back to specific changes whenever you can.

Highlight anything that moved the needle, even slightly. These are early signals of what's working and what you may want to scale.

Choose your 90-day themes

A road map is much easier to follow when it's organized around clear themes rather than a long list of unrelated tasks. Use the lessons from the first three weeks to pick two or three main priorities, for example:

- **Theme 1: Strengthen entity trust.** Continue improving your core brand pages, offsite profiles, and, where appropriate, Organization or Person schema so that search engines keep a clean, consistent record of who you are.

- **Theme 2: Expand AI-ready content.** Build more pages and passages that answer common questions clearly and match true user intent, especially in commercial and comparison searches.
- **Theme 3: Increase coverage across answer engines.** Track new prompts, add sources, and aim for more consistent citations across ChatGPT, Google AI Mode, Perplexity, Microsoft Copilot, and others.

Each theme should have one or more measurable outcomes you can check weekly, such as:

- Higher coverage on a specific set of prompts
- More citations for key pages
- More branded queries that mention your brand in AI answers

Map work to metrics

For every task on your 90-day road map, define the metric it's meant to influence; for example:

- **Updating entity pages and, where you use it, schema:** This can help search engines maintain accurate entity details, which supports more consistent brand information wherever those systems surface you.
- **Publishing new BoF content:** More coverage on commercial or comparison queries.
- **Improving entity consistency across profiles and directories:** Better recognition in search features and AI features that sit on top of those indexes.

When every task is tied to a measurable result, your road map becomes a performance plan rather than a simple to-do list.

Create a weekly schedule

Break your 90-day road map into weekly "sprints" so that it feels manageable. One simple structure looks like this:

- **Weeks 1-4:** Continue onsite optimization and entity cleanup based on the first 30 days. This isn't a repeat of the earlier weeks. It's the next phase, using what your baseline and quick wins revealed.

- **Weeks 5-8:** Publish and promote AI-ready content, especially high-intent and BoF assets.
- **Weeks 9-12:** Expand tracking, test new prompts, and double down on what has worked best.

Schedule one 30-minute review-and-plan session each Friday. During this time, you'll:

- Check your dashboards
- Update your tracking sheet and evidence library
- Record wins and setbacks
- Decide what to adjust for the next sprint

This small weekly ritual keeps your 90-day plan alive instead of letting it collect dust.

Deliverables for Week 4

By the end of Week 4, you should have:

- A 90-day road map with clear themes, tasks, and metrics
- A prioritized backlog of about 12 to 18 actions, with owners and due dates
- Weekly review time blocked on your calendar
- Updated dashboards and tracking sheets that reflect your new baselines

When Week 4 ends, you'll have a living road map built on real data and proven wins. The map becomes your operating system for AI SEO, keeping you accountable, focused, and moving forward, quarter after quarter, without overclaiming what any single tactic, including schema, can do on its own.

IN THIS CHAPTER

» Seeing how AI answers change what visibility really means

» Seeing how LLMs and AI platforms work with AI SEO

» Structuring pages, passages, and schema so search (and AI on top of it) can trust your content

» Seeking out signals of credibility

Chapter 4
Talk Like an AI SEO Pro

To master AI SEO, you need to think and speak like the systems that shape visibility. This chapter gives you the vocabulary and framework to do that so that you can analyze results, explain what's happening, and make smarter optimization decisions.

In this chapter, I start off with an explanation of AEO and GEO (so many optimization acronyms out there!). From there, I explain how to measure share of voice (SoV) in AI answers, why entities and knowledge graphs sit at the backbone of AI visibility, and how large language models (LLMs), the AI models that generate text, and AI platforms, the interfaces that display answers to users, work with retrieval systems to assemble final answers. I also spell out why citations matter alongside links, how fact hubs help you earn consensus across the web, and how schema and other structured data help search engines understand and feature your content.

I won't just show you how to talk like an AI SEO pro. You'll also think and optimize like one.

Sifting through AI Visibility Terms

When people talk about AI SEO, you see labels like answer engine optimization (AEO) and generative engine optimization (GEO). In practice, different people use them in different ways, and often as synonyms. There is no strict industry standard yet.

TECHNICAL STUFF

A quick comparison of the two terms is useful because they overlap, but they are not identical. AEO focuses on earning visibility inside answer experiences, such as brand mentions, recommendations, and citations. GEO focuses on helping generative AI systems understand and repeat your information accurately. In practice, you use both ideas to make your brand easier for AI systems to understand, trust, and recommend.

You may see the terms AEO and GEO occasionally, but you won't rely on them as rigid frameworks. Instead, you should focus on these two practical outcomes:

- Showing up as a recommended brand in AI answers
- Making sure AI systems repeat your facts accurately

The goal isn't to pick a label. It's to understand how your brand shows up onscreen and what AI systems seem to "believe" about you.

The following sections spell out important concepts that offer lenses you can use to evaluate and improve that visibility:

- Share of voice
- Entities
- Indexes and knowledge graphs

Measuring share of voice

Share of voice is a marketing term that measures how often a brand is mentioned. In AI, it shows how often and how strongly your brand shows up inside AI answers. The main question is straightforward:

> When someone runs a commercial query in an AI platform, are you one of the brands that appears in the answer?

Citations and links can provide additional evidence, but they are not the primary measure. What matters most is whether your brand is included in the answer and how prominently it appears.

You can evaluate SoV using four practical factors.

Are we present at all?

For each tracked query on each AI platform, record a simple yes or no. If your brand isn't present, you have zero SoV for that query on that platform.

Where do we appear in the answer?

If your brand is present, ask these questions to note your position and prominence:

- Are you listed first in a short set of tools?
- Are you buried in the middle of a long list?
- Are you mentioned only once, in passing, inside a paragraph?

Higher positions and clearer mentions usually attract more attention and more clicks.

How crowded is the answer?

An answer that lists 3 competing products is quite different from one that lists 30. Your relative share among all brands in the answer tells you how strong your presence really is.

Which AI platforms matter most?

Not every AI platform should count the same in your SoV score. You need a market-weighted view. For example, if you sell primarily in the United States, a mention in ChatGPT may be more valuable than a mention in an AI platform that only a small fraction of your target audience uses.

To build a market-weighted SoV score, you can:

- Assign each AI platform a rough weight based on usage in your target region
- Multiply your presence and position scores by that weight
- Summarize SoV across all AI platforms into one simple view

Over time, these actions provide a clear picture of your brand's SoV, such as:

- How often your brand appears in AI answers
- How strong your position is when it does appear
- How its presence compares to other brands in the same answer
- How all of this looks after you factor in which AI platforms your audience actually uses

This market-weighted SoV becomes one of your primary AI SEO metrics. It shows whether your brand is truly visible where customers are asking questions, not just whether your site is listed somewhere as a source.

Entities: The building blocks of AI SEO

Search engines and modern AI systems care about entities, not just keywords. An *entity* is a clearly defined person, organization, place, product, or concept that can be described with specific attributes.

Each entity can have the following elements, shown here with examples:

- **A name and type:** "Rankability" (software) or "Nathan Gotch" (person)
- **Attributes:** Location, founding date, or pricing tier
- **Relationships:** "Founded by," "headquartered in," or "competes with"

These relationships can be stored in a *knowledge graph*, which is a connected web of facts. When AI systems understand who you are and how you relate to other entities, your brand becomes easier to retrieve, mention, and trust.

To strengthen your entity, focus on consistent naming and descriptions, a clear entity home, and structured data and corroborating references.

Consistent naming and descriptions

Use the same brand name, spelling, and core description everywhere, such as on these examples:

- **Your website:** The About, Contact, and product or service pages
- **Profiles:** Google Business Profile, LinkedIn, or Crunchbase

- **Key industry directories or review platforms:** G2, Capterra, Yelp, Clutch, Avvo, Angi, or other category-specific sites

If you use variations, keep them minor and intentional. Significant differences in how you describe yourself can confuse both users and machines.

Clear entity home

Create an entity home page on your site; it's usually the About page or a dedicated brand page that includes verified facts such as these:

- Official brand name
- Location or service areas
- Founders or leadership
- Core products or services
- Key brand descriptors (for example, "AI SEO software for agencies")

This page becomes the primary reference for who you are. And now other pages can link back to it when they mention your brand.

Structured data and corroborating references

Add structured data (see Chapter 3) that defines your entity type, such as Organization, LocalBusiness, Person, or Product. This helps search engines understand the basics of who you are and how your pages fit together.

There's no solid proof that large language models (or LLMs; see the later section "Looking at LLMs and AI Platforms") read or assign special value to schema (see the later section "Integrating Structured Data and Schema") directly. Structured data and schema work together. Here are two ways to think about schema:

- It helps search engines understand and feature your content.
- It helps AI systems identify and retrieve important information from your site more reliably.

REMEMBER

Structured data is how information is formatted so that AI systems can easily read it, and schema is the vocabulary used to label that information.

Also, work to build references on reputable third-party sites. Consistent mentions on trusted domains help reinforce your entity in search engine indexes and knowledge graphs (see the next section).

When information about your brand is inconsistent or wrong, AI systems can easily infer the wrong story about who you are. Cleaning bad data matters just as much as adding new information.

Looking at the roles of indexes and knowledge graphs

Search engines use indexes to store pages and documents, and they use knowledge graphs to store and connect facts about the world. You don't see the graphs directly, but you see their effects in features like these:

- Knowledge panels that show brand summaries
- Rich result boxes that highlight entities and relationships
- Direct answers to factual questions, such as "Who founded Rankability?"

In a simplified view, a knowledge graph lets a system:

- Look up an entity, such as "rankability"
- Follow relationships, such as "founded by"
- Retrieve connected entities, such as "Nathan Gotch"

AI systems can then use those facts as input when they generate answers.

If your entity information is incomplete or inconsistent, AI systems can connect the wrong facts or skip your brand entirely. You'll be competing with entities that have clearer, more complete profiles in the graph.

To support your position in knowledge graphs and indexes, keep these guidelines in mind:

- Use schema and internal links to make your site structure clear to search engines.
- Maintain verified author and organization profiles on major platforms.
- Keep entity descriptions, addresses, and URLs consistent across the web.

Allowing SoV, entities, knowledge graphs, and indexes to work together

Think of entity clarity as your passport into AI SEO. Clear, consistent entity signals make it easier for AI systems to:

- Reference your brand confidently
- Quote you accurately
- Include your brand as a trusted option in answers

All of this still depends on strong traditional SEO. Search engines use their traditional indexes and ranking systems to decide which pages to crawl, store, and retrieve before AI models summarize them. When your pages rank well and are easy to understand, you increase your brand's chances of being pulled into the retrieval sets that power AI answers.

Think of the entity clarity process as a chain of events:

- **Entities feed knowledge graphs and search indexes:** Those graphs and indexes support retrieval.
- **Retrieval drives citations and brand mentions in answers:** Those mentions grow your SoV across AI SEO environments.

Once you see how these layers connect, you can make deliberate choices about where to focus your AI SEO work next.

Looking at LLMs and AI Platforms

To master AI SEO, you need to understand the three pieces that work together in most AI search experiences. Here, *experience* means the full interaction a user has with a search or chat tool, from the prompt to the displayed answer:

- **The retrieval system:** Decides which content to bring in
- **The large language model (LLM):** Gemini, ChatGPT, or Claude, for example, generates the wording of the answer
- **The AI platform:** Shows the final answer, such as Google's AI features, Microsoft Copilot, or Perplexity

Each part affects your visibility in a different way.

How retrieval and LLMs work together

When retrieval and LLMs work together, the setup is often called retrieval-augmented generation, or RAG. In plain English, RAG means the AI system first retrieves outside information, such as search results or web pages, and then the LLM uses that information to generate an answer. RAG matters for AI SEO because your pages can become part of the information the system retrieves.

When someone asks a question, the AI system doesn't usually hand the entire web page to the LLM. In many setups, long pages are split into smaller passages (see the later section "Working with Pages and Passages"). The retrieval system then selects the passages that look most relevant. The LLM can consider those passages only within its context window. A *context window* is the total amount of text the LLM can process at once.

Inside that window, the LLM:

- » Reads the selected passages as text tokens (see Chapter 2)
- » Combines what it sees with patterns from training
- » Predicts an answer that seems most likely to satisfy the query

The LLM isn't looking up facts in a neat database. It's predicting which words, ideas, and brand names are most likely to answer the query based on the passages it has in front of it. If your brand is missing, vague, or buried in those passages, the LLM has fewer reasons to recommend you, even if the full page is well-structured.

How the AI platform controls what users see

The AI platform decides how a particular answer appears on the screen. It can carry out these tasks:

- » Show a list of recommended brands
- » Hide sources behind icons or a Show More link
- » Limit how many names appear at the top of the answer
- » "Fold" long answers so that only the first part is visible

Two AI platforms might retrieve similar information and generate similar answers, yet one AI platform might clearly list brand names while another buries them in a long paragraph or hides them behind an icon. In that case, the first AI platform is far more valuable for your brand, even if both have technically pulled your content.

Even if an AI model looks at your content, your brand can stay invisible if the AI platform doesn't show it clearly.

Many AI platforms:

- » Limit how many brands or citations appear
- » Hide sources in icons or expandable sections
- » Truncate longer answers so that only the first few names are shown

If your brand's best mention is buried halfway down a dense paragraph, an AI platform may prefer a shorter, clearer passage from another site that solves the query faster. A short answer that names your brand and solves the query in one or two sentences has a better chance of being pulled into a visible list or card (a boxed answer element).

Your goal isn't just to get used as a source. Your goal is to get your brand name into the visible part of the answer where users actually look and click.

How to optimize AI answers

Your goal is to influence all three layers of the AI answer system:

- » **Retrieval level:** Your pages should rank well in traditional search and include passages that contain clear, self-contained mentions of your brand and what it's useful for.
- » **Model level:** Those passages should make it natural for the LLM to include your brand as a relevant answer for specific jobs, such as "AI SEO content optimizer for agencies."
- » **Platform level:** Those recommendations should appear as visible brand mentions in lists, cards, or summaries that users can act on.

Understanding these three layers helps explain why content structure matters so much in AI SEO. The next section looks at the relationship between pages and passages, and why passages often become the units that AI systems retrieve, interpret, and use in answers.

Working with Pages and Passages

Traditional SEO focuses on pages, but passages play a big role. You build topical authority, earn backlinks, and organize the whole page around a theme so that the page can rank in a search.

In AI SEO, pages and passages are used differently:

- **Pages** are the unit that search engines crawl, index, and rank.
- **Passages** are the units that many AI retrieval systems pick up and feed into models.

For AI SEO, long pages are often split into smaller passages behind the scenes. Retrieval systems then grab only a few of those passages and send them to the model. The model uses those passages to predict an answer. This means that visibility depends on both the strength of the page as a whole and the quality of the individual passages within it.

You can think of this as two levels of visibility:

- **Page level:** Your page's overall quality, authority, and relevance help you win retrieval.
- **Passage level:** The specific passage that gets retrieved shapes what the model "sees" and says about your brand.

If the retrieved passage doesn't clearly mention who you are or what you offer, the model has less reason to recommend your brand, even if the full page is excellent.

Writing brand-friendly passages

Strong passages are easy for AI systems to lift and easy for users to act on. They don't just explain a concept. They make it natural to recommend your brand.

To write a strong passage, focus on these necessities:

- **One main idea per paragraph:** Answer a specific question, such as "What is rankability?" or "Who is this tool for?"
- **Short, direct sentences:** Put the main claim in the first line and then add one or two supporting details.

- **Specific names, not vague pronouns:** Use your brand name and product name rather than "it" or "they" when you want the model to remember who-did-what.
- **Tight links between claims and evidence:** Place numbers, examples, or case study results close to the brand statement they support.
- **Simple formats:** Use bullet points or shortlists for "top tools," "steps," or "features" so that AI platforms can turn them into clear recommendations.

You can still use schema types such as FAQ, HowTo, or Article to reinforce structure for search engines (see the upcoming section "Integrating Structured Data and Schema"), but assume the visible on-page text has to stand on its own. The passage should already be clear and self-contained even if the schema is ignored.

Knowing why both levels matter

You still need strong pages. They help search systems see your site as authoritative, rank you in traditional results, and choose your content for retrieval.

You also need strong passages so that the information that reaches the model:

- States who you are
- Explains what you're good at
- Fits neatly into the answer formats that AI platforms like to show

When both page and passage levels support each other, you give AI systems more reasons to recommend your brand in answers, not just quietly cite your site in the background.

Getting Up to Speed on Signals of Credibility

Making your brand a source of authority is essential. AI systems prioritize brands that are recognized and trusted. Several signals can help you reach that goal: backlinks, citations, mentions, fact hubs, and consensus. Together, these signals can influence search results.

Striving for backlinks

A *backlink* is a link from another website to your site. In traditional SEO, backlinks are one of the major signals search engines use to judge authority, trust, and popularity. In simple terms, strong backlinks can help your pages earn higher positions in the blue links people see on search engine results pages.

In traditional search, users see ranked pages, not the backlinks that helped those pages rank. AI-driven search adds another layer. In AI answers, users see brand names, URLs, and data points that the system chooses to mention. In that context, citations and brand mentions (see the next section) become your visible proof of credibility.

Garnering citations and mentions

A *citation* in an AI answer is any reference to your brand, website, or published data, whether or not the AI platform shows a clickable link. Citations are a means to an end. A *mention* is a reference to your brand, product, person, or site, even without a clickable link. The goal is to have your brand clearly recommended in the answer.

Citations and mentions form the bridge between your content and the user's question inside AI features.

AI platforms such as Google's AI features and Perplexity usually display only a small number of brands or sources per answer. Securing one of those visible mentions is similar to winning a top position in traditional search.

Citations and mentions can come from these sources:

- Direct quotes from your content
- Named mentions of your brand or domain
- Summaries of your published data or findings
- Screenshots, visuals, or tables clearly attributed to you

The more often your brand appears in AI answers, especially in commercial and "Best Of" queries, the stronger your SoV becomes. That presence feeds trust and reinforces your position as an option to consider, and it often matters more than whether the answer shows a full link to your page.

Building a fact hub

A *fact hub* is a central source of truth on your site. It pulls together your brand's key data points, statistics, and definitions in one place. Fact hubs help both humans and machines confirm what's true about your brand and your topic.

To create a fact hub, follow these guidelines:

- » Identify recurring facts, numbers, and definitions across your content.
- » Publish a single, well-organized page that lists these facts clearly.
- » Include the source, date, and update history for important numbers.
- » Use a simple structure, such as tables and headings, and support it with schema for search engines wherever it makes sense.

Schema is designed for search engines. No solid proof exists that LLMs read or weigh it directly. The safe way to think about it here is that clear structure and schema help traditional search understand and feature your fact hub. Because AI systems often rely on those same search indexes for retrieval, a well-structured fact hub can indirectly support AI visibility.

When search engines and AI systems can find and verify your core facts in one place, they're more likely to treat that page as a primary reference and to pull those facts into answers.

Earning consensus across the web

AI systems tend to place more confidence in information that's consistent across multiple trusted sources. When several reputable sites report the same fact, the system has more reason to treat that fact as reliable.

You can build this kind of consensus by following these guidelines:

- » Use consistent terminology and data across your own site.
- » Publish your facts in places others can reference, such as blog posts, reports, or data studies.
- » Encourage partners, customers, or media outlets to cite or link to your key facts.
- » Update older content so that your numbers and claims match your current fact hub.

Consensus doesn't guarantee that your brand will appear in every AI answer, but it raises the odds that your facts are treated as dependable and that your brand is included when those facts are discussed.

Measuring signal impact

To see whether your work is paying off, track a few simple indicators:

- **Citation rate:** The percentage of AI answers in your tracking set that mention your brand
- **Fact coverage:** The number of your key facts that appear on other reputable sites
- **Fact "freshness":** The average age of the data in your fact hub and related content

These metrics help you see which topics and facts are gaining traction and which ones need more support.

When you combine citation strategy with fact-driven publishing, you move beyond chasing backlinks alone. Links still help your content get discovered, crawled, indexed, and trusted in traditional search. Fact hubs and consensus help shape what AI systems say after your content is retrieved. Citations and brand mentions then turn that trust into visible presence inside the answers your customers actually read.

Integrating Structured Data and Schema

Structured data helps search engines understand your content without guessing. It translates human-readable information into a machine-readable format and gives search systems clearer context about who you are, what your content covers, and how it connects to other entities.

Schema is the shared vocabulary from `Schema.org` that labels information in structured data, such as identifying a page as an article, product, organization, person, or FAQ. Search engines clearly use schema for elements like rich results and knowledge panels (see Chapter 3), and they rely on the same understanding when they determine what to index and retrieve. Many AI answers sit on top of those same indexes. That means structured data can help you qualify for crawling, indexing, and retrieval, which indirectly improves your chances of being included in AI answers.

TIP

There's no public proof that general LLMs give special extra weight to schema fields on your pages. You should treat schema as a way to clarify entities and page types for search engines, which then support AI systems by way of better retrieval and ranking.

The following sections cover the types of schema that are important to implement and describe how to keep an eye on your structured data and schema usage.

Identifying schema types

You can put many types of schema into practice. Think of schema as a labeling system to identify key facts about you and your brand, such as what your organization is, who the people involved are, which content sets up your credibility, and which products and services you may sell or review.

Organization schema

Organization schema gives data about a company or an organization. Include details such as these:

- Official business name
- Logo and contact information
- Headquarters location and, if relevant, founding date and founders' names
- Links to social media profiles and sameAs properties for entity alignment

TECHNICAL STUFF

sameAs properties are schema fields that tell search engines and AI systems that profiles, pages, and listings across the web all refer to the same organization, person, or entity.

Person schema

Person schema gives details about people. When used for content authors, include this information:

- Full name and role
- Credentials or job title
- Affiliated organization
- Profile photo and links to verified profiles

These schemas help search engines connect your content authors and organization to the proper entities in their indexes and knowledge graphs. That clearer understanding supports features like knowledge panels and author attribution, which in turn help AI systems that rely on those same sources.

Content schema

For most sites, *content* schema types provide useful signals about topical focus and basic credibility.

Here are some common types:

- **Article or BlogPosting:** For most written content
- **TechArticle:** For technical or instructional material
- **FAQ Page or HowTo:** For question-based or procedural guides

Each content type should include this information:

- A headline and short description
- The name of the author and publisher
- The date published and date modified
- The main EntityOfPage property to define the primary topic

These details improve clarity for search engines when they interpret and feature your content. Some AI-related tools that parse HTML or reuse search results can also benefit from this clearer structure, but the main audience for your schema here is still traditional search.

Product and service schemas

If you sell or review products and services, structured data helps define the specifics in a consistent way.

Product schema gives data about certain products. Include the following information:

- Product name, description, and image
- Brand, SKU, and global trade item number (GTIN) where applicable
- Offers, price, and availability
- AggregateRating and Review schema

It's also helpful to provide the following information:

- Rating counts and average scores
- Basic review details and, where allowed, references to verified reviewers

Service schema describes a service offered by an organization or a business. Provide attributes such as these:

- Service type
- Area served
- Provider details

When applied correctly, these schemas reinforce credibility for search engines, make your data easier to appear in search features, and help connect your business to accurate, verified information that AI systems may reuse through those results.

Using claim and evidence schema patterns

Fact-based and educational content can benefit from schema patterns that highlight verifiable information and how it connects to sources. There are two main approaches:

- **ClaimReview schema:** A schema type used when you are reviewing or fact-checking a specific claim, including the claim being reviewed, the review result, and supporting details.
- **Evidence markup:** A flexible approach that uses standard schema properties to connect claims to supporting sources and entities.

These approaches can be implemented using common schema building blocks:

- **CreativeWork with citation properties**: Use these to connect statements or content blocks to supporting sources, including URLs, titles, and access dates.
- **sameAs and About properties**: Use these to connect entities in your content to authoritative external identifiers such as Wikidata, LinkedIn, or Crunchbase.

REMEMBER

Historically, schema types such as Speakable were explored for text that can be read aloud by voice assistants. Support for these types is limited and often experimental, so treat them as optional extras, not core requirements.

Schema elements improve precision for search engines and can reduce the risk of entity confusion when your content is interpreted, summarized, or matched to queries.

Keeping data focused with checks and balances

Using structured data and schema should be part of your publishing workflow, not an afterthought.

Follow these best practices for quality control:

- **Version control:** Maintain this for all JSON-LD files, which are the script blocks that usually contain schema markup.
- **Markup testing:** Test your structured data regularly using Google's Rich Results Test and `Schema.org`-oriented validators.
- **Structured data checks:** Include structured data review in your publishing checklist.
- **Change log:** Keep a simple one that records updates to your schema with each content release.

Consistent and accurate structured data and schema markup make your site easier for search engines to interpret, index, and trust. Over time, that foundation supports both traditional rankings and the retrieval pipelines that many AI-generated answers depend on. Strong schema doesn't guarantee AI exposure on its own, but it increases your brand's odds of getting into the sets of pages that AI systems can pull from.

2 Measuring AI SEO

IN THIS PART . . .

Measure the metrics that matter to you. You track not only rankings, clicks, and traffic but also whether your brand appears, where it appears, which sources get cited, and whether the answer describes you accurately.

Build a dashboard to log your coverage, traffic, and key trends.

Look at what competitors are doing to set standards for how your content should be structured, supported, and presented.

Run experiments so that you can identify which changes are driving results.

IN THIS CHAPTER

» Evaluating what makes a good prompt and building an AI prompt database

» Tracking how often your brand is recommended

» Working with citations to improve your position

» Looking at behavior cues as a measurement

Chapter 5

Tracking the Metrics That Matter

AI SEO can feel slippery. One week your brand shows up in AI answers, and the next week it seems to vanish. Most analytics tools don't show you exactly what changed. Traditional SEO reporting focuses on clicks, rankings, and traffic. AI SEO tracking adds another layer because you're watching answers, citations, and coverage across many different AI platforms at once.

In Chapter 3, I explain how to set up a basic evidence library and a simple tracking sheet so you can see whether early changes make a meaningful impact. In this chapter, I show how to turn that foundation into a repeatable tracking process that feels stable enough to report on.

You start by building a useful prompt database, because prompts are the questions that trigger AI answers. Then you measure coverage, position, share of voice, citations, referral traffic, and softer behavior cues, such as self-reported wins. Together, these metrics help you understand whether your brand is becoming more visible where customers ask AI platforms for recommendations.

Looking at Prompt Protocols

In traditional SEO, you track keywords in search engines. In AI SEO, you track prompts in AI platforms. Prompts are how you trigger AI answers and citations, so the quality of your AI SEO tracking starts and ends with the prompts you choose. A well-built prompt database reflects the kinds of questions real customers ask when they research, compare, and evaluate solutions. Before you start collecting prompts, however, it helps to understand the intent behind them.

Working with prompts and intent

Not every prompt is equally useful for AI visibility tracking. Some prompts are primarily informational, meaning the user is looking for education or background information. Others are commercial, meaning the user is evaluating options, comparing solutions, or moving toward a purchase decision.

The wording of a prompt does not determine its intent. A prompt that starts with *what* or *how* can still be highly commercial. For example, "What are the best CRMs for small businesses?" is really a request for recommendations, not general education.

REMEMBER

For AI visibility tracking, commercial prompts are usually the most valuable because they create opportunities for AI systems to mention, compare, and recommend brands. Informational prompts can still be useful for content planning and topic research, but they are typically weaker indicators of brand visibility.

As you build your prompt database, assign each prompt an intent label, such as Informational or Commercial. Later in this section, you also organize prompts into tracking groups, such as Branded and Nonbranded Commercial prompts. Intent describes the searcher's goal. Prompt groups describe the prompts you want to monitor.

Developing helpful prompts for tracking

For tracking, focus on prompts that give the AI system a clear opportunity to recommend, compare, or evaluate brands. The two prompt types that create the most measurable visibility are branded prompts and nonbranded commercial prompts.

TECHNICAL STUFF

In SEO, you might see the term, prompt cluster. A *prompt cluster* is simply a group of related prompts that explore the same topic, product, service, or buyer need from different angles.

Branded prompts

Branded prompts name your brand directly, as in these examples:

- [your brand] review
- [competitor] versus [your brand]
- [your brand] alternatives

These prompts let you track how AI platforms "talk about" your brand. They help you measure visibility, sentiment, and positioning, giving you a baseline for how your products are described and how that changes over time.

Nonbranded commercial prompts

Nonbranded commercial prompts describe a problem, category, or solution without naming a specific brand. They matter most for AI SEO tracking because this is where AI platforms choose which brands to recommend.

Here are some examples:

- Who is the best plumber in Chesterfield, Missouri?
- Give me the top five affordable air fryers.
- What are the best CRMs for small businesses?

These prompts are where you track whether your brand appears, how often it's recommended, and how it compares to competitors. They usually sit in the middle or bottom of the funnel, meaning the searcher is already comparing options, prices, providers, or products and is closer to making a buying decision (see Chapter 12). In AI SEO, that entire journey can happen in a single chat window. If your brand doesn't appear in these moments, you may miss the sale.

Building an AI SEO prompt database

To understand how AI platforms recommend your brand, you need a list of real-world prompts people actually use. Having a database of these prompts makes it easy to see when your brand appears, how it's described, and where you might be missing out.

Start by picking one product, service, or category you want to track. As an example, use the category "SEO content optimization software." Then create a simple nonbranded prompt seed that describes it, such as "SEO content optimization tool."

A *prompt seed* is a starting prompt that you will reuse and expand, or grow, for different tests.

Next, convert this seed into natural language prompts that a human might use in an AI chat. You can brainstorm these by hand, but it's easier if you follow a consistent process.

To begin, set up a Google Sheet or an Excel file to store your prompts. Use the following columns in your prompt database:

- **Brand:** The brand you will track
- **Product:** The exact product or service you will track
- **Prompt:** The exact prompt text you will run
- **Prompt Source:** Where the prompt came from, such as Google Search Console, customer interviews, or synthetic prompts (where you ask AI to create a prompt for you)
- **Category:** A label to group similar prompts, such as Local, SaaS, or Ecommerce
- **Stage:** The stage of the buyer's journey, such as Solution Aware, Product Aware, or Most Aware, shown in these examples:
  - *Solution Aware example:* "What are the best SEO content-optimization tools for agencies?"
  - *Product Aware example:* "Rankability versus Surfer SEO, what is best for agencies?"
  - *Most Aware example:* "Does Rankability have a free trial?"
- **Intent:** A broad label, such as Informational or Commercial
- **Status:** Active, Paused, or Retired
- **Start Date:** The date you began tracking this prompt
- **Owner:** The person responsible for running and reporting on this prompt
- **Priority:** High, Medium, or Low
- **Cadence:** How often you will run the prompt, such as Daily, Weekly, Biweekly, or Monthly
- **Country:** The target country
- **Language:** The language of the prompt
- **Location:** For local prompts, the specific city and state
- **Notes:** Any extra context or observations

TIP

Use this database as your source of truth. It keeps your tests consistent and lets you build coverage charts and trend lines, which I cover later in this chapter. The rest of this section shows you how to use Google Search Console and synthetic prompts to build a stronger list for your database.

Using Google Search Console

Google Search Console is a free tool every site should use because it shows the real queries people use to find your site in Google. It helps you see impressions, clicks, average positions, and the exact language searchers already use before they reach you. *Note:* Earlier in this chapter, I use the term *prompts* when discussing AI visibility. Here, I use *queries* because that's the term Google Search Console uses for searches performed in Google Search.

TIP

After you have Google Search Console set up, choose Performance ➪ Search Results. Click Add filter, choose Query, and select a custom regular expression (regex) filter. These patterns use Google's supported regex syntax. Test them on a small date range first so you can confirm the filter is finding commercial queries, not pulling in a messy list of unrelated searches.

Step 1: Find question-based commercial queries.

First, look for question-based queries with commercial intent. These help you find prompts that sound conversational but still point toward a buying decision.

You can use patterns like these:

Local

```
^(what|which|best|top|how|should)\b.*(service|company|near me|pricing|cost|
affordable|review|comparison)
```

SaaS

```
^(what|which|best|top|how|should)\b.*(software|tool|platform|pricing|cost|
review|comparison|alternative|vs)
```

E-commerce

```
^(what|which|best|top|how|should)\b.*(buy|price|deal|cheap|affordable|review
|alternative)
```

Review the results and add relevant commercial queries to your prompt database. Skip obvious research-only queries that don't involve picking a provider or product.

Step 2: Find long-tail commercial queries.

Next, look for long-tail commercial queries. These often come from users who type full sentences, which is closer to how they interact with AI chat.

Local

^\S+(?:\s+\S+){5,}.*(service|company|near me|pricing|cost|affordable|review)

SaaS

^\S+(?:\s+\S+){5,}.*(software|tool|platform|pricing|cost|review|comparison|alternative|vs)

E-commerce

^\S+(?:\s+\S+){5,}.*(buy|price|deal|cheap|affordable|review|alternative|best)

This pattern looks for queries with at least six words that also contain a commercial term. You can increase the number in `{5,}` to focus on even longer queries.

Add any strong commercial queries from this list to your database as well. You're building a set of prompts that already prove there's demand in traditional search.

Creating synthetic prompts

To further fill out your database, use AI platforms themselves to expand your list with synthetic prompts. Synthetic prompts are AI-generated prompt ideas. They don't come directly from your analytics or customer data, but they resemble how real users might ask questions in an AI chat.

TIP

Pick an AI platform such as ChatGPT, Gemini, or Claude, and use a simple template like this one:

> Create ten synthetic prompts that use natural language and are likely to be used in AI platforms for this seed: "[SEED]".

Replace [SEED] with what you want the AI platform to create a prompt for. For example:

> Create ten synthetic prompts that use natural language and are likely to be used in AI platforms for this seed: "SEO content optimization tools".

The AI generates a list of prompts that feel conversational. Review them, remove anything that feels unrealistic or too generic, and add the good ones to your database with a prompt source of "Synthetic."

Repeat this process for each of your core products and services.

REMEMBER

Using Google Search Console plus synthetic prompts should give you at least 25 to 50 strong prompts to start with. Most should be nonbranded commercial prompts, with branded prompts added separately as baseline checks.

Measuring Metrics: Coverage, Position, and Share of Voice

Once you have a stable prompt list (see "Looking at Prompt Protocols," earlier in this chapter), you can start measuring how often and how strongly AI platforms recommend your brand, using the three core visibility metrics: coverage, position, and share of voice (SoV).

These metrics mirror traditional SEO ideas, but they use prompts and AI answers rather than keywords and search result pages.

REMEMBER

A key nuance in AI SEO tracking is that the answer itself is the primary object of analysis. Citations still matter, and you will track them (see the upcoming section, "How to track citations"), but the first question is always this: "What does the AI recommend in its answer?"

Coverage

Coverage, a simple yes-or-no metric, tells you whether your brand is showing up. For every prompt you test on an AI platform, ask this question: Is my brand present in the AI answer? The answer gives you a clear picture of where your brand is visible and where it's missing.

In your prompt database, add a Brand Present column and record each prompt check:

- Record 1 if your brand appears.
- Record 0 if it doesn't appear.

TECHNICAL STUFF

You can turn these checks into a coverage rate:

> Coverage rate (%) = (Number of Answers That Mention Your Brand ÷ Total Number of Answers Checked) × 100

For reliable coverage data, you need a decent sample size. That means:

- Running multiple commercial prompts from your database
- Testing the prompts across multiple AI platforms
- Repeating checks regularly, such as weekly

TIP

Some of the major AI platforms worth considering for tracking include Google AI Mode, Google AI Overviews, Gemini, ChatGPT, Perplexity, Claude, Grok, Microsoft Copilot, and DeepSeek.

You don't need to track all of these AI platforms to start. Pick at least three that matter most for your audience and industry. That gives you a clear picture of your brand's overall coverage without overwhelming your reporting process.

Position

Coverage tells you whether your brand shows up. Position tells you how visible that recommendation is. AI answers can vary from run to run, so treat position as a trend to measure over time, not as a permanent ranking.

REMEMBER

To measure position, ask this question for each answer where your brand appears: Where does my brand appear relative to competitors?

There's a big difference between being the first recommendation and being buried in slot seven.

In many cases, AI answers follow a list-style format with numbered or bulleted options. When that happens, you can:

- Count the options.
- Assign your brand a position such as 1, 2, 3, and so on.
- Note how many competitors appear in the same answer.

These are a few examples:

- **Prompt**: What are the best SEO content-optimization tools for agencies?
- **AI answer**: A list of six tools
- **Your brand**: Appears as number 3

In your prompt database, you record these entries:

- **Coverage:** 1
- **Position:** 3
- **Total brands in answer:** 6

Sometimes, the answer doesn't use a clean numbered list. In those cases, read the answer and count brand mentions in order. The first distinct brand you see is position 1, the second is position 2, and so on.

If your brand appears multiple times in the same answer, you still record the position of the first mention because that's the earliest point where a user might reasonably notice you.

Share of voice

Share of voice (SoV) combines coverage and position into a single visibility metric. The idea is to answer this simple question: Of all the brands that show up for these prompts, how much "space" do we own?

There are many ways to calculate SoV. For a practical AI SEO version, you can use a simple scoring model that rewards both coverage and stronger positions.

One straightforward approach works like this: For each answer where brands are listed, give each position a score, as in these examples:

- Position 1 = 1.0
- Position 2 = 0.8
- Position 3 = 0.6
- Position 4 = 0.4
- Position 5 or lower = 0.2

Then execute these actions:

- » For each prompt and platform combo, record your brand's score (or 0 if you don't appear).
- » Add up your scores across all prompts and platforms.
- » Add up the scores for all brands (including competitors) across the same prompts and platforms.

Calculate:

AI SoV (%) = (your total score ÷ total score for all brands) × 100

The result is one simple number you can track over time in a chart. When your AI SoV increases, it means that, across your prompt set and platforms, your brand is appearing in more answers (better coverage), you're moving into stronger positions, or both.

TIP

The AI SoV score makes SoV a useful headline metric for stakeholders. It rolls up the details into a trend line while still letting you drill down later into individual prompts and answers to see what has changed.

Noting Citation Growth and Traditional Rankings

Tracking AI answers is the priority, but citations still play a critical role in how those answers are formed. Whenever an AI system uses retrieval, it leans on external sources to shape its response. Those sources become your citations.

There are three main reasons to track citations.

How citations influence AI answers

When you ask an AI platform a question, one of two things usually happens:

- » **If the answer is simple and well covered in its training data, the model can respond without retrieval.** In those cases, you often don't see citations. For example, the query "What is the sun?" is so basic that the model can answer from its internal knowledge.

- **If the query is more current, commercial, or open-ended, the AI often calls external sources to improve accuracy.** The query "What are the best SEO tools right now?" usually triggers retrieval, and you often see citations under the answer if the surface chooses to show them.

The citations gathered through retrieval are the sources the AI system used to improve its answer and reduce the risk that it invents false information, also known as hallucination. The key point is that whenever retrieval is involved, you have some ability to influence the answer by becoming one of those cited sources.

Many major AI systems lean on public search engines or their own web indexes as a part of retrieval, as in these examples:

- Google AI experiences can draw from Google Search results and related indexes.
- Microsoft-backed systems often rely on Bing and other Microsoft properties.
- Other AI systems combine search application programming interfaces (APIs), their own crawlers, and third-party providers for web results.

The exact setups change over time, but the pattern stays the same. If you rank well in traditional search and appear on trusted third-party sites, you increase your odds of being used as a retrieval source. That, in turn, raises your chances of being surfaced or supported in AI answers.

How citations send referral traffic

While the main reason to care about citations is their influence on AI answers, they can also send referral traffic.

AI platforms usually provide a link to at least some of their sources beneath the answer. Though the total number of visitors is usually small compared to organic search, these clicks come from highly motivated users. They are already deep in research mode and are choosing to leave the AI platform to learn more.

Even if this traffic is a small percentage of your overall visits, it's worth measuring, especially if you see high engagement or conversion rates from these referrals.

How to track citations

You can track citations using the same basic structure you use for AI answers: coverage and position.

Citation coverage

For each prompt and platform, add citation fields to your database and ask these two questions:

Is our website used for retrieval?

Record yes or no in a Website Cited column.

In a perfect world, your own website would appear frequently as a source. In practice, AI systems rarely rely on a single site. Your realistic goal is to become one of the recurring sources that show up across multiple prompts and platforms.

Is our brand present on third-party retrieval sources?

Record yes or no in a Brand on Third-Party Source column. Many AI answers are shaped by consensus. It isn't enough for your own site to say you are the best. The AI looks across multiple domains to see which brands are mentioned repeatedly and in what context.

TIP

Track brand coverage on the most common retrieval sources for your industry, such as review sites, directories, comparison posts, and niche publications.

If you notice that competitors are heavily represented on these sources and you aren't, you have a clear list of outreach and content opportunities. You can turn those gaps into a prospect list for link building, public relations, and content placements that support both AI SEO and traditional SEO. I cover this process in Chapter 7.

Citation position

As with AI answers, position matters for citations. It's better to be the first or second source listed than to sit near the bottom of a long list.

TIP

When you review an AI answer, read the citations under it and record where your domain appears.

For each prompt and platform, note these details:

- Whether your site is cited
- Its position in the citation list (for example, first, third, or fifth)
- Any key third-party sites that mention your brand

Over time, you can summarize your citation tracking with these metrics:

- Citation coverage rate for your own site
- Citation coverage rate for key third-party domains that feature your brand
- Average citation position across prompts and platforms

REMEMBER

This list gives you a clear view of how often you're part of the evidence stack, meaning the set of sources AI systems use to support their answers. It also shows whether your traditional SEO and digital PR work are influencing AI SEO, not just traditional rankings.

Spotting Patterns via Self-Reported Wins and Soft Signals

Tracking used to feel simpler. You watched keyword rankings, organic traffic, and the number of queries you ranked for. AI SEO changed that. Traffic alone no longer tells the full story, because lots of influence now happens inside chat windows you cannot see.

You can still track referral traffic from AI answers, but that only captures the small group of people who click. Many users read the answer, remember the brand, and come back later by way of a different path. That's where self-reported wins and soft signals come in:

- **Self-reported wins** are direct comments from customers or prospects saying they found you through an AI platform. For example, a lead might write, "ChatGPT recommended you" in a form field.
- **Soft signals** are behavior clues that suggest AI visibility is helping, even when you can't prove the full path. For example, branded searches may rise after your brand starts appearing more often in AI answers.

REMEMBER

Think of this main section as your pattern-spotting layer. You will use what customers tell you, plus a few behavior clues, to connect the dots that hard numbers miss. The next few sections walk you through these patterns.

Understanding journey compression

In AI chat, the searcher can move from "I have a problem" to "I picked a vendor" in a single conversation. This shortcut is called *journey compression*. The searcher asks for options, reads comparisons, asks follow-up questions, and then either clicks once or searches your brand name directly.

Traditional analytics often give credit to the last touch, such as direct traffic, branded search, or email. To catch journey compression from AI SEO, you can:

- **Add a simple self-reported field on forms.** Examples are "How did you first hear about us?" or keep "AI SEO" or "AI platform" as a visible option.
- **Listen for AI mentions on sales calls and support tickets.** This is a soft signal. For example, ask, "Did any AI platforms help you research options?" when it feels natural.
- **Tag these notes in your CRM (customer relationship management system) so you can review them every quarter.** For example, create tags such as AI Mention, ChatGPT, Perplexity, or Copilot.

Over time, you'll start to see patterns, such as "Perplexity plus YouTube" or "ChatGPT then Google then our blog."

Watching branded search with context

Branded search matters. When more people search for your brand name, it usually means awareness is growing. In an AI SEO world, branded search often reflects invisible AI influence. Someone sees you in an AI answer, forgets to click, and then later types your brand name into Google or goes straight to your site.

REMEMBER

A *branded search* is a search query that includes your brand name. A branded prompt is an AI prompt that includes your brand name. The key difference is that searches are entered into search engines, while prompts are entered into AI systems.

TIP

You can track branded search most accurately in Google Search Console and Bing Webmaster Tools. Watch queries that contain your brand name, core product names, and common misspellings.

Treat branded search as a supporting signal, not a single source of truth. When you see a lift in branded search at the same time your SoV improves in AI answers, you can reasonably suspect a connection.

Factoring in the recency effect

Humans tend to remember what they saw or heard most recently. Many AI systems also change how they behave as they pick up fresh content and new retrieval signals from the web.

That recency effect shows up in a couple of ways:

- **Recognition:** Prospects mention "I just saw you in ChatGPT" or "Perplexity recommended you" more often immediately after you ship a big campaign or land a new roundup mention.
- **Increased visibility:** You notice a short-term bump in AI coverage or citations after a major launch, a conference, or a strong PR win.

Log these events in the same change log you created for your evidence library in Chapter 3. Then compare the dates of those events with your AI tracking runs in your prompt database. You'll start to see which activities reliably produce fresh AI mentions, citation gains, or both, and which ones barely move the needle.

Looking for category legitimacy

Category legitimacy answers this simple question: Do AI systems and humans treat you as a credible option in your space?

You can look for these elements:

- **Inclusion:** Your brand appears in "top X" or "best tools for Y" style answers and listicles.
- **Association:** Your brand appears alongside established category leaders, not just in narrow or long-tail questions.
- **Recognition:** Buyers repeat language from AI answers, such as "I saw you listed as an alternative to [big competitor]."

TIP

Maintain a shortlist of prompts that reflect your ideal category, such as "best [category] tools for agencies" or "top [category] providers for small business." Track how often you appear, which competitors surround you, and whether your position improves over time. The more consistently you appear in these category-level conversations, the stronger your category legitimacy becomes.

IN THIS CHAPTER

» Estimating AI SEO traffic inside Google Analytics

» Capturing screenshots and prompts in a reusable evidence library

» Building a simple Looker Studio dashboard for AI SEO

» Using change logs and quick checks to keep your numbers honest

Chapter 6

Setting Up Your AI SEO Dashboard

If you're taking AI SEO seriously, you need proof that your work is paying off. Screenshots, scattered exports, and "a gut feeling" don't help when your boss or client asks, "What did we get from this?" A basic AI SEO dashboard gives you a single place to see your coverage, traffic, and key trends without digging through ten different tools.

In this chapter, I show you how to connect your AI SEO work to Google Analytics (GA) so you can estimate AI-driven traffic. GA is the focus here because it is free, widely used, and connects cleanly with Google Search Console and Looker Studio. I also show you how to set up and maintain an evidence library, build a starter Looker Studio dashboard, and use change logs and sanity checks so you can trust the numbers before you make decisions or share results.

For the purposes of this chapter, you need access to a Google account, a Google Analytics 4 (GA4 is Google's current analytics platform for measuring website traffic, user behavior, and conversions) property, a Google Search Console property, and Looker Studio.

Tracking AI Traffic with Google Analytics

AI platforms don't send traffic with a neat label called AI SEO. In GA4, visits from platforms such as ChatGPT or Perplexity usually appear as referral traffic from domains such as `chatgpt.com` or perplexity.ai. Some platforms do not pass referral data, so GA4 only shows part of AI-influenced traffic. The setup in this section gives you a useful estimate, not a complete count of every AI-influenced visit.

In this section, you set up GA4 so it groups known AI chatbot referrals under a clear AI channel. That gives you a starting point for estimating AI-influenced traffic on your site.

Log in to the right Google account

Before touching GA4, make sure you're signed in to the Google account that has access to these two properties:

- Google Analytics 4
- Google Search Console

If you use the wrong account, you won't see your GA4 or Search Console data, and your Looker Studio report will be empty later.

Create an AI channel group in GA4

This section shows you how to create a custom channel group that catches traffic from the main AI chat platforms. Think of a channel as one bucket of traffic and a channel group as the system that decides which bucket each visit goes into. Follow these steps to set up a custom channel group:

1. **Open GA4, then click Admin.**
2. **In Admin, go to Data display and click Channel groups.**
3. **Click Create new channel group.**
4. **Name the group something simple, such as AI.**
5. **Inside this group, add a new channel and enter the following settings:**
   - *Channel name:* AI Chatbots
   - *Dimension:* Session source
   - *Match type:* Matches regex

6. **In the Value field, paste this regular expression:**

```
^(?:www\.)?(?:chatgpt\.com|chat\.openai\.com|claude\.
  ai|perplexity\.ai|gemini\.google\.com|bard\.google\.
  com|copilot\.microsoft\.com|poe\.com|you\.com|character\.
  ai|meta\.ai|chat\.mistral\.ai|huggingface\.co|replika\.
  ai|chat\.deepseek\.com|grok\.com|openrouter\.ai|together\.
  ai|cohere\.com|groq\.com|janitor\.ai|crushon\.ai|cursor\.
  sh|codeium\.com|ai\.google\.dev|spicychat\.ai|talkie-
  ai\.com)$
```

   This pattern groups referrals from common AI platforms into your newly created AI Chatbots channel so you can see their traffic at a glance. GA4 uses Session source, meaning the domain a visitor came from, to classify traffic. Review your reports periodically and update your list of sources as new AI platforms appear. ***Note:*** In this setup, the AI Chatbots label refers to visits from AI platforms that pass a referrer domain into GA4.

7. **Save the channel.**

   Click Save.

8. **Prioritize your AI group.**

   On the Channel groups screen, drag your AI group toward the top of the list so GA4 evaluates it before other rules.

9. **Save the group.**

   Click Apply, and then click Save group.

Checkpoint: In GA4, choose Reports ⇨ Acquisition ⇨ User acquisition and look for the Session default channel group dimension. After GA4 detects traffic from the sources you defined, you should see AI Chatbots appear as one of the channels.

Understand what this AI channel captures

The custom channel group doesn't capture every AI-influenced visit. It focuses on sessions where someone clicked a link inside an AI chatbot and that platform passed its domain as the referrer.

You're not measuring every AI-influenced visit here. You're measuring a clean subset that still tells an important story:

- » Which pages receive AI chatbot traffic
- » Which platforms send it
- » How those visitors behave compared to other channels

That's enough to start, especially when you combine it with your evidence library and Looker Studio dashboard, discussed later in this chapter.

Give the AI channel time to fill in

GA4 will group new sessions only after you save the channel group. It doesn't rewrite old data. Plan to:

- » Wait at least a week before drawing conclusions.
- » Use a 28-day window or longer when you review AI channel performance.
- » Compare the AI Chatbots channel against GA4's built-in default channels, such as Organic Search and Direct, in your acquisition reports.

After the AI channel has been running for a few weeks, you'll have a baseline you can reference whenever you publish new AI SEO optimizations.

Building an Evidence Library

AI traffic numbers are useful, but they don't tell the whole story. Chapter 3 introduces the basic idea of an evidence library. This section gives you the fuller setup: a reusable archive that proves when AI systems mention your brand, cite your content, and send visitors to your site.

Think of this as a simple, shared archive of these items:

- » AI answers where your brand appears
- » Screenshots that show your citations and placements
- » Prompts you used to trigger those answers
- » Notes on what has changed over time

Later, you can plug this evidence sheet into Looker Studio using Google Sheets so your screenshots and logs are tied to charts.

Create a simple folder and sheet

Using a shared workspace that your team already uses, such as Google Drive, create these two items:

- **Folder:** Name it something like AI SEO Evidence Library.
- **Google Sheet:** Inside that newly named folder, create a Google Sheet named AI SEO Tracking Sheet.

In the Google Sheet, add columns such as these:

- Date Captured
- AI Platform (ChatGPT, Gemini, Perplexity, and so on)
- Prompt Used
- Our Brand Present? (Yes/No)
- Our URL Cited? (Yes/No)
- Answer Position (for example, list item 3, first citation, or sidebar)
- Screenshot URL (a sharing link to the image stored in your Google Drive folder)
- Notes

You'll connect this sheet to Looker Studio later to calculate your brand's citation rate and visualize trends.

Capture answers on a regular cadence

Establishing a consistent process for tracking AI answers gives you a clear view of how your brand shows up over time. Anchor prompts are the priority prompts you test repeatedly. By capturing responses to the same prompts on a regular basis, you can move beyond one-off checks and start building a reliable data log.

Pick a short list of anchor prompts you care about. Anchor prompts are the foundational prompts you most want AI systems and searchers to associate with your brand, products, services, or expertise. Examples include these:

- "best [your category] tools"
- "[your brand] review"
- "[your core problem] for [ideal customer]"

Once a week, run these prompts in your target AI platforms and capture the results by following these steps:

1. **Take a screenshot that clearly shows the whole answer and any citations.**
2. **Upload the screenshot to your evidence library folder.**
3. **Paste the link into your Google Sheet.**
4. **Log whether the answer links to your site.**

Over time, this log becomes a time series of what AI platforms show for your priority prompts.

In the sheet, use the name of the AI platform, such as ChatGPT or Perplexity, as the label for each entry.

Use logs when you ship changes

Anytime you ship a meaningful AI SEO change, such as:

- » Publishing a new fact hub page
- » Updating schema for your company or product
- » Earning a prominent citation from another trusted site

Log a quick entry in your sheet in a Notes column or a separate Change Log tab. (See the later section, "Monitoring Change Logs and Sanity Checks.") Include these items:

- » The date
- » A description of the change
- » The URLs affected

REMEMBER

Those notes can help when you look back at your Looker Studio dashboard and notice a jump in citations or AI traffic. You can then connect improvements to specific actions instead of guessing.

Getting Looker Studio Started

To open Looker Studio, go to `lookerstudio.google.com` and sign in with the same Google account that has access to your GA4 and Search Console properties.

After your GA4 channel group and evidence library are in place (see the previous sections), you can pull everything into a single Looker Studio report. This report becomes your AI SEO Visibility dashboard, as shown in Figure 6-1.

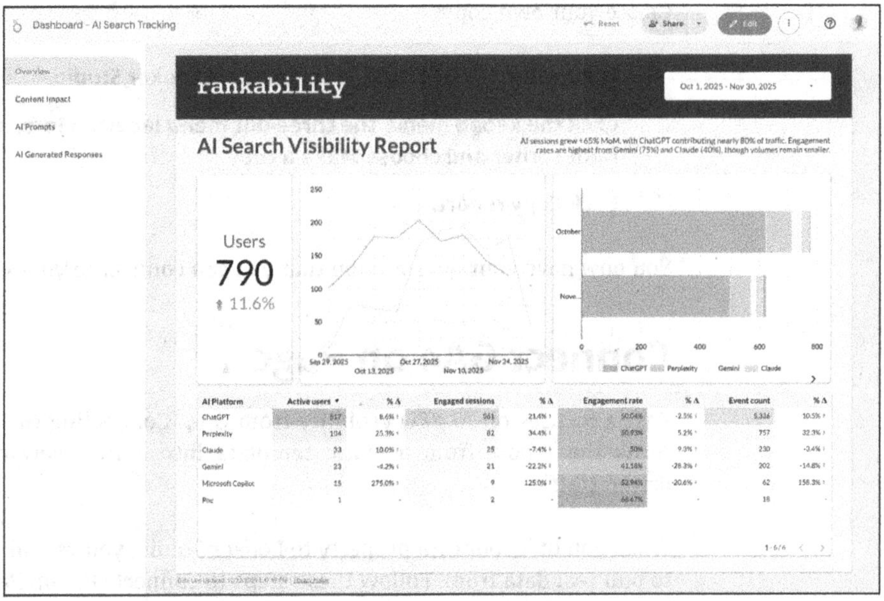

FIGURE 6-1: A basic AI SEO-Tracking dashboard built in Looker Studio, showing estimated AI-driven users, trends over time, and traffic by AI platform.

Source: Screenshot of a Looker Studio dashboard, used under fair use for educational commentary.

The goal isn't perfection. You want a simple report that answers questions such as these:

- » Which AI platforms send traffic?
- » Which pages receive that traffic?
- » What types of queries feel more like prompts?
- » How often do AI answers link back to you?

The next six sections walk you through getting a Looker Studio dashboard up and running.

Copy the AI SEO Tracking template

At this point, you have the raw data. The next step is turning that data into charts and dashboards that are easier to review and share. Rather than building a report from scratch, start with a prebuilt Looker Studio template.

REMEMBER

Here you use the Looker Studio report template, not the AI SEO Tracking Sheet you created earlier. The tracking sheet stores your evidence, while the Looker Studio template turns GA4, Search Console, and sheet data into charts.

Create your own copy:

1. **Open your AI SEO Tracking template in Looker Studio.**
2. **Click the kebab menu, the three-dot menu labeled More, in the upper-right corner and choose Make a copy.**
3. **Click Copy report.**

You now have your own version that you can connect to your data sources.

Connect GA4 on Page 1

Page 1 focuses on AI SEO visibility from GA4. Connecting GA4 on Page 1 is what turns the report from a static template into a live view of your actual AI-driven traffic.

When you link your GA4 property to Looker Studio, you're telling the report where to pull real data from. Follow these steps to connect GA4 on Page 1:

1. **On Page 1, click Add data from the toolbar, and then select your Google Analytics 4 property.**
2. **After the GA4 property is connected, a Resource menu appears on the top bar. If you don't see it, refresh the page.**
3. **Choose Resource ⇨ Manage added data sources and confirm that your GA4 property is listed.**

REMEMBER

At this point, you're checking that Looker Studio can see your GA4 property. If the Resource menu is visible and your GA4 property appears under Manage added data sources, the report is connected to the right data source.

Add an AI platform field

On Page 1 of your Looker Studio report, you want to see not only AI Chatbots as a channel, but also which AI platforms are sending visitors. Create a calculated field that groups the referral sources.

The calculated field is named AI Platform because that short label is easy to scan in a dashboard. In plain-language explanations, think of each value as the AI platform that sent the referral.

1. **In the top menu bar, choose Resource ⇨ Manage added data sources, and then click Edit for your GA4 source.**
2. **Click Add a field and name it AI Platform.**
3. **Paste the formula at `www.dummies.com/go/aiseofd` into the formula box.**
4. **Save the field and verify that AI Platform appears as a dimension you can use in charts.**
5. **On Page 1, confirm that charts now show AI chatbots traffic and can be broken down by AI Platform.**

Review AI landing pages on Page 2

Page 2 focuses on the pages that receive AI-driven traffic. While Page 1 shows which AI platforms send visitors, Page 2 helps you see where those visitors land and which content attracts the most AI referrals.

After connecting your GA4 property on Page 1, Page 2 should populate automatically. Use it to identify:

- » Top landing pages from AI Chatbots traffic
- » Pages gaining the most AI-driven sessions
- » Content that appears to attract citations, recommendations, or referrals from AI systems

Checkpoint: Page 2 should display landing-page performance metrics based on the GA4 data source you connected earlier.

Connect the Search Console and create prompt buckets

Page 3 shows how people search in Google before AI answers appear, especially long queries that look more like prompts. To connect Google Search Console and create prompt buckets (see Chapter 5), follow these steps:

1. **Go to Page 3 in your report.**
2. **Choose Resource ⇨ Manage added data sources, and then add your Search Console site.**
3. **With Search Console selected, click Add a field in the data panel.**
4. **Name it AI Prompt Bucket (see Figure 6-2) and paste this formula:**

```
CASE
  WHEN REGEXP_MATCH(Query, ".*(buy|purchase|for sale|order|
  pricing|cost|deal).*")
       AND REGEXP_MATCH(Query, "^(?:\\S+\\s+){9,}\\S+$")
  THEN "Extreme Long-Tail Commercial"

  WHEN REGEXP_MATCH(Query, "^(?:\\S+\\s+){9,}\\S+$")
       AND REGEXP_MATCH(Query, "^(how|what|why|who|where|
  when|best way to|guide|steps to|tutorial|explain|
  examples).*")
  THEN "Extreme Long-Tail Informational"

  WHEN REGEXP_MATCH(Query, "^(give me|show me|help me|
  explain|list|step by step).*")
  THEN "Instructional Prompt"

  ELSE "Other"
END
```

   This formula is just a starting point. You can adjust the word-count threshold or keyword patterns to better fit your niche.

5. **Save the field and confirm that AI Prompt Bucket appears in your field list.**

You can now build charts that show how much of your Google traffic comes from long, prompt-like queries and whether they lean toward commercial or informational use.

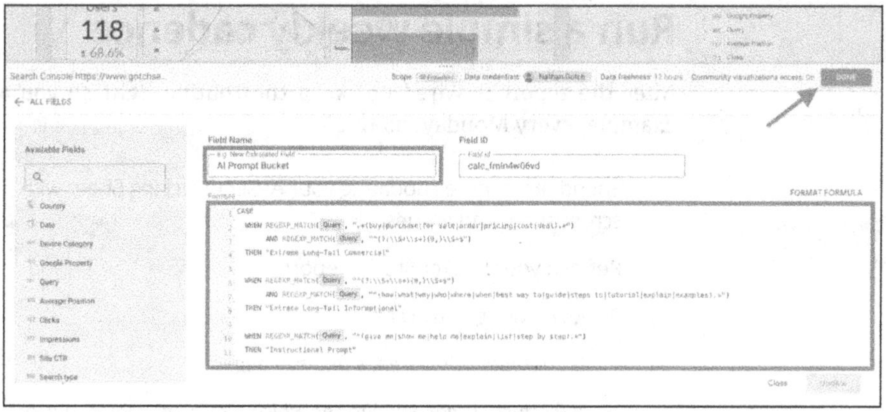

FIGURE 6-2: Creating the AI Prompt Bucket calculated field in Looker Studio allows your queries to be grouped into readable categories instead of forcing you to wrangle a messy list of individual prompts.

Source: Screenshot of Looker Studio, used under fair use for educational commentary.

Connect your evidence library and calculate the citation rate

Page 4 ties your evidence library to your dashboard and shows what percentage of AI answers link back to your site. To connect your evidence library and create a citation rate, follow these steps:

1. **Choose Resource ⇨ Manage added data sources, add a Google Sheets source, and select your AI SEO Tracking Sheet.**
2. **For each scorecard or chart on Page 4, click the pencil icon and confirm that the data source is your sheet.**
3. **Add a new calculated field named Citation Rate and paste this formula into the formula box:**

```
IF(
  SUM(CASE WHEN UPPER('Our URL cited?') IN ("YES","NO")
   THEN 1 ELSE 0 END) = 0,
  0,
  SUM(CASE WHEN UPPER('Our URL cited?') = "YES" THEN 1
   ELSE 0 END) /
  SUM(CASE WHEN UPPER('Our URL cited?') IN ("YES","NO")
   THEN 1 ELSE 0 END)
)
```

4. **Adjust the field name to match the exact column header in your sheet.**

   This formula calculates the percentage of AI answers in your evidence log that link to your site out of all answers where you marked Yes or No.

Checkpoint: Page 4 should now show Citation Rate % and other metrics fed from your evidence sheet.

Run a simple weekly cadence

After the report is wired up, keep the routine light so you actually use it. For example, every Monday, do this:

1. Spend ten minutes updating your AI SEO Tracking Sheet with new screenshots and entries.
2. Refresh your Looker Studio report.
3. Review these three areas:
   - *AI Chatbots traffic trends and top pages*
   - *AI Platform breakdown to see which platforms matter most*
   - *Citation Rate and any changes in prompt buckets*

Capture one or two notes and add them to a change log (see the next section). That's enough to spot patterns without turning AI SEO tracking into a full-time job.

Monitoring Change Logs and Sanity Checks

Data is useful only if you can trust it. Maintaining a change log and conducting a few quick checks can help you avoid chasing phantom wins or losses.

Keep a simple change log

A change log is a running list of meaningful changes that can influence AI visibility. You can keep the log in one of these two places:

- On a tab inside your AI SEO Tracking Sheet
- In a separate document linked from your report

Include columns such as these:

- Date
- Type of Change (content, schema, links, product, or algorithm news, for example)
- Short Description
- URLs Affected
- Person Responsible

Whenever you ship a notable change, log it. This turns your dashboard into a story, as in these examples:

- "Our citation rate jumped the week we shipped this fact hub."
- AI chatbot traffic dropped after we changed our navigation and internal links.

Without this information, you're stuck guessing why the traffic, citations, and visibility lines go up and down.

Run sanity checks before you report results

Before you share screenshots with a client or leader, do a quick, 5-minute sanity check:

- **Channel totals versus overall traffic:** Make sure the sum of major channels looks reasonable compared to your total users.
- **Time range:** Confirm that the date range is correct and matches your narrative.
- **Spikes and drops:** Look for odd, one-day spikes. Check to see whether they're caused by bot traffic, internal testing, or a tracking issue.
- **Data freshness:** Confirm that GA4, Search Console, and your Google Sheet have recent data.

If something looks off, investigate before you either claim a win or panic about a drop.

Use your dashboard to guide, not to obsess

Your AI SEO dashboard is a decision-support tool. Use it to:

- Confirm that your AI SEO projects are moving the right numbers.
- Prioritize which pages and prompts need work.
- Show progress to collaborators and stakeholders.

You don't need perfect attribution. You need consistent tracking, simple logs, and a few honest checks so that you can make better decisions every week.

IN THIS CHAPTER

» Noting that AI winners don't always mean Google winners

» Finding citation gaps that reveal the evidence AI systems trust

» Discovering why AI picks certain sources

» Looking at market share

Chapter 7

Using Competitive Intelligence for AI SEO

Competitive intelligence used to mean checking to see who outranked you in Google and reverse-engineering their content and links to understand why they were ranking you.

In an AI SEO world, that's not enough. A competitor can sit below you in traditional search and still be the first brand recommended when someone asks an AI platform for the best option in your category.

So the competitive question changes to this: Who do AI systems recommend, and what evidence do they use to justify that recommendation?

In this chapter, I show how to use the measurement system discussed in Chapter 5 but aim it at competitors. You'll track these elements:

- **Share of voice (SoV):** Who shows up most often and where they appear in the answer

- **Citations:** Which sites and pages AI systems treat as credible evidence
- **Entities:** Why some brands are easier for machines to understand and trust

Seeing Why AI Winners Aren't Always Google Winners

Google rankings still matter, but AI answers often behave more like a recommendation engine. To understand the difference, it helps to look at how AI systems actually choose what to show:

- AI platforms may summarize multiple sources into a single list.
- AI platforms may lean on review sites, directories, and best-of lists even when those sources don't rank first for you.
- AI platforms may reward brands with clear positioning and strong third-party proof, even if their SEO is only average.

Rather than ask "Who ranks?," start with these:

- Who appears?
- Who appears early?
- Who gets supported by citations?
- Which sources keep showing up across prompts and AI platforms?

That's competitive intelligence for AI SEO.

Benchmarking competitors with share of voice

You don't need a new system for competitor tracking. You'll reuse the same prompt database and scoring model from Chapter 5 and then layer in competitor labels.

Pick a realistic competitor set

Start by identifying five to ten brands you can track consistently. If you start with too many, the process becomes hard to manage. If you start with too few, you miss important context. In your prompt database, use three categories to organize competitors:

- **Direct competitors:** Same-buyer decision set
- **Adjacent competitors:** Related tools that AI might still recommend
- **Category leaders:** The names that shape the category narrative

Track the competitors in one simple sheet. Create columns for these items:

- **Brand:** Name of competitor
- **Type:** Direct, Adjacent, or Category Leader, for example
- **Website:** The associated URL for easy reference
- **Category:** Description of what the competitor does

Extend your existing prompt database

Your Chapter 5 prompt database tracks your own visibility. In this chapter, you extend that same database so it can compare your brand against competitors. Keep the original commercial prompts because they reveal who appears for the buyer intents you already care about. Then add competitor-branded prompts and nonbranded commercial prompts to expose gaps you would miss if you only tracked your own brand:

- **Competitor-branded prompts (a small set):** Some examples are "[Competitor] review," "[Competitor] versus [Your Brand]," and "Alternatives to [Competitor]."
- **Nonbranded commercial prompts (neutral category prompts):** Examples are "Best [category] tools for [segment]" and "Best [category] providers in [location]."

Keep it tight. You're not trying to map the whole Internet, you're simply building a repeatable benchmark.

Record competitor presence the same way every time

On your tracking sheet, add columns like these: Prompt, AI platform, Brand, Present? (1/0), Position (1, 2, 3 . . . or None), and Notes (optional).

WARNING

AI answers can change. The same prompt may produce a different answer later in the same day or week. Don't overreact to one run. Track the same prompts on the same AI platforms over time so you can see patterns instead of noise.

REMEMBER

If the answer is a list, position is obvious. If it's a paragraph, position is the order of first mention.

Turn presence into share of voice

Use the same SoV scoring model from Chapter 5. In Chapter 5, the score shows your visibility. Here, the same score becomes a competitor benchmark: it shows how much answer space each brand owns across the prompts and AI platforms you track.

Break your SoV data into views, meaning smaller cuts of the data, so you can see which gaps deserve action:

- **By AI platform:** Compare visibility across interfaces and features, such as ChatGPT, Google AI Mode, Google AI Overviews, and Perplexity. Track Google AI Mode and Google AI Overviews separately when possible because they behave differently.
- **By intent stage:** Analyze performance at each stage of the buyer's journey (Solution Aware versus Product Aware versus Most Aware, for example).
- **By prompt cluster:** Track performance by query type, for example, Best Tools, Alternatives, Versus, or local prompts.

What you're looking for is a short list of gaps you can actually fix, like these:

- "We show up in alternatives prompts, but not in best-tools prompts."
- "We're visible in one AI platform and invisible in another."
- "Competitor A dominates early mentions for solution-stage prompts."

Turning AI answers into a competitor score

In this section, I show how a single AI answer becomes a competitor benchmark. Instead of relying on one screenshot or one impression, you turn each answer into numbers you can compare over time. For example, you track one prompt on one AI platform:

- **Prompt:** "Best AI SEO tools for agencies"
- **AI platform:** ChatGPT

TIP

If you want ChatGPT to retrieve current web sources, run the test with Search enabled. Otherwise, the answer may rely mostly on training data instead of fresh web retrieval.

The answer lists five tools. Your brand appears in Position 3. Competitor A is in Position 1. Competitor B is in Position 2.

Using the same scoring weights from Chapter 5 (where earlier positions earn higher scores), your visibility score for this single prompt might look like this:

- **Competitor A:** 1.0
- **Competitor B:** 0.8
- **Your brand:** 0.6
- **The remaining two competitors:** 0.4 and 0.2

Now repeat this process across 20 prompts. When you total the scores, you get a clearer benchmark than a one-time screenshot can provide. You see not just "Did we show up?" but also "How much of the category are we occupying inside answers?"

These two insights usually show up fast:

- **You might be present but still losing visibility.** If you're always in Position 4 or 5, your SoV stays weak even if you appear often.
- **One prompt cluster can carry the whole score.** If Competitor A dominates "best tools" prompts but is absent from "alternatives" prompts, you've found both their investment and your opportunity.

This is why competitive AI tracking works best when you score consistently, and break results down by prompt cluster and AI platform rather than treat all mentions as equal.

Citation Gap Analysis: Finding the Evidence That AI Systems Trust

REMEMBER

Citation patterns vary by AI platform. Perplexity may cite one domain, while Google AI Overviews may cite another. Track citation gaps by surface so you don't assume one source matters everywhere.

SoV tells you who wins. Citation gaps tell you why. (For more information on citations and tracking AI, check out Chapter 5.)

The following four sections detail how to collect citation sources, group sources, build a source matrix, and turn noted gaps into a target list you can act on.

Collect recurring citation sources

TIP

Recurring citation sources are important because they act as signals of authority and trust for AI systems and search engines when evaluating your brand or content. Record these sources in a Citation Sources tab inside the same competitive tracking sheet you created earlier in this chapter. To collect recurring citation sources, follow these steps:

1. **Pick 10 to 20 priority commercial prompts and 3 to 5 AI platforms you care about.**
2. **For each prompt, run it and record the source domains shown in citations or references in your Citation Sources tab.**
3. **Track the date, prompt, AI platform, source domain, page type, and whether your brand or a competitor appears on that source.**

TIP

After a few runs, you see the same domains repeat. List those repeating domains in a short Core Evidence Sources section at the top of your Citation Sources tab so you can find them quickly.

Group sources by type

To make recurring citations actionable, organize the sources you track into meaningful categories. Each category calls for a different next step:

- **Review platforms: Sites where users leave ratings or testimonials.** Improve these by earning more real reviews, responding to reviews, and keeping your profile complete.
- **Directories and marketplaces: Listings of companies or tools.** Improve these by claiming your listing, choosing the right category, and making your description match your official positioning.
- **Media and niche publications: Articles, blogs, or news coverage relevant to your category.** Improve these by pitching useful data, expert commentary, or original research.

- **Best of listicles and comparisons: Selected lists that rank or recommend tools or brands.** Improve these by building comparison pages, strengthening proof points, and reaching out when your brand is missing or misrepresented.
- **Brand sites: Your own site and competitors' websites.** Improve your own pages by adding clearer passages, proof, and facts that AI systems can reuse.

In other words, don't treat every source the same. A review platform needs a review program. A directory needs a complete profile. A listicle may need an editorial pitch or a stronger comparison asset. Matching the action to the source type keeps your competitive work practical.

Build a simple who's-featured-where matrix

A who's-featured-where matrix helps you see at a glance which sources mention your brand versus competitors so you can prioritize where to focus your efforts. Build the matrix in the same competitive tracking sheet, either as a new tab or as part of your Citation Sources tab. Follow these steps to create the matrix:

1. **Create rows for the sources you track.**
2. **Set up columns for your brands and for your competitors' brands.**
3. **Fill in the matrix. In each cell, use Y/N to indicate meaningful presence.**
4. **Prioritize the gaps.**

   Add a Priority column and mark each gap High, Medium, or Low. Give High priority to sources that match all three of these conditions:

   - Frequently cited by AI platforms
   - Already favorable to competitors
   - Realistic for you to influence, such as a profile you can claim, a review site you can earn reviews on, or a publication you can pitch

Turn gaps into a target list

After you identify the sources where competitors appear, but your brand does not, turn those gaps into a target list. Add these columns to your Citation Sources tab or create a new Target List tab:

- Source and URL
- Type (review site, directory, and listicle, for example)

» Priority (high, medium, low)

» Play (profile, reviews, editorial pitch, contribution)

This is where competitive intelligence becomes a roadmap. Each row tells you which source matters, why it matters, and what action to take next.

Seeing Why AI Picks Certain Sources

After you map the gaps (refer to the previous section), you can reverse-engineer the reasons AI favors certain sources so that you can take action on closing them.

Find AI-ready passages

Take advantage of what competitors have already done. For prompts where competitors beat you, follow these steps:

1. **Open the cited pages.**
2. **Identify the two or three sentences that might be lifted into a recommendation.**

   Strong passages usually:

   - Say what it is and who it's for and then specify the outcome in plain language.
   - Use scannable formatting.
   - Include proof or specificity (reviews, numbers, or named use cases, for example).

TIP

3. **Take action:** Rewrite or adapt these insights for your key pages so that your recommendable paragraph is obvious.

Check entity clarity

You're not doing advanced entity engineering here. You're simply checking to see whether competitors made it easy to understand who they are.

Here are some quick checks:

» Do they have a clearly stated About or Company page that answers the basics, such as what the company does, who it serves, where it operates, and what makes it credible?

- Are brand and product names consistent across the website, LinkedIn, and other major listings?
- Do they use basic structured data, like Organization or Product?
- Do they link out to canonical (generally accepted) profiles consistently?

TIP

To take action for your brand, tighten your entity home, naming consistency, and core structured data (see Chapter 4) so that you're easier to trust and easier to cite.

Compare reputation footprints

This section talks about assessing how your reputation compares to competitors and identifying where you need to strengthen it. Commercial answers lean on third-party proof to signal trustworthiness. Here's how to compare your reputation with your competitors:

- **Evaluate review volume:** Compare how many reviews you have versus each competitor on the platforms that matter most in your category. A large gap tells you where trust signals may be weaker.
- **Review recency:** Check whether competitors have recent reviews or whether their last meaningful review is months or years old. Recent reviews can make a brand look active and trusted.
- **Check for proof near the main offer:** Look for testimonials, logos, ratings, case studies, or short proof points near the top of important pages. If competitors show proof faster than you do, their pages may be easier for buyers and AI systems to trust.

REMEMBER

If a competitor has a clear lead, don't treat it like a mystery. Build a review-and-profile strategy: earn more reviews on the platforms that matter, update the profiles AI platforms already cite, and make your proof easier to find on your own site.

Tracking Market Share across AI Platforms

AI market share almost never looks the same across AI platforms. Treat each surface like a separate market because it may cite different sources, show different competitors, and format answers differently. The goal is to see where you lead, where you're close, and where you're absent so your next actions are specific.

Build a simple scorecard for each AI platform in your competitive tracking sheet. This could also become a figure that shows one row per surface and the key metrics in columns. Include these items:

- Your SoV
- Top competitors' SoV
- Your average position
- Your citation coverage (how often you're a cited source)
- Notes (big gaps)

Then label each AI platform with Lead (you're ahead), Chasing (close behind), and Absent (rarely shows).

Prioritize where to push first using these three filters:

- **Audience fit:** Which AI platforms your buyers actually use
- **Pipeline signals:** Which AI platforms show up in attribution and sales calls
- **Reachability:** Whether the core cited sources are ones you can influence

IN THIS CHAPTER

» Seeing why AI SEO experiments may fool you

» Designing a repeatable test

» Looking at what the test results actually mean

» Turning experiments into clear next steps rather than random wins

Chapter 8
Conducting Experiments That Don't Fool You

AI search invites testing. You can easily tweak a page, rerun a prompt, and feel that you have proved something because the answer changed.

The problem is that AI systems change, too. Models update, interfaces shuffle citations, and small prompt-wording shifts can create apparent wins, meaning changes look successful but may have nothing to do with your work.

In this chapter, I describe how to run AI SEO experiments that don't fool you. I show how to lean on the baselines and tracking habits you set up in Chapter 3, use your prompt database from Chapter 5 as the backbone, and read results through the same lens you built in Chapter 5: coverage, position, share of voice (SoV), citations, and a few soft signals. You'll also use the competitive gaps from Chapter 7 to decide what to test next.

The goal is simple: Build a lightweight way to test ideas, distinguish luck from skill, and choose your next moves with more confidence.

Why AI SEO Experiments Can Fool People

AI experiments are fragile because AI answers are not fixed outputs. Even if you run the exact same prompt twice, you can get different answers due to normal variation.

On top of that, the environment changes in ways you don't control, such as in these examples:

- Model upgrades or model switches
- User interface (UI) changes that hide, show, or reorder citations
- Retrieval changes where the retrieval system pulls evidence from different sources
- Personalization differences (logged in versus logged out, device, plugins, location)

A quick spot-check is fine for curiosity. An experiment is different: An experiment is a structured comparison that helps you answer a single question:

> Did our change move results beyond normal variation and platform drift?

TECHNICAL STUFF

Platform drift occurs due to changes in the AI platform or underlying AI system rather than changes caused by your work.

If you design around this question, your experiments become far more honest.

Putting Experiments to the Test

Experiments matter because AI SEO results move for many reasons at once. A test, or experiment, gives you a clean way to isolate one change, measure what happened, and avoid giving yourself credit for normal AI variation. In the next sections, I show how to design a test, run it consistently, and read the results without overreacting to random movement.

Design the test

You don't need an experimentation department. You need a repeatable design that protects you from obvious traps. In this chapter, test and experiment mean the same basic thing: a planned comparison between what happened before and after a specific change. Most AI SEO tests can follow the same design.

TIP

Use the Chapter 5 prompt database as the place to tag the prompts you will test and use your AI SEO experiment tracking sheet or change log as the place to record the hypothesis, shipped change, dates, results, and conclusion.

Pick a single hypothesis

Focus on testing one specific idea about how AI systems interpret or rank your content. Start by writing a single sentence that names these elements:

- The change you'll ship
- The prompts you expect to move
- The AI platforms you care about, such as ChatGPT, Google AI Mode, Claude, Perplexity, Microsoft Copilot, Grok, or a local, shopping, or vertical surface that matters to your audience
- The metric(s) you expect to improve

Here are some examples:

- "If we publish a comparison page for Brand A, we should improve coverage and average position for Brand A comparison prompts on ChatGPT and Perplexity."
- "If we clean up the key digital assets, known as entity signals (for example, the About page, naming consistency, and key profiles), we should improve SoV for solution-stage prompts on Google AI Mode or Google AI Overviews."
- "If we improve our presence on the top-cited review sites, we should increase citation coverage and SoV for 'best tools' prompts across AI platforms."

Where should your hypotheses come from? Start with the biggest gaps you can find (explained in Chapter 7), as in these examples:

- The prompt clusters where competitors dominate SoV
- The recurring citation sources where competitors are present and you're missing
- The AI platform where you're absent even though it matters to your buyers

REMEMBER

A single hypothesis keeps experimentation tied to strategy, not to random ideas.

Build a small experiment prompt set

AI answers can vary based on phrasing, context, and constant model updates. That makes it difficult to tell whether a change you made caused a result or the system simply shifted on its own.

To reduce that noise, create a fixed set of prompts you can reuse for every experiment. This strategy gives you a consistent baseline so that you can measure true movement instead of guessing.

TIP

Use your prompt database from Chapter 5 rather than creating a new system.

For each experiment, first tag a small set of prompts with an Experiment ID, such as EXP_03_ComparisonPage, and then follow these steps:

1. **Select five to ten prompts from your existing database.**
2. **Assign each prompt a role:**
   - *Direct:* Prompts that point straight at the asset you're changing, like "[Your Brand] versus [Competitor]" or "Your Brand versus Competitor"
   - *Related:* Prompts in the same topic or intent cluster that should benefit indirectly, for example, "best [category] tools for [segment]"
   - *Control:* Prompts in a similar category that you aren't touching during the test window

   These roles help you separate movement caused by your work from changes that may happen on its own because the AI platform or underlying system changed.

TIP

Keep the set small on purpose to make results easier to interpret. You're aiming for repeatability, not completeness.

Freeze prompts (prompt hygiene)

Prompt hygiene means using the same set of prompts every time so that you can see whether your work moved the results.

Follow these guidelines to keep tests honest:

- Use exactly the same wording each time for a given prompt.
- Run prompts on the same AI platforms you chose at the start.
- Keep prompts close to how a real buyer would ask the question.
- Save new prompt variants for a future experiment.

WARNING

If you keep changing the question midtest, you can't trust the answer shift.

Choose AI platforms and set a cadence

Pick the three to five AI platforms that matter most to your audience. Then test across the same surfaces for direct, related, and control prompts.

Set the cadence before you start. Here's a simple schedule that works for many teams:

- **Baseline window:** One to two weeks, depending on how often you run the prompts
- **Follow-ups:** Two to four weeks after the change goes live
- **Longer, optional check:** Six to eight weeks for changes that take time to be discovered and cited

TIP

You can adjust timing to match your cycle, but decide it upfront so you measure every experiment consistently and avoid changing the schedule based on the results you see.

Create a change log entry

Clean prompts don't help if you don't record what changed. Without a clear record, you can't connect movement in AI answers to a specific action. You'll just see that results improved or dropped without knowing why.

In your experiment change log, for each experiment, record these elements:

- **The date:** And time, if it matters
- **What changed:** Page, profile, directory listing, fact hub, or review campaign, for example. (A *fact hub* is a page that gathers your key facts, statistics, and definitions in one reliable place.)
- **The type of change:** Comparison page, entity cleanup, profile update, or PR mention, for example
- **The hypothesis:** No more than a single sentence
- **The Experiment ID:** The short label you use to connect the prompt set, change log entry, and results, such as EXP_03_ComparisonPage

Creating a change log prevents this classic problem: "We changed ten things, and something moved."

Control for drift without obsessing over it

You can't stop model and UI changes, but you can keep them from confusing you.

Add these two simple habits when conducting experiments:

- **Record visible version info when it's shown.** Note details such as the model name, mode label, logged-in state, date, and surface version if the AI platform displays them. These details help you spot whether a result changed because your work improved or because the surface itself changed.
- **Tag major AI platform events in your change log when they're publicly announced.** For example, record a major model upgrade, a new search mode, or a citation display change that happens during your test window.

Focus on time periods, not isolated runs. If both the test prompts and control prompts move in the same direction around the same time, suspect platform drift.

Run the test

After a test is live, the main job isn't cleverness. It's consistency.

Use this run checklist every time you capture results:

- Run the same frozen prompts (filter by Experiment ID).
- Use the same AI platforms.
- Keep locale and language consistent (or note differences).
- Keep the environment consistent when possible (logged-in state, device, extensions).
- Capture the full answer and the citation section.
- Log these items for each prompt:
  - *Coverage:* Present or absent
  - *Position:* First mention or list position
  - *Citations:* Which domains show up
  - *Quick notes:* Whether something unusual happened, such as missing citations, a login change, a location mismatch, or an answer that failed to load

That's enough structure to make your results comparable without turning this into a research project.

Reading Results without Getting Fooled

AI answers are noisy. Your goal is to detect repeatable movement, not to celebrate one mention. The following four sections show how to read results without getting fooled.

Evaluate using the core metrics stack

To recognize whether your changes had an impact, measure against several core metrics. For most AI SEO experiments, this means tracking these aspects:

- **Coverage:** Did you show up more often for the prompts you targeted? Track this info for direct prompts first and then related prompts.
- **Position:** Did you move higher in lists or get mentioned earlier in narratives? Compare average position before-versus-after for each prompt role.
- **Share of voice:** Did your share improve relative to competitors in that prompt cluster and AI platform? SoV helps you avoid "we improved" stories when competitors improved more.
- **Citations:** Did your site show up more often as a cited source? Did the key third-party sources you influenced start appearing more in citation lists? Track domains and page types, not just raw counts.

TIP

- **Soft signals:** Which patterns show up in self-reported mentions, branded search, or targeted referrals? Use soft signals as support, not proof. Here are some examples:
  - Self-reported mentions: Prospects or customers say things such as, "We found you via ChatGPT," "Perplexity recommended you," or "Google's AI answer mentioned your brand."
  - Branded search lift: More people search for your brand, product name, or comparison terms tied to the experiment topic.
  - High-intent referral spikes: More visitors arrive from pages you targeted, such as comparison pages, review profiles, or cited third-party sources.

  Soft signals can strengthen the story when your core metrics move, but they shouldn't override them.

Look for patterns, not single wins

A positive result, such as improved share of voice, position, citations, or coverage, is more believable when it shows up in these places:

- » Across multiple prompts tagged direct in your experiment prompt set
- » Across at least two scheduled follow-up runs
- » On more than one AI platform your buyers use

You can use simple internal rules, like these:

- » "We care when at least three direct prompts move in the same direction."
- » "We care when the movement holds for two consecutive follow-up runs."

These rules prevent you from overreacting to a single lucky ranking, citation, or visibility spike.

Compare test movement to control movement

Comparing test movement to control movement is where your control prompts pay off. Control prompts give you a comparison group. If the prompts you targeted improved, but the controls stayed mostly flat, your change is more likely to matter. If everything moved together, the platform may have changed instead.

Ask yourself these questions:

- » Did direct prompts improve more than controls?
- » Did related prompts move in the expected direction?
- » Did control prompts shift at the same time because of platform drift?

If both groups move similarly, treat the result as likely noise or a platform change. If the test group improves while controls stay mostly stable, you can be more confident that your work had an impact.

Drawing Conclusions and Taking Action

After you read the results, you need to decide what they mean and what to do next. This section shows you how to apply simple outcome labels, record the conclusion in your experiment tracking sheet, and turn real wins into repeatable playbooks.

Keep outcome labels simple

When you're running multiple experiments over time, your change log can easily become cluttered with long, detailed labels. Keep outcome labels simple so that you can scan your experiment history later. Here are some examples:

- **Clear win (scale it):** The expected metrics moved, the trend held across follow-up runs, and there's no major downside on the AI platforms that matter.
- **Inconclusive (keep, watch, refine):** Some movement shows up, but it's inconsistent, too small, or too dependent on one AI platform. Keep the change live, extend the window, or tighten the prompt set.
- **Weak or negative (rethink or roll back):** Little positive movement or clear harm to SoV or position occurs on important prompts. Decide whether to roll back, revise the asset you changed, or test a different optimization approach.

Write the outcome label into your AI SEO experiment tracking sheet, along with a sentence summarizing what happened and what evidence supported the outcome.

Turn wins into playbooks

Experiments compound only when you turn wins into repeatable actions.

TIP

When something works, write a short, internal playbook that includes this information:

- **A clear name:** "Comparison page playbook for AI recommendations," for example
- **What you shipped:** The change
- **Which prompt roles you tracked:** Direct, related, control
- **Which AI platforms you tested:** The surfaces included in the experiment, such as ChatGPT with Search, Perplexity, Google AI Mode, or Google AI Overviews

- **Which metrics improved and by how much:** The specific measures that moved, such as coverage, average position, SoV, citation coverage, or branded search lift
- **The conditions that seemed to matter:** "Worked best on solution-stage prompts" or "Needed strong review site presence," for example

Then add the playbook to your standard workflows so that future campaigns start with proven moves. Now you're turning the results you discovered into action.

REMEMBER

Failures matter, too. Record this information in the same experiment tracking sheet or change log:

- What you changed
- What you expected
- What actually happened
- What you would do differently the next time

Those notes essentially become guardrails that can save you from repeating expensive mistakes.

3

Building an AI-Friendly Website

IN THIS PART . . .

Create a topic game plan based on how buyers make decisions.

Set an AI readiness check by auditing your site, prioritizing problems, providing actions for your team, and ranking which issues to fix first.

Build pages that make it easy for AI systems to retrieve.

Find out how to create bottom of funnel pages that answer purchase-critical questions.

Be the source of truth so that AI systems see you as a topical authority.

Improve underperforming pages and check to see whether your fixes are working.

Put media, such as images and video, to work to lend structured support to your content.

IN THIS CHAPTER

- Using customer awareness stages to pick the right topics (and the right page types)
- Creating a topic plan
- Finding topics from buyer demand signals and then qualifying what's worth building
- Clustering topics into a simple roadmap you can ship

Chapter 9

Building Your Topic Game Plan

Time to turn abstract into action! This chapter and the other chapters in Part 3 are where you start building the pages that make AI systems likely to recommend you. In this chapter, I walk you through the buyer-intent thought process to build a topic game plan that produces pages AI answers can pull from and cite.

A topic game plan has two jobs:

- **Help buyers choose you:** The business outcome
- **Help machines understand and trust you:** The AI outcome

When you build the right topics in the right order, you usually see two things happen: Your classic SEO improves, and your brand starts showing up more often, and more accurately, in AI answers.

Sorting Out Customer Awareness Stages

Not every person is looking for the same kind of answer. Customer awareness stages provide a framework for examining where someone is in their journey, from vague curiosity to active decision-making. When people search in AI chat, they often skip the slow-paced journey of "Read ten articles" and jump straight to "Give me the best option." Accommodating the various customer awareness stages — Unaware, Problem Aware, Solution Aware, Product Aware, and Most Aware — can help interpret the intent of the consumer. The stages tell you what kind of content the user needs and what kind of answer the AI is likely to generate.

Zero-click behavior is part of this shift, too. Sometimes the AI answer gives the searcher enough information that they never visit a website. That does not make awareness-stage content useless, but it means you should judge those pages by more than raw traffic. Look at whether they clarify the next step, earn brand mentions, support internal links to commercial pages, or help AI systems describe the topic accurately.

REMEMBER

A good topic plan isn't "Let's write a bunch of blogs." It's "Let's build the pages that match how buyers decide." You use awareness stages to choose what to publish first and to decide which pages deserve the most depth.

The following sections walk you through the five customer awareness stages.

Unaware

Users can search at the Unaware stage, but their searches are usually broad and messy because they haven't yet clearly defined the problem or the solution. The search often shows up as curiosity-driven queries, vague symptoms, or general "learn about" searches.

Take a look at these examples:

- "Why is my traffic down?"
- "How does SEO work?"
- "Basement water problem"

TIP

How do you treat Unaware searches in your plan? Avoid building your SEO roadmap around Unaware topics, because they usually convert poorly and rarely trigger brand mentions in AI answers. Instead, use Unaware topics as short support pages that define the problem and link to the next awareness-stage page.

Problem Aware

In the Problem Aware stage, users know something is wrong, but they don't yet know the solution category. These searches are often framed as symptoms, drops, errors, or questions asking, "Why is this happening?"

Here are some examples:

- "Why does my basement keep flooding?"
- "My leads dropped this month. What should I check first?"

TIP

To help a user clarify what the problem is, try out these content types:

- **Diagnostic guide:** It can point to a how-to-fix-it page.
- **Common-causes explainer:** This is usually an article that introduces solution categories.
- **Checklist:** Completing this document can help users name the problem.

Problem Aware prompts matter because they're often the first touchpoint. The win here isn't just topical authority. The win is moving the user forward.

Keep these points in mind:

- **Use Problem Aware pages to guide the next click.** Build them so that they naturally funnel into Solution Aware and Product Aware pages by way of strong internal linking, such as "If you're dealing with X, here are your options," "Compare these approaches," "See pricing," or "See the best tools for agencies."
- **Set expectations on traffic.** AI answers now satisfy many broad diagnostic searches directly, so these pages may get fewer visits even when they rank well.
- **Treat Problem Aware pages as decision-shapers that create clarity, reduce confusion, and tee up the commercial pages that convert.** These pages are still worth building — just build them strategically. Built well, they can still drive leads, assisted conversions, and AI mentions, but be sure to measure them beyond raw traffic, such as engaged sessions, internal clicks to BoF pages, and branded searches.

Solution Aware

In the Solution Aware stage, users know the solution category, but not which provider, product, or method.

Take a look at these examples:

- "Best sump pump repair options in Chicago"
- "Best SEO content optimization tools for agencies"

TIP

Test out these content types:

- "Best/top" lists that are built credibly
- Use-case pages, such as "for agencies," "for e-commerce," or "for local services"
- Pricing and what-it-costs pages
- Buyer guides that compare approaches, not just products

In the Solution Aware stage, AI answers tend to produce commercial shortlists. That makes these topics prime opportunities for improving your AI visibility.

Product Aware

In the Product Aware stage, users compare specific options.

Here are some examples:

- "Rankability versus Surfer"
- "Zoho CRM versus HubSpot for a small team"
- "Brand A alternatives"

TIP

Try using these content types:

- Comparisons (A versus B)
- Alternatives pages
- "Best for X" pages that explain fit

REMEMBER

Product Aware queries tend to generate AI answers with brand mentions and citations. This level of visibility makes Product Aware content excellent for tracking and for wins you can show stakeholders.

Most Aware

In the Most Aware stage, users know you. They're in decision mode and want specifics before they buy.

Here are some examples:

- "Does Rankability have a free trial?"
- "Is [Brand] worth it?"
- "How much is [Brand] per month?"

TIP

Put these content types to use:

- Clear pricing pages
- FAQ pages
- Proof pages (case studies, testimonials)
- How-it-works onboarding pages

The Most Aware stage is where accuracy matters most. When the brand is in the query, AI systems often shift into direct-retrieval mode and pull answers straight from the brand's own site (pricing, features, trial terms, positioning, or constraints, for example). That means your site becomes the source the model trusts at the exact moment the buyer is ready to convert.

If your pages are vague, inconsistent, or outdated, AI can repeat the wrong price, wrong features, or wrong terms and that can cost you sales. Your job is to make the truth easy to retrieve and hard to misunderstand by keeping your pricing, plan details, FAQs, and proof pages current, explicit, and internally consistent.

Creating Your Topic Plan

If you want your topic plan to translate into rankings, leads, and AI mentions, you need these two items:

- **A keyword research template** that keeps your decisions consistent
- **A knowledge base** that makes your research faster, smarter, and easier to reuse

Creating a keyword research template

A keyword research template is your single source of truth for what you're building, why you're building it, and what it maps to on your site. Use Google Sheets, Airtable, or Notion, or your internal system, but keep the columns consistent so that your team can filter, sort, and ship.

These are columns to include (your exact build):

Priority	Keyword Difficulty	Opportunity
Source	Cost-Per-Click	Primary Keyword
Cluster	Current Position	Status
Keyword	Current URL	Keyword Variation
Volume/Impressions	Intent	Secondary Keyword
Exclude	Notes	

Here's how to use the most important columns in practice:

- **Priority:** A simple label (P1, P2, P3) or a number. This is your build order.
- **Source:** Where it came from (GSC, gap, Reddit, Rankability, or Ahrefs, for example). It helps you validate and repeat what's working.
- **Cluster:** The topic group or decision area the keyword belongs to. (One cluster is equal to one roadmap unit.)
- **Pillar:** A pillar page is the main commercial page that anchors a cluster and receives links from supporting pages.
- **Keyword:** The exact phrase you're tracking.
- **Volume/Impressions:** Uses volume (from SEO tools) when you have it; uses impressions (from Google Search Console) when you don't. (GSC is often more accurate than third-party volume.) Search *volume* is an estimate of how often a keyword is searched, and *impressions* are real counts of how often you appeared in search results.
- **KD:** A keyword difficulty score. Don't set your clock by it, but don't ignore it.
- **CPC:** Your cost-per-click. High CPC usually signals buying intent and commercial value.
- **Current Position, Current URL:** Where your fastest wins hide.

- **Intent:** Prevents wasted content (see the upcoming section "Qualifying with primary filters").
- **Opportunity:** A quick label that shows where you now stand, based on Current Position.
  - *Low-hanging fruit:* Positions 2–15, so you're already close. Small improvements can nudge you into the top results.
  - *Existing:* Positions 16–50, where you're on the board, but you need meaningful upgrades (content depth, on-page, internal links, and likely some authority) to break through.
  - *Clustering opportunity:* Position 51 and beyond, where you're barely visible. This is usually a sign that you need stronger topical support via a cluster (a combination of pillar, supporting pages, and internal linking).
  - *Untapped:* When you aren't even ranking in the top 100 and have no traction yet. Treat this situation as a net-new target that needs a full-page build and cluster support.
- **Primary Keyword:** The lone keyword that the page is built around.
- **Keyword Variation, Secondary Keyword:** Helps you build pages that cover the topic, not just one phrase.
- **Status:** Your production pipeline (Backlog, Briefed, Drafting, Editing, Published, Updating, Consolidating).
- **Exclude:** A simple check box or Y/N option. If this field is excluded, it stays visible, but it stops clogging your pipeline.
- **Notes:** A tactical option. Add context like "Needs case study," "Needs schema," "AI answer keeps citing competitor," or "Refresh quarterly."

TIP

Optional entity columns can help when AI retrieval is part of the goal. Add Primary Entity for the main brand, product, place, or concept the page should reinforce, and Related Entities for the supporting people, tools, services, locations, or competitors that help machines understand the topic.

REMEMBER

If a topic isn't in the template, it doesn't exist. That's how you prevent random "good idea" topics from hijacking the roadmap.

Developing a knowledge base

Keyword lists are helpful, but they're no longer sufficient for AI-assisted content planning. A knowledge base turns your topic plan into an asset that feeds content creation, optimization, and AI visibility.

Why it matters

A knowledge base:

- **Speeds up research:** Because you're not starting from scratch every time
- **Improves accuracy:** Because you store facts, definitions, and brand truths one time only
- **Makes AI output safer:** Because you control what gets ingested and reused
- **Improves internal consistency:** Because you benefit from entities, terminology, positioning, and product details

What you need for ingestion

At minimum, your knowledge base should offer:

- **Basic information:** Services, pricing ranges, coverage areas, guarantees, differentiators
- **Proof:** Case studies, testimonials, before-and-after results, screenshots showing results
- **Entities:** Products, methods, standards, tools, people, locations, brands
- **Policies:** Stipulations of what you do and don't do, and who you do and don't serve
- **FAQs:** Sales objections and questions related to the Most Aware stage
- **Source notes:** Information about where facts came from, plus Last Updated fields for freshness

Using a client knowledge base

A client knowledge base helps content reflect approved facts, positioning, proof, and terminology.

The goal is not simply to collect information. The goal is to integrate that information into your content workflow, so it becomes the foundation for planning, writing, editing, and reviewing content.

PUTTING ChatGPT PROJECTS TO GOOD USE

ChatGPT projects are a way to organize your work into focused, reusable workspaces. You can group conversations, files, and instructions around a specific goal, so projects are perfect for keeping research, drafts, and references together.

Use a project to store these items:

- Your keyword research template link
- The knowledge base artifacts (documents, screenshots, briefs, link lists)
- Your cluster roadmap (one folder per cluster with everything needed to write and update; see the future section "Enhancing Your Work with Clusters and a Roadmap")

Create a knowledge base for each client and use it as the source of truth for content creation. The practical outcome is simple: Every page you publish reflects the client's real-world details rather than generic assumptions, which produces these results:

- **Every piece of content carries the client's unique nuances.** The content might consist of offers, service areas, differentiators, policies, proof, or terminology, for example.
- **Accuracy remains consistent across pages.** The reason is that the same approved facts and positioning get reused rather than rewritten from memory.
- **Writers and editors work faster.** No one is repeating their research of basic information or guessing at brand details.
- **AI-assisted drafts are safer.** They're grounded in client-approved inputs, which reduces errors and mismatched claims.

The point is not the knowledge base itself. The point is building a repeatable workflow where content quality, accuracy, and efficiency improve as the knowledge base becomes more complete over time.

Finding Topics

Topics are the individual ideas, questions, or themes that your audience is searching for or thinking about — each one can become a page, an FAQ, a guide, or another piece of content. Finding topics is about collecting demand signals. You want more inputs than you'll publish, because the filtering is where the strategy happens.

In the following several sections, I walk you through the process of finding topics.

Probing for prompts

Start by mining the information that buyers and customers have already given you: These inputs usually map to topics with the highest intent because they stem from true decision-making moments.

Use these prompts to pull topic ideas from your knowledge base (client knowledge base, call notes, support logs, onboarding docs, competitor notes, and FAQs, for example). The next five sections go into detail on what prompts to use.

Sales call questions

Use common questions and objections from sales calls to generate topics that address decision-making moments and guide prospects toward action, such as in these examples:

- "List the 25 most common questions prospects ask before they buy, using their exact wording wherever possible."
- "What objections come up most often on sales calls? Group them by theme and suggest one page topic per objection."
- "What questions do prospects ask just before they request pricing, a demo, or a proposal? Turn each into a BoF keyword/topic."

Churn: Reasons to cancel

Churn is the loss of customers through cancellations or non-renewals. Looking at why customers leave can uncover topics that reduce friction, set realistic expectations, and help future customers decide whether your product or service is the right fit. Here are some examples:

- "Summarize the top reasons customers cancel. For each reason, suggest a prevention page, an FAQ answer, and a how-it-works clarification section."
- "Identify the top ten expectation gaps that lead to cancellations. Turn each into a page topic that sets expectations clearly."
- "What features or outcomes do churned customers say were missing? Convert each into an educational page topic that clarifies fit."

Onboarding friction

Analyze where users struggle during onboarding to uncover topics that help them succeed and reduce early confusion. For example:

- **List the top onboarding sticking points.** For each, propose a Help page title and an outline with the key sections to include.
- **Where do users get confused during setup?** Convert each confusion point into a searchable question and recommended page type (FAQ, guide, or checklist, for example).
- **What are the top ten steps users delay or skip in onboarding?** For each, write a how-to topic that removes friction.
- **Extract all terms customers ask to define.** Prioritize terms that affect buying decisions and propose a single glossary or FAQ entry per term.
- **List the biggest misconceptions prospects have about your category.** For each misconception, write a myth-busting topic and the internal link to the next-step commercial page.
- **What do prospects misunderstand about pricing, timelines, or outcomes?** Turn each into an FAQ question that's specific and measurable.

Content from competitor comparisons

Analyze the competitor comparisons prospects make naturally to identify content that helps them evaluate your solution. For example:

- "List all competitors, tools, or services that prospects mention without being prompted. For each, recommend whether we need a comparison page, an alternatives page, or a best-for page."
- "What phrases do prospects use when comparing us to alternatives? Output them as keyword targets (for example, *X versus Y, X alternatives,* or *best X for Y*)."

- "Identify the top five most common comparison themes (price, features, speed, support, outcomes). For each theme, propose three supporting topics that help the pillar page convert."

Output format prompt (so that it's immediately usable)

Use a standardized output format to turn topic ideas into a repeatable process for content planning. After you run the prompts from the previous sections, use the following output-format prompt to standardize the results:

> "Output the results as rows for my keyword research template with these columns: Source, Cluster, Keyword/Topic, Intent, Opportunity Label (Low-Hanging Fruit, Existing, Clustering Opportunity, Untapped), Notes, Recommended Page Type."

This strategy turns a collection of topic ideas into a structured content-planning workflow that you can repeat whenever you need the next cluster. *Note:* This prompt uses a shortened export format — it creates a first-pass topic list that later gets copied into the full keyword research template.

Examining visibility and opportunity signals

Look to see where your site is already visible, which queries are underperforming, and where the biggest opportunities lie, such as with Google Search Console.

Pull these elements:

- Queries with a high number of impressions and a low number of clicks
- Keywords sitting in positions 2–15 (often one push away)
- Pages ranking for the mismatched keywords (clues to an intent mismatch)
- Branded and nonbranded queries that reveal cluster gaps (missing topics or page types inside a cluster that prevent the cluster from fully answering the buyer decision)

These signals tell you where you are already in the conversation. The next step is figuring out where competitors are gaining visibility that you aren't so that you can close the gaps and build clusters that win.

Identifying competitor keyword gaps

Use gap analysis to find the topics competitors dominate — and that you don't. The goal isn't to copy their content. It's to identify the page types and decision questions your market expects you to answer.

You can run a keyword gap analysis using any platform that identifies missing opportunities, such as Ahrefs, Rankability, or Semrush. The tool matters less than the output: a clear list of missing commercial topics and the pages that win them.

Focus on these items:

- **Commercial pages:** Service and pricing, and "best," "versus," or "alternatives" wording
- **Supporting pages:** Ones that reinforce their cluster authority — use cases, FAQs, proof pages, implementation guides
- **Patterns across multiple competitors:** When several competitors cover the same topic, usually a category requirement

Here's how to run a quick workflow for a keyword gap analysis:

1. **List your top 3–10 competitors for the cluster you're building.**

   Keep it tight: Use direct competitors, not huge publishers, unless they're dominating the search engine results page (SERP).

2. **Run a keyword gap analysis in your tool of choice. For example:**

   - *In Ahrefs:* Use Content Gap (Ahrefs version of keyword gap analysis) or compare domains to find keywords that competitors rank for — and you don't.
   - *In Rankability:* Compare your domain against competitors and export the missing keywords/pages.
   - *In Semrush:* Use keyword gap analysis to surface missing and weak keywords across competitors.

3. **Filter for commercial intent first.**

   Prioritize keywords containing modifiers like these:

   - Best, top, review
   - Versus, compare, alternatives
   - Pricing, cost
   - For [use case], for [industry], near me (where relevant)

4. **Tag each gap keyword so that it turns into a build plan.**

   Decipher these elements:

   - *Likely page type:* Pillar, comparison, alternatives, pricing, use-case, FAQ/proof
   - *Cluster:* Which decision group it belongs to
   - *Opportunity label:* Existing versus Untapped (based on your current rankings)

5. **Map gaps to pages, not just keywords.**

   If multiple gaps share the same intent and SERP format, they often belong on one strong page with sections rather than several thin pages.

REMEMBER

If you see one competitor ranking for a topic, it might be a one-off. If you see three competitors ranking for a topic, that's a signal the market expects it, and AI systems are more likely to reuse it in answers.

Looking at user-generated content

User-generated content, or UGC, is created when people say what they mean, and it refers to content created by your users, customers, or community. UGC includes reviews and ratings on forum posts, such as Reddit and Quora. Use it to extract these items:

- **Natural language questions:** These work perfectly for second-level headings (H2s), FAQs, and sections featuring People Also Ask (PAA) wording. See the upcoming section, "People Also Ask" for more information.
- **Pain points and objections:** These elements might show what customers are worried about, what they're skeptical of, or what would block a purchase.
- **Terms and analogies real people use:** Make your content sound human and improve query matching.

UGC works best for discovering phrasing and subtopics you might miss with tools. After you extract ideas, validate them with these two aspects:

- **Intent:** Is it informational, investigative, comparison, or transactional?
- **Business value:** Does it lead toward your offer, or is it mostly curiosity?

UGC indicates how people talk. Keyword tools help you scale it into a complete list so that you can build out clusters, prioritize, and create a roadmap with confidence.

Generating keywords from scratch

Build keywords from scratch whenever you want to expand beyond what you already rank for, especially when you're building a new cluster or entering a new niche.

Here are some practical workflow steps for keyword expansion:

1. **Start with seed keywords that match your offer.**

   Pick 5–20 targeted seeds, not vague informational terms; for example: "content optimization tool," "SEO agency software," "sump pump repair Chicago," or "basement waterproofing cost."

2. **Expand each seed into commercial modifiers.**

   Look for keywords that signal evaluation or action: pricing, cost, quote, near me, best, top, reviews, versus, alternatives, competitors, for agencies, for small business, or for e-commerce (use cases).

3. **Use the phrase *Also rank for* to see what Google thinks the page is about.**

   When you find a competitor page that's ranking well, pull the terms it ranks for that you didn't think to include and the subtopics Google associates with that intent.

   This strategy helps you avoid building pages that are too narrow or that miss expected sections.

4. **Group keywords by parent topic.**

   If multiple keywords share the same parent topic and intent, they usually belong on a single strong page (divided into sections), not five weak pages.

5. **Validate with the search results (SERP).**

   Before finalizing a keyword and adding it to your roadmap, double-check to determine the answers to these questions:

   - *Which page types rank?* Service pages, listicles, product pages, guides
   - *Which formats win?* Pricing tables, comparisons, local pages, templates
   - *Which angles repeat?* Speed, trust, guarantees, "What's included?"

This is how you align with "What Google expects" without guessing.

For each seed, end with one pillar keyword (commercial) and 3–10 support page keywords (pricing, comparisons, alternatives, use cases, or FAQs, for example).

Expanding topic coverage with query fan-out and People Also Ask

Query fan-out is a technique for rapidly expanding coverage around a high-value keyword, or head term. Query fan-out is how you build coverage fast without relying on tools alone. People Also Ask (PAA) is a box in the Google search results that contains expandable questions related to your query.

The following sections detail these two strategies.

Query fan-out

In query fan-out, you take one high-value head term and deliberately expand it into the questions and modifiers buyers use across the decision journey.

Start with a head term, and then fan it out by intent:

- **Problem clarification (Problem Aware):** These queries reflect users trying to understand or diagnose a problem before they know the solution. Examples:
  - Why is . . .
  - Common causes of . . .
  - How to fix . . .
  - Signs you need . . .
- **Evaluation (Solution Aware):** These queries show users exploring solution options and weighing alternatives. Examples:
  - Best . . .
  - Top . . .
  - What is the best . . .
  - How to choose . . .
- **Comparison (Product Aware):** These queries reflect users comparing products, services, or brands. Examples:

- [A] versus [B]
- [category] alternatives
- Best alternative to . . .

» **Action (Transactional/Most Aware):** These queries indicate that users are ready to take action or make a purchase. Examples:

- Cost
- Pricing
- Near me
- Quote
- Trial
- Is it worth it?

People Also Ask

When you click a question in the PAA box, Google reveals a short answer and often adds more related questions underneath. It's basically Google showing you the follow-up questions searchers commonly have.

To find PAA, you're not just locating the box, you're extracting and mapping the questions Google associates with your topic. Follow these steps to find PAA:

1. **Open an incognito/private browser window (optional, but helps reduce personalization).**
2. **Google your pillar keyword (the main commercial query for the cluster).**
3. **Scroll until you see the People Also Ask box.**
4. **Click to expand 6–10 questions (with each click usually revealing more).**
5. **Copy the questions into your keyword template.**

TIP

If you want to be thorough, repeat this process for a few close variants (like "best," "cost," "versus," and "alternatives" versions of the query).

Put PAA questions to good use. PAA questions are often perfect as:

» **H2s on your pillar page:** To address the core decision-making questions buyers need answered

PREVENTING FAN-OUT FROM TURNING EVERYTHING INTO BLOG POSTS

Fan-out produces a lot of keyword ideas fast. The risk is that you'll default to "Write a blog post" wording for every question, which creates thin content and cannibalization.

Fan-out works best when you assign a page type to each query before you write anything. Here are some page-type guides:

- Pricing/cost/quote: Pricing page or cost guide
- Best/top/reviews: Listicle or buyer guide
- Versus/alternatives: Comparison and alternatives pages
- Near me/city: Local landing page
- How-to/steps: Implementation guide or standard operating procedure page
- Is it worth it?/does it work? Proof page, FAQ, or decision page

- **FAQ blocks:** To remove friction immediately before conversion
- **Supporting pages:** For when a question needs true depth to answer well

REMEMBER

A simple rule makes deciding whether a PAA question should become a section or a separate page easy:

If the question can be answered well in 3–6 paragraphs, it's probably a section on an existing page.

If it needs a full explanation, examples, steps, and proof, it probably has its own page.

Qualifying and Prioritizing Topics

Finding topics is easy. Deciding what's worth building next is the skill.

This step is where you stop collecting keywords and start building a pipeline you can ship. The goal is to prioritize every topic into one of these three outcomes:

- **Build now:** It has the highest impact and the highest probability.
- **Build later:** It's a good idea, but the timing isn't right.
- **Don't build:** It has the wrong intent or a low value, or it's too difficult right now.

When you qualify a topic, you're answering these three questions (with a few examples thrown in):

- **Will it drive the right outcome?** Revenue, leads, trials, calls
- **Can our brand realistically win the topic?** Authority, competition, proof, resources
- **Is the click worth it?** Organic CTR potential in a search engine results page (SERP) full of features

That third entry matters more than ever. Even if you rank, the SERP can steal the click. Many results pages now satisfy the query directly, which means visibility doesn't always translate into traffic.

Qualifying with primary filters

Primary filters are used to quickly qualify whether a topic is even worth pursuing. Apply the following filters to decide.

Relevance to the offer

This is the most important filter because it determines whether the traffic can turn into money. What you're asking is this: How close is this searcher to taking action?

Here's a simple ladder (ranking queries by distance to action) you can use:

- **Bottom of funnel (BoF):** Pricing, cost, hire, demo, trial, Near me, quote, best, reviews, versus, alternatives
- **Middle of funnels (MOFU):** How to choose, what's best for, tools for, services for, agency software
- **Top of funnel (TOFU):** Definitions, broad how-to, general education

Follow this rule: Build your strategy around BoF first and then fill in what supports those pages. (Chapter 12 discusses creating BoF pages.)

Intent

Intent is what prevents you from creating the wrong page for the keyword. Each keyword should map to a clear page format, such as a guide, comparison, or pricing page, based on what the searcher is trying to accomplish.

TIP

When you're first building a prompt database, keep intent classification simple by using two broad categories: Informational and Commercial. This makes prompt tagging fast and consistent. As your database grows, you can break those categories into more specific intent labels. For example, informational prompts might be divided into educational, how-to, or definition intents, while commercial prompts might be divided into comparison, alternatives, pricing, or review intents. Start broad, then add more granularity only when it improves your reporting.

Follow this decision rule: If you can't confidently name the page type (that is, if you can't answer the question, "What job is it supposed to do for the user?"), don't build it yet.

The following examples show solutions for what users want:

- Best [category]: Listicle/buyer guide
- [brand] pricing: Pricing page
- [A] versus [B]: Comparison page
- How to fix: Troubleshooting guide or SOP page
- Near me/city: Local landing page

Competition

This is where most keyword lists fall apart. Teams pick topics based on volume and then run into SERPs they had no chance of beating. You should ask this question: Do we have enough authority and trust to rank?

Use these checks to see whether you can realistically win a ranking:

- **Who's ranking?** Are they giant brands, government sites, major publishers, or niche specialists?
- **What kind of pages win?** Are they product pages, directories, listicles, service pages, or guides?
- **What's the minimum bar?** Are they depth, proof, reviews, pricing clarity, expert authorship, tooling, or location signals?

If you don't pass the win test, you have three smart options:

- **Start with easier entries in the same cluster:** Long-tail commercial.
- **Build support first:** Proof pages + internal links + coverage.
- **Park it as a longer-term play:** Do this while you build authority.

Keyword value

Cost-per-click (CPC) is a practical "what this traffic is worth" signal when volume is misleading. It reflects the perceived commercial value of that keyword.

High CPC usually means there's money on the other side of the click: Businesses believe that the click can turn into money.

CPC alone isn't enough: You need intent to interpret it correctly. Combine CPC with intent to decide whether the keyword belongs in your roadmap:

- High CPC + BoF intent = Build sooner.
- High CPC + informational intent = Treat as support unless it funnels well.

Organic CTR potential

Organic CTR potential is the missing piece in most topic plans. The *organic click-through rate* (or organic CTR) is the percentage of searchers who click on a search engine result.

Two keywords can have the same volume and intent, but the SERP can dramatically affect how many clicks your page earns. You need the answer to this question: If we rank, will we get clicks?

Also factor in brand bias in both search and AI-generated answers. Some systems tend to surface or cite well-established brands and entities that appear frequently across trusted sources. This can reduce visibility for newer or less established brands, even when content quality is strong.

This doesn't mean you should avoid those topics. It means you should adjust your CTR expectations and evaluation criteria based on how brand-skewed the result space is. In more biased environments, ranking alone may not translate into proportional traffic, and you may need additional authority signals (third-party mentions, reviews, citations, and entity consistency) before visibility reflects effort.

TIP

Scan the SERP for features that compete for attention: AI answers, ads, local packs, shopping results, featured snippets, PAA, video carousels, top stories, and knowledge panels.

Follow this guideline: The more features above the fold, the lower your expected CTR, even with strong rankings.

REMEMBER

If CTR potential is low, the topic can still be worth building if it directly supports BoF pages via internal linking, helps you show up in AI answers (citations, recommendations), or is essential for trust (pricing, policies, FAQs).

Measure the low-CTR topic differently. Instead of expecting traffic alone, track whether it assists conversions, earns internal clicks to BoF pages, improves lead quality, or supports AI mentions.

Prioritizing topics based on current rankings

Your current ranking position tells you whether the topic is a quick win or a longer build. Use your ranking to quickly identify which topics will deliver the fastest returns and then score and prioritize them to focus your efforts where they'll matter most.

Categorize each topic based on your current ranking to see which opportunities will deliver the fastest results. Use Opportunity labels (see the earlier section "Creating a keyword research template") to develop a plan:

- **Low-hanging fruit (positions 2–15):** Fastest ROI, usually refresh + internal linking + proof
- **Existing (16–50):** Needs meaningful improvements and stronger cluster support
- **Clustering opportunity (51+):** Needs pillar + support + internal linking to move
- **Untapped (not in top 100):** Net-new build, treated as a full cluster play
- **Secondary filters (volume/impressions, relevance to offer, intent, CTR potential, KD):** Supporting signals used to refine and size opportunities after primary filters are assigned

Setting up a simple scoring system

To keep your team from debating, set up a simple scoring system to follow:

1. **Score each topic from 1-5 across these criteria:**
   - Impact
   - Relevance to offer (BoF proximity)
   - Win probability
   - Competition fit (authority and SERP reality)
   - Monetization
   - CPC/keyword value
   - Click opportunity
   - Organic CTR potential (SERP features)
   - Speed
   - Opportunity label (low-hanging fruit scores higher)
2. **Total the scores to create a single rank for each topic.**
3. **Sort by total score and sanity-check against your cluster roadmap (see the next section, "Enhancing Your Work with Clusters and a Roadmap").**

When scoring is complete, follow these priority rules to prioritize topics consistently:

» **Low-hanging fruit + BoF:** Positions 2–15, commercial intent

» **BoF + high CPC:** Even if untapped

» **BoF with high CTR potential:** Cleaner SERPs can outperform higher-volume cluttered SERPs

» **Competitor-owned commercial gaps:** Category expectations

» **Support pages that strengthen the cluster:** Especially when SERP CTR is low

» **Informational pages only when they move people forward:** Internal links to BoF, objection handling, proof

REMEMBER

The best topic isn't the one with the highest volume. It's the one that matches intent, maps to your offer, offers a realistic path to winning, and has enough click opportunities to justify the work.

Enhancing Your Work with Clusters and a Roadmap

Once you have a prioritized keyword list, avoid the urge to treat it like a queue of unrelated articles. The goal is to group keywords into decision-based clusters and then ship one cluster at a time so that you build momentum (rankings, leads, and AI visibility) rather than scatter effort across 50 half-finished ideas.

Clustering is how you turn a messy keyword list into a build plan. You're not grouping keywords because they look similar. You're grouping them because they represent the same buyer decision, which usually means they belong in the same cluster and often on the same page.

WARNING

Avoid overlap across clusters. As a rule of thumb, one topic should have one primary page unless the intent clearly differs. That prevents redundant pages, conflicting signals, and cannibalization that can confuse both search engines and AI retrieval systems.

A strong cluster does three things. It

- Gives you one clear pillar page to win the commercial term
- Gives you support pages that capture adjacent intent (pricing, versus, alternatives, best-for)
- Creates an internal linking path that helps both buyers and bots understand the full decision

Creating clusters using ChatGPT

ChatGPT can help speed up cluster creation, but it won't replace SEO judgment. It's best used for producing a first draft that you can quickly refine. ChatGPT can:

- Detect keyword families and repeated modifiers ("best," "cost," "pricing," "near me," "versus," "alternatives," "reviews," "for [use case]").
- Infer intent and suggest the correct page type (pillar, pricing, comparison, alternatives, use-case, FAQ).
- Recommend which keywords should be on a page with sections versus separate pages.
- Draft cluster names that read like real decisions.

Your job is to validate the output with SERP reality and your business goals.

To produce accurate, useful clusters, provide context — not just keywords. Include the following inputs to give to ChatGPT:

- Your offer (1–2 sentences)
- Your ICP (who you want)
- A shortlist of core products or services
- Your keyword list (P1/P2)
- Any must-win clusters (if you already know them)

Building and judging your cluster

For this section, I provide a prompt code you can use to build your cluster. Use the prompt code formula found on `www.dummies.com/go/aiseofd` and swap in your own details.

After you create a prompt with your specifics, judge the information that's returned as follows:

- **Cluster names that read like decisions.**

  Good:

  - "Choose the best content optimization tool for an agency."
  - "Hire sump pump repair in Chicago and compare options."

  Weak:

  - "Content optimization keywords"
  - "Sump pump related terms"
- **A single pillar that's clearly commercial.**

  If ChatGPT gives you two pillars inside one cluster, that's usually a sign you're mixing two decisions. Split the cluster.
- **Support pages mapped to intent (not random blogs).**

  The best clusters usually include these elements:

  - **Pricing/cost:** Transactional
  - **Alternatives and comparisons:** Comparison intent

* **Best-for/use-case:** Investigative
* **Proof and FAQs:** Most Aware conversion support

ChatGPT can draft clusters fast, but you validate them with one quick check. If the pillar keyword and the support keywords don't naturally flow into this sentence, the cluster is off:

> "If someone is trying to [pillar decision], they'll also ask [pricing], [versus], [alternatives], [best for], and [is it worth it]."

TIP

If the cluster name doesn't sound like a decision a buyer would make, rename it until it does. That lone change usually improves the entire roadmap.

Focusing on one critical cluster at a time

If you try to build ten clusters at a time, you end up with a bunch of pages that feel unfinished and fail to reinforce each other. Follow these steps to help narrow your focus:

1. **Pick one critical cluster.**
2. **Build the pillar asset first (see the next section "Building a pillar asset").**
3. **Ship the pages that help it win: supporting pages, proof, and internal links.**
4. **Validate cluster completion. Only after the cluster is complete enough do you start the next one.**

REMEMBER

Focusing on one critical cluster at a time is how you create compounding returns, because each new page strengthens the cluster instead of starting over.

Producing a pillar asset

A cluster works only if it has a clear center of gravity. That's your pillar asset: the one page designed to rank for a commercial keyword and convert the visitor. Everything else in the cluster exists to support that page, not compete with it.

Think of the pillar as the page that answers the buyer's core question:

> "If I'm going to choose a solution, why should I choose you, and what do I need to know to decide?"

What makes a pillar page a pillar? A *pillar* isn't automatically the longest page — it's the page that:

- Targets the primary commercial term
- Covers the decision criteria the buyer needs to move forward
- Acts as the hub for internal linking (support pages feed it, and it routes people to deeper answers)
- Gives AI systems a single, unambiguous place to understand what you do, who it's for, and why you're credible

When you build a pillar page, you're building for two readers at one time: a human buyer and an AI retrieval system. Provide the following information to satisfy both:

- **Clear promise and positioning (above the fold):** Make it obvious: who it's for, what problem it solves, and what outcome can be expected. Avoid clever. Be specific.
- **A fast path to conversion:** Give them a next step that matches their intent: call, form, quote request, demo, trial, consult, or "see pricing" or "compare options" if they're not ready.
- **The core decision content:** The Choose You section. This is what most pages skip, and it's why they don't convert. Help readers understand what they'll receive (scope and deliverables), how to evaluate their options (criteria, trade-offs, and red flags), what they'll pay (or how pricing works), and what to expect throughout the process (timelines, first steps, and measures of success).
- **Proof and trust signals:** In the flow, not buried. Buyers and AI systems both lean on trust. Add reviews and testimonials, case studies and outcomes, credentials, standards, certifications, or guarantees or risk reducers (if you have them).
- **Internal links to deeper pages (decision support):** Link to pages that answer high-intent questions without bloating the pillar: pricing/cost, comparisons, alternatives, "best for" use-cases, or FAQs and objections.

TIP

Write the pillar so that a buyer can make a decision without leaving the page, while providing links to supporting resources where they can verify details or learn more. That balance usually produces the best conversion rate.

Your pillar format should match the dominant page type in the search results. These are four common winners:

- **Service page:** "sump pump repair Chicago"
- **Use-case page:** "content optimization tool for agencies"
- **Commercial guide:** "best [category] for [use case]"
- **Category page:** "SEO content optimization software"

If you pick the wrong format, you'll fight the SERP rather than fit it.

Once your pillar exists, supporting pages do two jobs: Win additional commercial keywords, and push authority and conversions back into the pillar.

To make your cluster more effective, include supporting pages that capture related questions and searcher intent. High-leverage adjacent intent (the type of topics that supporting pages should target) usually looks like this:

- **Cost and pricing:** "how much," "pricing," "cost"
- **Shortlists:** "best," "top," "reviews"
- **Comparisons:** "versus," "compare," "X versus Y"
- **Alternatives:** "alternatives," "best alternative to . . ."
- **Variants:** locations, industries, use-cases
- **FAQs and objections:** "is it worth it," "does it work," "how long," "what's included"

REMEMBER

The pillar isn't just a page. It's the anchor that makes the cluster operate like a decision path rather than a pile of content.

Launching a simple cluster roadmap

Use the following build sequence for most clusters. It keeps you focused, prevents cannibalization, and compounds authority:

1. **Ship the pillar (commercial keyword).**

   Get the core page live first. Until it exists, your support pages have nowhere to concentrate authority or send conversions.

2. **Ship the decision helpers (2–4 pages).**

   Build the pages that remove the biggest buying friction: pricing, cost, best-for, use case, alternatives, or comparisons.

   These are the pages that tend to perform well in both classic search and AI-assisted discovery because they map to decision moments.

3. **Add proof and FAQs.**

   Proof and FAQs are conversion accelerators. They also reduce retrieval mistakes because they give explicit, scannable answers to common questions.

   Link it all together.

   Make the cluster navigable and unmissable by keeping these points in mind:

   - Every support page links to the pillar with intent-matching anchor text.
   - The pillar links out to the support pages where deeper detail lives.
   - Comparisons and alternatives cross-link where it's genuinely helpful.

Following this roadmap clarifies the difference between "We published content" and "We built a cluster that wins."

IN THIS CHAPTER

» Running a fast readiness checkup to find what's broken and how widespread it is

» Reading crawl results through an AI-retrieval lens so that you fix what actually blocks visibility

» Using a simple scoring model to turn issues into a prioritized fix-first list

» Passing a minimum AI-ready checklist so that you know whether you're eligible for AI answers

Chapter 10

Conducting an AI-Readiness Checkup

You can't optimize for AI answers if bots can't reliably crawl, render, and trust your pages.

Lots of AI SEO advice starts with content formats, entities, and wording that says, "Write passages the model can lift." That's helpful, but it skips the part that decides whether you'll even be seen: Most AI search systems still rely on classic crawling, indexing, and retrieval to gather evidence. If your pages can't be fetched consistently or your main content isn't readable at first pass, your best AI-ready content never makes it into the evidence set.

That's what this chapter is for.

Rather than rebuild, you'll run an audit workflow that ends with a short, prioritized fix list. You'll identify the problems, label them in a way your team can act on, and rank what to fix first based on impact, reach, and effort.

If you read the entire chapter, you'll know what's broken, how bad it is, and what to fix first.

Here's what you'll walk away with:

- A crawl findings summary (the "what")
- A prioritized fix list (the "what first")
- A minimum AI-ready pass-fail checklist (the "are we even eligible?")

This chapter covers triage and decision-making only. Chapter 11 is where you can implement the fixes.

Crawling Your Site and Reading the Findings

Understanding crawling is important because, before you can interpret the findings, you need to understand what you're looking at. *Crawling* is the process of using a bot (similar to how search engines and AI systems navigate the web) to visit your site's pages, follow links, and record what it encounters. It's essentially a simulation of how machines discover and interpret your site. This section is about learning to read what a crawl is telling you; not fixing anything yet. Your job is to turn a pile of warnings into a clear story:

- What's broken
- How widespread it is
- Whether it threatens AI visibility
- Where it probably lives (template, plugin, server rule, migration leftovers)

Start with the right crawl scope (so that you don't drown)

Before you run any crawls, decide what you're crawling and why. You'll run two types of crawl passes:

- **Wide lens (whole-site crawl):** Use this to spot systemic problems that repeat across templates, categories, and navigation.

- **Money lens: (most-important-pages crawl):** Pick your ten most important pages and audit them like your revenue depends on it, because it does. Here are some examples: home page, core service pages, pricing page, Best and Alternatives pages, top converting landing pages, and main category pages (if e-commerce).

TIP

If you're unsure which pages matter most, use your analytics (or a tool such as Rankability) to choose the set. The point is focus.

REMEMBER

A whole-site crawl tells you what's happening across the site. A money-page crawl tells you whether your business-critical pages are even eligible to show up in AI answers.

Set up your crawl lenses

A crawl is only as useful as the lens you use to view your site. The same site, viewed through different lenses, will show different problems.

Lens 1: User-agent choice

A *user agent* is the label a crawler sends when it visits your site. In plain English, it tells the server who is requesting the page. Different user agents can receive different responses, which means the same page may appear differently depending on who's asking for it. To see whether your site serves different content or access levels to different crawlers, run two passes:

- **Baseline lens:** Googlebot (or the closest available option in your crawler)
- **Reality check lens:** A generic bot user-agent (if your site behaves differently for unknown agents)

The baseline crawl shows how a major search engine is likely to access your site. The reality-check crawl helps reveal whether security rules, bot management tools, or other configurations treat less-recognized crawlers differently.

Why it matters for AI: If security settings treat bots outside the major search engines as suspicious, you might accidentally block systems that power AI answers, research tools, or citation engines.

TIP

If you're using Cloudflare or another web application firewall (WAF), assume that bot management can create false positives. Your crawl results might be telling you about security rules, not your content.

Lens 2: Render mode choice

Render mode determines how your crawler views a page. By comparing a page before and after JavaScript runs, you can see whether important content is available immediately or only after the browser assembles the page. Check important pages in both modes:

- **HTML-only:** The content visible in the raw page, before any JavaScript runs.
- **Rendered (JavaScript):** The page content that appears after scripts execute and the page is fully assembled.

Why it matters for AI: Many retrieval systems act more like fast fetchers than full browsers. If your key content only appears after heavy client-side rendering, you're making it harder for those systems to reliably extract and use your content as evidence.

REMEMBER

If your important content isn't present in HTML (or server-rendered), it's harder to extract, chunk, and cite consistently.

Lens 3: Scope and limits

Define how much of your site you're going to crawl and how deep you want to go. Don't try to be perfect. Just be consistent.

TIP

For example, an e-commerce site may generate a separate URL for every color, size, sort order, and filter combination. If your crawler follows every version, your crawl can balloon from hundreds of useful pages to thousands of low-value URLs. Set limits so the crawl shows real site problems instead of endless URL variations.

Launch a whole-site crawl

You don't want to crawl every possible URL variation your site can generate. Follow these steps:

1. **Start with a whole-site crawl using sane limits.**
2. **Avoid the traps that can explode a crawl, like infinite calendars, parameter combinations, and faceted filters that create endless near-duplicate pages.**

3. **Make a second pass with extra attention on your top pages.**

   These are the pages that matter most to revenue or conversions, so treat them like a separate audit. If you can, check them in both modes: HTML-only (what a fast retriever might see) and rendered (what appears after JavaScript runs).

TIP

Use the right tools for the job. You're not "doing technical SEO" here. You're doing triage, which means gathering evidence and making decisions. Here are some tools to consider:

- **Screaming Frog:** Your primary diagnostic tool, used to surface status codes, indexability signals, canonical tags, redirect chains, duplicates, internal links, and crawl depth.

  TECHNICAL STUFF

  Canonical tags are HTML signals that point search engines to the preferred version of a page. After this point, I use canonicals as shorthand for those tags.

- **Siteliner:** Gives you a quick reality check on duplicate content and thin pages.
- **Rankability:** Keeps you focused on what matters by anchoring the audit around your Top 10 most important pages.

REMEMBER

Tools won't fix SEO or AI search visibility. They help you find opportunities, but it's your job to decide what's worth focusing on. (More on this in the next chapter.)

How to read crawl output without becoming overwhelmed

Most crawls spit out hundreds (or thousands) of issues. An *issue* is anything the crawler flags as unusual, inconsistent, or potentially problematic based on predefined rules, such as missing tags, duplicate pages, or redirect chains. Most so-called issues are just noise. The trick is to sort findings into a few meaningful buckets.

A finding deserves attention when it repeats across a template, affects a money page, blocks crawlability or rendering, or creates confusion about the correct source URL. If it affects one low-value page and doesn't block discovery, leave it for later.

REMEMBER

When in doubt, keep findings that repeat, block access, hide content, or affect revenue pages. Park isolated cleanup items until the high-impact work is done.

TIP

Create a simple Crawl Findings Summary sheet with columns for Issue, Finding Type, Example URL, URLs Affected, Money Page Impact, AI Retrieval Risk, and Notes. As you review the crawl, write a short description of the specific problem in the Issue column (for example, "Product pages blocked by robots.txt" or "Pricing content missing from HTML"). Then assign each finding to one of the following Finding Type categories:

- Indexing and access
  - Robots directives
  - Noindex tags
  - Blocked resources
  - Authentication walls
- Rendering and missing content
  - Thin or empty HTML
  - JavaScript-only content
  - Delayed content
  - Hidden text
- Canonicalization and duplicates
  - Incorrect canonicals
  - Duplicate clusters
  - Parameter variants
  - Near-identical pages
- Redirects and status code waste
  - Redirect chains
  - Redirect loops
  - Soft 404s (see the next section)
  - Broken internal links
  - Excessive redirects
- Architecture and discoverability
  - Deep important pages
  - Orphan pages
  - Weak internal linking
  - Inconsistent hubs

After everything is sorted, you can compare like with like. At that point, your findings stop being a list of random warnings and become a set of patterns you can evaluate and prioritize. It becomes decision-making, not Whac-A-Mole.

For every issue you keep, answer these six questions in plain English:

- What is it? (Name the problem without jargon.)
- How do you spot it?
- Which report, column, or pattern revealed it?
- Why does it matter for AI retrieval?
- Does it block fetching, reduce trust, or make passage extraction inconsistent?
- Where does it usually live? (Examples: template, plugin, server rules, migrations, CMS settings, security layer)

Those answers become the short notes in your Crawl Findings Summary. Later, you'll use the same notes to score severity, reach, commercial impact, and effort.

High-impact issues and how to interpret them

Not all issues are worth your time. This section lists the most common problems you'll see that are *high-leverage:* They tend to affect important pages, repeat across the site, or directly impact whether AI systems can access and trust your content. Notice the pattern: what it is, how to spot it, why it matters, and where it usually lives. Think of these as abbreviated versions of the notes you capture in your Crawl Findings Summary.

These are the issues to prioritize (the examples in this list use four visible labels so they stay easy to scan. Use the other two questions from the previous section, "Which report, column, or pattern revealed it?" and "Does it block fetching, reduce trust, or make passage extraction inconsistent?" as notes in your crawl sheet):

- **Blocked by `robots.txt`**
  - *What it is:* Crawlers are told, "Do not enter."
  - *How to spot it:* Look for "Blocked by `robots.txt`" flags, missing crawl coverage, or entire folders not crawled.

- *Why it matters for AI retrieval:* If a bot can't fetch a page, it can't use it as evidence.
- *Where it usually lives:* In `robots.txt` rules, security settings, or staging rules carried into production.

REMEMBER

Blocking bad bots sounds smart until you block the bots that help you get discovered.

» **Noindex on important pages (or mixed index signals)**

- *What it is:* A page exists but tells bots not to index it or sends conflicting signals.
- *How to spot it:* Indexability status shows noindex, or headers conflict with meta tags.
- *Why it matters for AI retrieval:* Many systems pull from sets of indexed pages or trusted caches. Conflicting signals reduce stability and trust.
- *Where it usually lives:* In CMS plugins, templates, HTTP headers, or staging or dev settings.

TIP

When you see noindex, don't assume that it's intentional. Verify whether it's on purpose or a leftover setting.

» **Redirect chains and loops**

- *What it is:* A URL hops through multiple redirects before landing, or never lands cleanly.
- *How to spot it:* Look for reports showing more than one redirect before the final page loads, such as 301 → 301 → 200, or loops. A 301 means permanent redirect, and 200 means the final page loaded successfully.
- *Why it matters for AI retrieval:* Chains waste crawl budget, slow discovery, and reduce reliability.
- *Where it usually lives:* In site migrations, old http-to-https rules, www versus non-www rules, old page slugs, or canonical mistakes.

» **Soft 404s and thin Not Found pages**

- *What it is:* A page looks like an error to Google even if it returns 200 or it's effectively empty.
- *How to spot it:* Look for soft 404 indicators, very low word count, thin-content patterns, and high broken internal links.
- *Why it matters for AI retrieval:* These pages don't make good evidence. They also break internal pathways for discovery.

- *Where it usually lives:* In deleted pages, poor redirects, expired listings, search pages, or thin tag archives.

» **Thin or empty HTML (content missing on initial load)**

- *What it is:* The raw HTML contains mostly navigation and placeholders, though the real content is injected later by JavaScript.
- *How to spot it:* An HTML-only crawl shows little main content, but rendered crawl shows full content.
- *Why it matters for AI retrieval:* If a system can't extract clean passages reliably, it can't cite you reliably.
- *Where it usually lives:* In SPA builds, heavy JavaScript frameworks, delayed hydration, lazy-loaded content, or gated sections.

REMEMBER

If the content isn't there when the bot looks, it might as well not exist.

» **Canonical confusion**

- *What it is:* The page claims that a different URL is the "real" version, or canonicals are inconsistent across variants.
- *How to spot it:* The canonical points to a different URL than expected, or it changes based on parameters.
- *Why it matters for AI retrieval:* AI systems need a stable source of truth, so to speak. Canonical confusion fragments signals and can push the wrong version into the evidence set.
- *Where it usually lives:* In templates, parameter handling, pagination, internationalization, or e-commerce filters.

» **Duplicate clusters**

- *What it is:* Multiple URLs contain the same (or nearly the same) content.
- *How to spot it:* Look for duplicate content reports (Siteliner helps here), nearly identical title tags and meta descriptions, and URL parameter variations.
- *Why it matters for AI retrieval:* It dilutes authority and increases the odds that a weak or wrong variant gets selected.
- *Where it usually lives:* In tag archives, faceted navigation, location pages, printer-friendly versions, or tracking parameters.

» **Money pages are too deep or are orphaned**

- *What it is:* Your most important pages are buried or not linked internally.
- *How to spot it:* Look for high crawl depth for key pages, orphaned URL patterns, and weak internal link counts.

- *Why it matters for AI retrieval:* Bots discover and prioritize what your architecture emphasizes. If money pages are hard to find, you're telling machines they're not important.
- *Where it usually lives:* In weak navigation, missing hub pages, or blog posts that never link to commercial pages.

REMEMBER

A page that converts well for humans can still be invisible to bots if it's orphaned or buried.

Note AI retrieval red flags

In your Crawl Findings Summary sheet, add a column called Red Flag. Mark Yes when a finding creates one of the following outcomes:

- **Fetch failure:** Blocked, gated, noindex, persistent 4xx/soft 404.
- **Render failure:** Main content is missing from HTML-only view.
- **Truth ambiguity:** Canonicals and duplicates hide the source of truth.
- **Discovery weakness:** Money pages are buried, orphaned, or not reinforced.
- **Extraction weakness:** Content exists but isn't structured into clean, extractable sections.

These red flags are the findings most likely to prevent you from showing up in AI answers, even if your content is good.

Create a crawl findings summary

Before you move on to triage (see the next section), capture a short summary. Keep it short and simple.

Your summary should include these elements:

- The top five to ten systemic issues you found
- Where each issue occurs (for example, specific page templates or site sections)
- Whether money pages are impacted
- Which issues could prevent AI systems from accessing or using your content (such as fetch or render failures)

REMEMBER

If you can't explain the problem simply, you can't prioritize it confidently.

Deciding What to Fix First

After you've crawled the site and labeled the findings, your job is to make decisions. I'm not saying to "fix everything" or "clean up all warnings." Just decide what to tackle first so that your site becomes reliably crawlable, renderable, and trustworthy.

Think of this process as triage. You're sorting issues into these areas:

- Stop-the-bleeding problems (blocks crawling, indexing, or rendering)
- Performance drags (waste crawl budget, weakened trust, fragmented signals)
- Nice-to-have cleanup (real, but not urgent)

REMEMBER

The goal isn't a perfect audit. The goal is a Top 10 Fixes page that turns findings into action.

Group findings into issue clusters

Before you score anything, combine repeated problems into one cluster. Most crawl reports show the same root issue hundreds of times.

Here are some examples of issue clusters:

- "Legacy redirects create chains across old blog URLs."
- "JavaScript renders main content on service pages, and HTML is thin."
- "Canonical tags are inconsistent on parameter URLs."
- "Internal links point to noncanonical URLs sitewide."
- "Tag pages create duplicate clusters and thin content."

Clustering is how you keep your fix list small and executable. (See Chapter 9 for more on clusters.)

TIP

If the fix would be made in one place (a template, a rule, a plugin setting), treat it as a single issue, even if it affects 5,000 URLs.

Score each issue with the 4-factor triage model

You're not trying to create the perfect score. You're trying to answer a single question:

> "If we fix this, will it noticeably improve crawlability, retrieval eligibility, or revenue pages — and can we ship it soon?"

To do that, give every issue cluster four quick ratings from 1 (low) to 5 (high). Then add them up. Higher totals get fixed first.

Here are the four factors to consider, along with scoring criteria (ratings are 1 through 5, but I've noted 1, 3, and 5 to show the general scale. Use 2 or 4 for issues whose score falls between these examples):

- **Severity (damage): How much does this hurt you?**
  - 5 = Bots can't crawl, index, or see the content (blocked, noindex, missing HTML)
  - 3 = Bots waste time or become confused (redirect chains, broken links, duplication)
  - 1 = Mostly cosmetic or minor
- **Reach (size): How big is the mess?**
  - 5 = Sitewide or multiple templates
  - 3 = One template or one section
  - 1 = Just a few pages
- **Commercial impact (money): Does this affect pages that make you money?**
  - 5 = Hits money pages or conversion paths
  - 3 = Hits high-traffic supporting pages
  - 1 = Hits low-value pages
- **Effort (time): How fast can you ship a true improvement?**
  - 5 = Quick win (hours)
  - 3 = Medium lift (up to a week)
  - 1 = Rebuild-level project

After each issue cluster has been scored, you can calculate the priority score. Just add them up:

Priority Score = Severity + Reach + Commercial Impact + Effort

That's it.

Here's an example so that everything clicks:

- **Issue cluster:** "Service pages are missing main content in HTML-only mode."
  - *Severity:* 5 (bots may not see the content)
  - *Reach:* 3 (service template)
  - *Commercial impact:* 5 (money pages)
  - *Effort:* 3 (likely a template change, not a rebuild)
  - *Total:* 16 (goes near the top of the fix list)
- **Issue cluster**: "A handful of old blog posts have duplicate titles."
  - *Severity:* 2 (minor duplicate-title issue)
  - *Reach:* 1 (a handful of old posts)
  - *Commercial impact:* 1 (low-value supporting content)
  - *Effort:* 5 (quick title cleanup)
  - *Total:* 9 (fix later)

TIP

If two issues tie, fix the one that affects money pages first. If they still tie, fix the one you can ship faster.

Use AI eligibility blockers as automatic escalators

Some issues should jump to the top, even if the score looks similar.

AI eligibility blockers are problems that prevent an important page from being fetched, rendered, indexed, trusted, or discovered. Move an item into your Top 10 (see the next section) if it causes any of these problems:

- Key pages can't be crawled (robots or WAF blocks).
- Key pages aren't index-eligible (noindex or conflicting signals).

- Key content is missing in HTML-only mode (render risk).
- Canonicals point away from the real page (source-of-truth failure).
- Money pages are buried or orphaned (discovery failure).

These are the problems that prevent you from being used as evidence in AI answers.

Create your Top 10 Fixes page

When you're ready to create your Top 10 Fixes page, remember that a crawl report is simply information; a Top 10 Fixes list is a plan.

TIP

Think of the Top 10 Fixes page as the one you can hand to a developer, a client, or your team and they instantly know what to fix, why it matters, and what to do next.

TIP

Limit it to one page on purpose. If it spills into three pages, it stops getting used.

For each of the following items, write it in plain English and include just enough detail to take action:

- **Issue name:** What's wrong, stated simply
- **Bucket:** The fix-it category where the issue belongs (HTML/Rendering, Architecture/Internal Links, Speed/Redirects/404, or Schema/FAQ/Fact Hub)
- **Why it matters:** One sentence that ties to crawlability, retrieval, or revenue pages
- **Scope:** A rough count of URLs affected plus two or three sample URLs
- **Priority score:** The number from your triage model
- **Owner:** Who's responsible for fixing it
- **Notes:** Dependencies, risks, or anything else that can slow down the fix

TIP

If you can't describe the issue and why it matters in a single sentence, it's not ready to be prioritized.

Build your prioritized fix list

After you have your Top 10 Fixes page, add only the next-best opportunities until your working fix list reaches 20 items.

Why the cap matters:

- A 60-item fix list becomes a maybe-someday list
- A 10–20 item fix list becomes a shipping plan

When you hit 20 items, you're done. Everything else waits for the next audit cycle.

REMEMBER

This fix list is a lever, not a museum exhibit.

Tag every item to a fix-it bucket

By marking each item with a fix-it bucket, you create a bridge from triage to implementation. These are the same buckets used in Chapter 11, where you learn how to implement the fixes. Every fix item must map to exactly one of these categories:

- HTML/Rendering
- Architecture/Internal Links
- Speed/Redirects/404
- Schema/FAQ/Fact Hub

If an item doesn't clearly fit, it's probably too vague or too broad. Rewrite it until it fits.

Pick the first sprint

Choose your first sprint of fixes (your action plan): three to five fixes you can focus on immediately to generate some quick wins.

To turn your audit into momentum, pick items that:

- Remove eligibility blockers first.
- Improve money pages first.
- Are high impact and low effort.
- Can be shipped independently (minimal dependencies).

REMEMBER

You're not trying to "do technical SEO." You're trying to make your site reliably usable as evidence. That's what unlocks everything else.

Producing a Minimum AI-Ready Checklist

Before you start chasing AI answers, you need to know whether your site is even eligible. This checklist is pass-fail on purpose. These aren't "nice-to-have best practices." These are the gates that determine whether bots can reliably fetch your pages, understand what's on them, and trust them enough to use as evidence.

If you fail any gate, don't panic: You just found your fastest path to progress. (The fixes live in Chapter 11.)

REMEMBER

You can't win AI visibility with clever content if your site fails the basics of crawl, render, and trust.

Setting up the checklist

Create a small checklist in the same place you keep your crawl findings. A spreadsheet works best because you can add one row for each of your ten most important pages and one column for each gate. Mark each cell Pass, Fail, or Needs Review, and add a short note when something fails. If you already created a crawl findings sheet earlier in this chapter, add a new tab called AI-Ready Checklist so the audit stays in one place.

At each gate, perform a simple pass-fail test to see whether a page meets a requirement for crawlability and AI visibility. Include these gates in your checklist:

- **Gate 1: Your important content is present in the HTML (or server-rendered).**

  Pass if: The main content is visible in the raw HTML, not just after heavy JavaScript runs.

  Fail if: The HTML is mostly placeholders, and your real content appears only after rendering.

  Why this matters: AI systems need extractable passages. If there's nothing to extract when the bot looks, you're not a reliable source.

- **Gate 2: Key pages return a clean 200 status code.**

  Pass if: Your money pages return 200 consistently.

  Fail if: You see 3xx loops, 4xx, 5xx, or "Soft 404" behavior on important pages.

TECHNICAL STUFF

The xx label refers to redirect status codes, such as 301 and 302.

Why this matters: Inconsistent fetching means inconsistent evidence. Even one unstable hop can knock you out of the retrieval set.

- **Gate 3: You're not blocking crawlers by accident.**

  Pass if: Key pages are crawlable and not blocked by `robots.txt` or security rules.

  Fail if: Your crawler reports "blocked," "access denied," or you see inconsistent results that point to bot protection.

  Why this matters: Blocked pages don't get used. Also, bot protection tools can unintentionally block legitimate systems that support AI answers.

- **Gate 4: You're not telling bots "don't index this" on pages that matter.**

  Pass if: Important pages are index-eligible (no unintended noindex, no conflicting directives).

  Fail if: Money pages are noindexed, or you see mixed signals between meta tags and headers.

  Why this matters: You're sending "do not trust/use this" signals to systems that rely on indexing and caching.

- **Gate 5: Canonicals are sane and consistent (clear source of truth).**

  Pass if: Canonicals consistently point to the correct primary URL.

  Fail if: Canonicals frequently point to unexpected variants, parameter URLs, or other pages.

  Why this matters: AI retrieval prefers a stable source. Canonical confusion fragments signals and increases the odds the wrong page gets selected.

- **Gate 6: Money pages are easy to discover within a few clicks.**

  Pass if: Important pages are reachable quickly from navigation, hubs, or strong internal links.

  Fail if: Money pages are buried deep, weakly linked, or orphaned.

  Why this matters: If your own architecture doesn't treat a page as important, bots won't either.

- **Gate 7: You have no systemic redirect chains.**

  Pass if: Redirects are mostly one hop (or rare).

  Fail if: Redirect chains and loops are common, especially on internal links.

  Why this matters: Chains waste crawl budget, slow discovery, and reduce reliability.

» **Gate 8: Internal links don't routinely lead to dead ends.**

Pass if: Broken internal links and soft 404s are rare and isolated.

Fail if: Large sections of the site link to 404s, soft 404s, or outdated URLs.

Why this matters: Dead ends break discovery paths and weaken trust across the site.

» **Gate 9: Structured data is valid where you use it.**

Pass if: Schema validates and matches what's on the page.

Fail if: Schema is broken, inconsistent, or fails to reflect the visible content.

Why this matters: You're not trying to add schema everywhere. You're trying to avoid trust-eroding errors.

TIP

Run these tests on your ten most important pages first (money pages). This is your eligibility test: If you fail multiple gates, you'll gain bigger wins fixing foundations than publishing more content.

Tagging your results

Use this final pass as a cross-check, not a second fix list. If a failed gate (a pass/fail check that determines whether a page is eligible for reliable AI retrieval) already appears in your Top 10 Fixes list, keep it there. If it doesn't, add it now because a failed gate means the page may not be eligible for reliable AI retrieval.

If you passed most gates, that's outstanding! Your pages are eligible. Move forward with confidence.

If you failed any gates, those failures become your highest-priority fix items.

Now tag every failed gate into a single fix-it bucket:

- HTML/Rendering
- Architecture/Internal Links
- Speed/Redirects/404
- Schema/FAQ/Fact Hub

This chapter tells you what's broken and what to fix first. Chapter 11 shows you how to build it right.

IN THIS CHAPTER

» Turning your prioritized fix list into clear build tickets, with *done* defined up front

» Shipping clean HTML patterns that bots can reliably crawl, retrieve, and quote

» Strengthening site structure and internal links so that your most important pages get found and digested faster

» Implementing speed fixes, redirects, 404 reclamation, and structured content patterns (FAQ blocks and fact hubs) the right way

Chapter 11

Establishing Foundations That Bots (and Models) Love

Results give you a place to start. If you haven't read Chapter 10, take some time to look it over. In that chapter, I show you how to crawl your site, figure out what matters for AI retrieval, and turn a long list of issues into a prioritized fix list. Based on those results, in this chapter, you can fix the top problems in a way that machines can consistently understand. In other words, you want to show bots and models that your content is accessible, clearly structured, connected to related pages, and backed by stable facts.

This chapter is about implementation. Not "It looks fine in the browser" and not "It's technically valid." Instead, you build pages that are structured, predictable, and easy for crawlers and retrieval systems to fetch, parse, and reuse as evidence.

Here's the shift: You're not just doing SEO cleanup. You're laying a foundation that helps your site get crawled, retrieved, and cited.

This chapter shows you how to:

- Structure pages so that bots can extract the right sections and claims.
- Design internal links so that important pages are discovered and understood faster.
- Implement speed and redirect fixes that improve crawl depth and freshness.
- Use schema, FAQ blocks, and fact hubs as repeatable systems.

And you won't leave with vague advice. You'll have rules of thumb, good-versus-bad examples, and checklists you can use to verify the build before it ships.

Focusing On Which Issues to Fix First

A prioritized fix list matters only if it turns into shipped fixes. The easiest way to get stuck is to open your site, see a couple dozen problems, and decide to "clean up everything." That's how one clear priority becomes ten half-finished projects.

Instead, work on these two tasks:

- Pick the top three issues from your Chapter 10 fix list.
- Turn each one into a build ticket that's easy to execute and easy to verify.

You don't just want to document the problem — you want to prove that the issue is fixed so that bots and models can rank, retrieve, and summarize your content.

Pick your top three issues

Start with issues that affect the pages most likely to drive revenue or visibility. In most cases, the top issues have one or more of these traits:

- They block or weaken access to an important page.
- They repeat across a template, so one fix improves many pages.
- They affect pages tied to commercial prompts, citations, pricing, products, services, or locations.
- They are small enough to finish and verify before you move to the next two priorities.

A simple rule works well: pick the fixes with the highest expected impact, the widest reach, and the lowest reasonable effort. Save cosmetic cleanup for later.

Create a build ticket

Before you even consider touching code, turn each of your top three issues from your fix list into a build ticket. A *build ticket* is a short, actionable task that tells you exactly what to fix and what *done* looks like. A fix is *done* when it's fully implemented and verified to work in practice.

A build ticket can live in whatever system you already use. A simple spreadsheet works fine for solo work. A project management tool such as Asana, Trello, Jira, ClickUp, or Monday works better when several people need to assign, review, and approve the fix.

TIP

Use the same short format every time. If a ticket can't be understood in one quick read, it's too vague.

To set up your build ticket, answer these criteria questions:

- **Goal:** What should improve when this task is complete? Choose one primary outcome and then list any secondary wins.

  Examples: Better crawl reliability, clear retrieval, higher citation odds, steadier indexing, improved UX, better conversion.
- **Surface area:** Where will the change happen? List the exact templates, components, and systems involved.

  Examples: Blog post template, service page template, navigation, routing rules, CMS fields, schema generator, caching.
- **Acceptance criteria:** What does *done* mean in plain language? Then attach the relevant build-validation checklist from later in this chapter that matches the kind of fix you're shipping.

Examples: "Main content shows up in view source," "No redirect chains," "FAQ answers visible on-page and match the schema," "Hub page links to every spoke."

- **Risk level:** Tag the ticket so that you know how carefully to implement it and how to roll it out. Use the following tags:
  - *Low:* Copy, headings, internal links, small HTML structure changes
  - *Medium:* URL changes, routing, navigation changes, canonical and redirect updates
  - *High:* Rendering strategy, caching, major template refactors, JavaScript-heavy behavior changes

REMEMBER

Don't "clean up everything." Ship the top three issues, validate them with the checklists in this chapter, and then go back for the next three. Results compound when your implementations are consistent and complete, not when you attempt a big rewrite.

Creating Clean, AI-Friendly HTML

This section isn't about audits — it's about how you use patterns to build pages. Your goal is to make sure your most important content is immediately visible in HTML, clearly structured, and easy for bots to extract.

Bots don't see your page the same way humans do. If a crawler can't fetch and parse your core content quickly and consistently, you're forcing it to do extra work just to understand what a human sees instantly. Some systems do that work. Many don't. And even when they do, anything inconsistent increases the chances of partial indexing, weak retrieval, and missed citations.

Core build guidelines

Use core build guidelines when you build or update the pages that matter most to your business, such as pricing pages, service pages, product pages, location pages, pillar pages, and other pages you want bots to crawl, retrieve, and cite. You can apply the same ideas to lower-priority pages but make them required for pages that affect revenue or AI visibility. The guidelines include:

- **Put the main content in server-rendered HTML whenever possible.** If the HTML a bot receives at first is mostly empty and JavaScript has to add the real page content later, crawlers and retrieval systems may not see the page consistently.

- **Use semantic structure.** Your page outline should still make sense even if someone ignores the visual design. The headings, lists, tables, and definitions should carry the structure:
  - H1/H2/H3 for hierarchy
  - Lists for sets and steps
  - Tables for comparisons
  - Definition-style blocks for terms and entities
- **Write retrieval-friendly passages.** Keep paragraphs short and self-contained. Name the entity. State the claim clearly. Avoid "pronoun soup."
- **Keep important text visible:** Avoid putting key answers only behind complex JavaScript, click-to-open sections, or content that appears after the page loads.

If an important answer appears only after someone clicks a closed dropdown, tab, or other hidden section, bots may extract it inconsistently or treat it as less important, especially if that text is not in the HTML that loads first.

How pages load

You don't need to be a developer to make the right call for loading pages. You just need to understand what the bot receives first. Pages can deliver content in two common ways:

- **Server-side rendering (SSR):** The HTML arrives with actual page content. This is best for crawl, retrieval, and quickly showing visible content to users. Bots can parse it immediately, and so can systems that store passages for later use.
- **Client-side rendering (CSR):** The HTML arrives mostly empty, and content appears after JavaScript runs. This is risky because many crawlers and retrieval systems don't reliably wait, render, and execute everything. Even when they do, rendering budgets and timeouts vary.

WARNING

If your page renders one item on the server and then changes it on the client, bots can see inconsistent versions. Known as a *hydration pitfall*, it's anything that causes a mismatch between server output and client output during page loading. The disconnect can lead to partial indexing, wrong extraction, or missing passages. Consistency matters more than cleverness.

SSR VERSUS CSR: WHICH TO USE AND WHEN

The way your pages load determines whether bots can immediately access your content or have to work to reconstruct it. Follow these guidelines.

If you use React, Vue, Next, Nuxt, or SvelteKit, aim for SSR on these elements:

- Money pages (services, product, pricing, location pages)
- Core informational pages you want cited
- Hub pages that control internal linking and discovery

If you must use CSR, treat the initial HTML like a minimum viable page. Make sure it still contains these elements:

- **The H1:** The main page title that names the page topic
- **A first-answer paragraph:** A direct, plain-language answer near the top
- **Primary body copy:** At least the key sections, not just headings
- **Internal links to related pages:** Actual links in the HTML

If the H1, first-answer paragraph, primary body copy, and internal links aren't present in the HTML that loads, you're gambling with crawl and retrieval.

TIP

Use view source as a quick reality check. In your browser, right-click the page and choose View Page Source. Then search for the H1, the first-answer paragraph, and a few lines of body copy. If you can find them there, a basic crawler is more likely to see them without rendering JavaScript.

Good and bad HTML structure

Use the examples in this section to check whether your page structure explains itself. The good examples make the page topic and sections clear. The bad examples force bots and readers to infer too much.

» **Good — machine-readable and chunk-friendly:**

- One H1 that matches the page's main topic
- H2s that map to user intents and questions

- Short paragraphs that can stand alone
- Lists and tables where comparisons matter
- Definition-style blocks for entities and key terms

» **Bad — hard to parse, unclear hierarchy:**

- Multiple H1s
- Headings used for styling, not hierarchy
- Giant paragraphs with multiple claims and unnamed pronouns (*it* or *they*, for example)
- Important answers hidden inside collapsible (accordion) sections that users must click to expand

Retrieval-friendly passage pattern

Your content should work in small chunks. Use this pattern near the top of key sections, especially on pages you want retrieved and cited:

» **Sentence 1:** Name the entity and make the claim.

» **Sentence 2:** Explain who the entity, product, or service is for or when it applies.

» **Sentence 3:** Add proof, constraint, or the next step.

Here's a sample structure:

» "[Entity] is [category] that [does what]."

» "It's best for [audience/use case] when [condition]."

» "The key differentiator is [proof/metric/example]."

This structure reduces ambiguity and makes passages easier to lift accurately.

Build-validation checklist (HTML)

To prevent problems, double-check these elements in your build ticket before you ship:

» **The page source (view source):** Contains primary headings and core body copy, not just placeholders

- **H1:** Exactly one allowed
- **The H2/H3 hierarchy:** Makes sense when skimmed without CSS
- **Core answers:** Are visible without clicking accordions or tabs
- **Key tables and lists:** Rendered as real HTML (not images)
- **Internal links:** Are real <a href> links in the HTML

TECHNICAL STUFF

An <a href> link is a standard HTML link that points directly to another URL. Chapter 10 shows why JavaScript-only links can be harder for bots to follow.

- **Critical content:** Not blocked by cookie gates or geo pop-ups
- **Canonical tag:** Exists and points to the intended URL

Working with Smart Architecture and Internal Links

Architecture is how bots and retrieval systems find and make sense of your site. Internal links are how you direct attention and explain relationships between pages.

If your content is clean but your structure is chaotic, you still lose. Bots won't reliably discover the right pages, and retrieval systems won't be confident about which pages are "about" what. The goal isn't a bigger site — it's a site that's easy to navigate, easy to map, and hard to misunderstand.

Setting up a good architecture

Use this list as your mental model for a bot-friendly site:

- **Important pages are reachable in three clicks or fewer from the home page.** If humans struggle to reach the page, bots will too. Also, pages that sit deep in the site tend to get crawled less often.
- **Every cluster has a clear hub and spokes.** A hub page (pillar or category) defines the topic. Spoke pages cover the subtopics and link back to the hub (see the later section "Using a hub-and-spoke pattern").
- **Internal links define how pages connect.** Internal links use descriptive anchors (clickable link text) that reveal topic and intent.

- **Anchor text is a label.** It tells machines what the destination is about before they even fetch it.
- **Navigation and breadcrumbs reflect true hierarchy.** Your site should have an obvious map, of sorts, that matches both your URL structure and your content relationships.

Making internal links work for you

Internal links should work like street signs, not decorations. Each link should help explain where a page fits in your site and what the next logical step is for the reader. Follow these guidelines to create strong links between pages:

- **Link for meaning, not just for SEO.** A strong internal link answers this question: "What should the reader do next, and why?" (Bots follow meaning, too.)
- **Use anchors that describe the destination in plain language:**
  - *Good:* "Sump pump repair in Chicago"
  - *Bad:* "Click here" or "Learn more"
- **Put the most important internal links where they'll be seen:**
  - In the main body content (not only in footers)
  - Near relevant passages (right where the concept is introduced)
- **Avoid orphan pages.** Crawl paths stop at orphans. That's also where topical authority breaks. Every important page should have:
  - At least one link to it from a relevant hub page
  - Two to five links out to closely related pages (so that it stays inside a cluster)

Differentiating good and bad internal links

Check out these examples of good and bad internal links:

- **Good internal links:**
  - "If you need sump pump repair, see our repair service page for pricing, common failure signs, and scheduling."
  - "Compare options in battery backup versus water-powered backup."
  - "For maintenance, use the seasonal sump pump checklist."

» **Bad internal links:**

- "We offer many services. Click here."
- Footer-only links to key services
- Random cross-links between unrelated posts

TIP

The good examples do one important thing: They tell both humans and machines what the destination will deliver.

Using a hub-and-spoke pattern

You don't need a complicated model. You need consistency and clear relationships between pages. A *hub-and-spoke pattern* is a way of organizing content so that one main page (the hub) connects to several detailed subpages (the spokes). This arrangement helps both users and bots understand which pages belong together and how topics are broken down.

Here's an example of a hub-and-spoke pattern at work:

» **Hub page:** Should introduce the main category and then route users (and crawlers) to more specific pages. Sample hub page: "Sump pump services." Provide links to repair, installation, battery backup, cost, FAQ, and emergency service.

» **Spoke page:** Covers one focused subtopic in depth. Each page links back to the hub and links sideways to two or three closely related spokes. For example: The repair page links to cost and battery backup.

This structure does two things at one time:

» **It improves discovery.** Bots can move through the cluster quickly.

» **It clarifies relationships.** Retrieval systems can see which pages belong together.

Build-validation checklist (architecture and links)

Use this checklist after you update navigation, breadcrumbs, hub pages, or internal links. Copy it into the build ticket and confirm each item before you mark the ticket complete. Make sure:

- Every money page is linked from at least one hub page.
- Hub pages link to all priority spokes.
- Breadcrumbs exist on deeper pages (and match the URL structure).
- Important pages aren't buried behind search, filters, or infinite scroll.
- Internal links are crawlable HTML anchors, not JavaScript-only click handlers.
- Anchor text is descriptive and varies naturally, not the same anchor repeated sitewide.

Structuring with Schemas, FAQs, and Fact Hubs

Schemas, FAQs, and fact hubs are how you turn content into structured, reusable information. Rather than just publish pages, you define what your content is, and what it says, and how individual facts can be reliably extracted and reused.

This section is about implementing those structures, not validating them. (For validation and diagnosis, see Chapter 10.) Here, you implement patterns that make your content easier to reuse accurately.

Knowing which schema to use

You don't need to memorize dozens of schema types (see Chapter 4). Schema works best when it labels the main purpose of the page. Use the following as a simple decision guide on when to use certain types of schema for certain situations:

- **Is this your brand/business entity home?** Use Organization (or LocalBusiness, if local) on the Entity Home/About/Contact page.
- **Is this a specific product or plan page?** Use Product (and Offer, when appropriate).
- **Does the page contain Q&A that users actually ask?** Use FAQPage only when the questions and answers are visible on the page.

REMEMBER

Do *not* add schema for content you don't visibly show. If it's not on the page, it doesn't belong in the markup. Invisible Q&A and phantom offers create trust issues and extraction mismatches.

Using FAQ blocks

An FAQ block is one of the simplest structured systems you can ship because it does three jobs at one time: Clarify commercial intent, remove friction for humans, and give machines clean, extractable answers. Follow these guidelines to create a usable FAQ block:

- **Follow a simple FAQ block pattern:**
  - Keep answers brief and literal.
  - Put pricing, timing, guarantees, and constraints in plain language.
  - Avoid marketing fog — bots prefer directness.
- **Use this format:**
  - *Question:* [Commercial question] (See the next bullet.)
  - *Answer (no more than three sentences):* Direct answer, context, and proof/constraint/next step
- **Try these commercial FAQs:**
  - "How much does it cost?"
  - "Which factors affect price?"
  - "How fast can you schedule?"
  - "Do you offer emergency service?"
  - "What brands/areas do you serve?"
  - "What's included (and what isn't)?"

TIP

To keep your Q&A easy for machines to use without losing accuracy, follow these FAQ writing rules:

- Start each answer with a direct response.
- Add one sentence of context.
- Add one sentence of proof or the next step.

Here's an example of an FAQ block:

> Question: How much does sump pump repair cost in Chicago?
>
> Answer: Most sump pump repairs in Chicago cost between $150 and $600, depending on the part, accessibility, and whether the service is an emergency. The diagnostic fee is applied to the repair if you approve the work. For an exact quote, schedule an inspection.

Setting up fact hubs

A *fact hub* (see Chapter 4) is a single page that gathers the most important, verifiable information about a topic in one place with these elements:

- The claim
- The entity it refers to
- A date (and Last Updated)
- A source link or internal reference
- Notes or definition boundaries

Why it works: It gives systems a single location to confirm what's true, and then your other pages can link back to it. Rather than repeat numbers across 15 or so pages and let them drift out of sync, you centralize the source of truth and distribute it via internal links.

TIP

To create a fact hub layout, use this simple structure:

- **H1:** [Brand/topic] facts and statistics
- **Intro paragraph:** What this page is and how often it's updated
- **Table:** Claim | Value | Applies To | Source | Last Verified | Notes
- **Sections for common clusters:** Company facts, product facts, pricing facts, performance/stat facts, and definitions (what you mean by *key terms*)

When thinking about internal linking for fact hubs, follow these guidelines:

- Every time you cite a key number or claim elsewhere, link the claim text back to the Fact Hub row or section.
- Fact hub links out to the full-context pages (case study, methodology, or documentation, for example).

This strategy creates a clean verification path:

Claim → source of truth → supporting evidence

Build-validation checklist: Schema, FAQ, fact hub

Use this checklist after you add or update schema, FAQ blocks, or a fact hub. Copy the items into the build ticket so the publisher, marketer, or developer can verify that the structured content matches the visible page. The checklist is as follows:

- » The Organization (or LocalBusiness) schema exists on the entity home page.
- » The Product schema exists on true product/plan pages (not blog posts).
- » The FAQPage schema is used only when Q&A is visible on the page.
- » FAQ answers are short and direct and match the page copy exactly.
- » The fact hub exists for key claims and is linked from pages that repeat those claims.
- » The fact hub includes Last Updated and source notes for numbers.

IN THIS CHAPTER

» **Building clear, official pages buyers and AI can quote**

» **Creating comparisons and reviews that help close the deal**

» **Noting how commercial topics build depth**

Chapter 12

Creating Bottom of Funnel Pages That Win Answers

Search is changing fast. Rather than list dozens of links, AI systems now deliver a single answer or a very short list. That means your bottom of funnel (BoF) pages — content aimed at people who are ready to make a decision — must do more than attract clicks; they have to finish the decision. If your page doesn't clearly answer the buyer's question and support it with proof, the buyer will choose the competitor who does. BoF is no longer about traffic: It's about clarity, trust, and being the final answer.

In this chapter, I show you how to build BoF content that wins decisions. First, you take control of your message by creating clear, official pages that define your pricing, policies, and answers. Then you use comparisons and reviews to help readers choose your solution with confidence. You also see how to use commercial content clusters to create a cohesive asset.

Controlling the Narrative

AI tools and buyers want clear, official answers. Your job is to publish short, quotable pages that make decisions easy. Use literal titles, a one-sentence summary near the top, and simple structure so that people and machines find the same facts fast.

When you leave gaps in your official information, other sources supply the missing information for you. Review sites, affiliates, forums, and outdated blog posts often become the voice of your brand. That leads to confusion, lost trust, and inaccurate AI summaries that spread quickly. Here's what that looks like in practice:

- **Local business:** A directory site lists your "typical prices," and AI repeats them, even though your diagnostic fee changed last quarter. Potential customers think your prices are outdated or inconsistent and stop calling.
- **E-commerce store:** A blogger's summary of your return policy outranks your product pages, and AI tells shoppers that returns aren't free, even though they are. The result is fewer purchases and more customer service complaints.
- **SaaS company:** A comparison site claims that you charge extra for single sign-on (SSO). Your current plans include it, but because there's no clear pricing or FAQ line to quote, AI keeps spreading the wrong details. Buyers who care about security choose another platform.

Each of these problems happens because the brand never published a clear, quotable source of truth. When that happens, someone else controls your narrative.

Building Your Answer Set

At the bottom of the funnel, buyers are looking for answers before they make a final decision. Your *answer set* is the small group of pages that delivers those answers to pricing, policy, and news questions. These three pages are your source of truth. Keep each one short, factual, and easy to quote.

Pricing

Your Pricing page is one of the most visited pages on any website. It's also one of the first places AI systems look when answering "How much does it cost?" If you hide or skip pricing, people and machines will guess, and that rarely helps you. Be upfront and make your pricing simple to understand.

Here's what to include on your Pricing page:

- **Clear prices or honest ranges:** If you charge a fixed rate, list it. If pricing varies, show a realistic range rather than say "Contact us." Transparency builds trust.
- **What's included and what's not:** Spell out exactly what buyers get for the price and any extras that cost more.
- **Ways to compare:** Add a short chooser (for example, "Choose this, if this") or table that helps people pick the right option for their situation.
- **A one-line summary:** Start with an "In short" line that gives a fast, quotable answer to the pricing question. For example:

  In short, most services start around $500, and full packages range between $2,000 and $5,000, depending on scope.

Figure 12-1 shows a real-world pricing table layout that illustrates clear feature-tier segmentation.

TIP

If you can't publish exact prices, publish *something*. A range or starting-at price still shows honesty and helps buyers determine whether they're a fit.

REMEMBER

Buyers don't expect the lowest price — they expect clarity. Be the business that answers the question directly.

Policies and FAQs

Your Policies and FAQ pages should answer every post-purchase question clearly and consistently. Together, they build buyer confidence and give AI systems a single, trusted source to quote. When buyers cannot find refund, warranty, or support details, they turn to other sources, and AI tools may repeat outdated or incorrect information. Clear, human-written answers prevent that confusion and reduce support tickets.

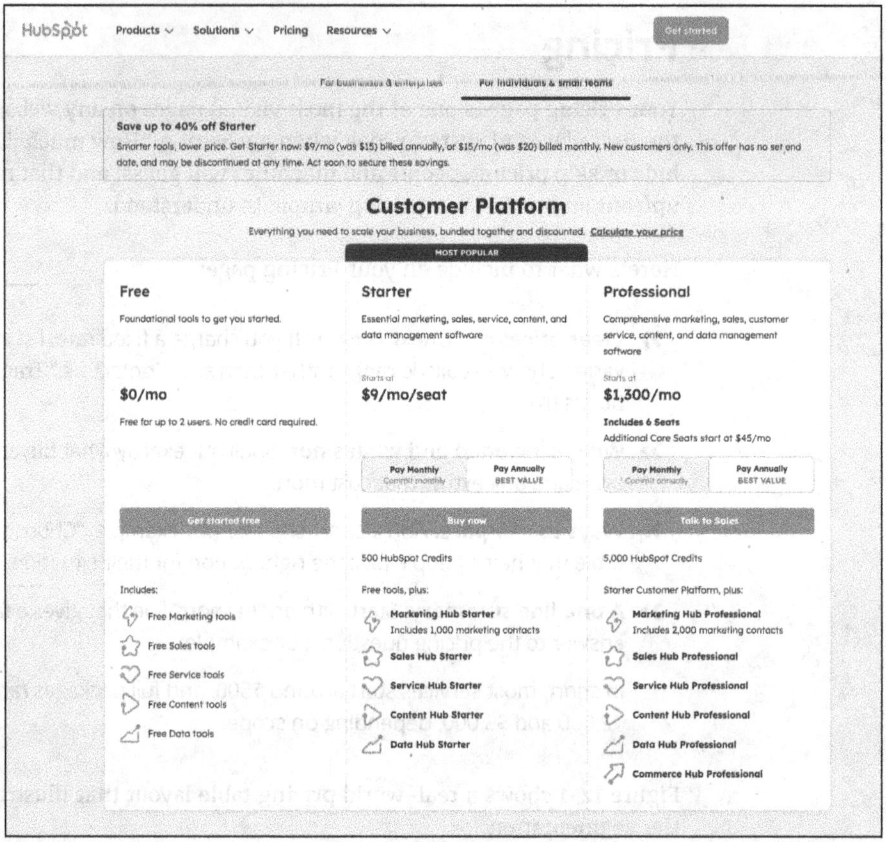

FIGURE 12-1: A clear, user-friendly pricing table from HubSpot.

Source: Screenshot of hubspot.com, used under fair use for commentary.

Taking notes from other brands

It helps to look at what others have done before you. Here are some brands that have conquered the usefulness of their Policies and FAQ pages:

- Nike places top tasks like Returns & Exchanges and Orders & Payment at the top of the page, helping users act fast.

  Figure 12-2 shows Nike's clean, action-first support menu that helps users reach top tasks fast.

- Google Support lets users pick a product or topic before showing answers, so both people and AI find the right content.

  Figure 12-3 shows Google Support's product-chooser layout.

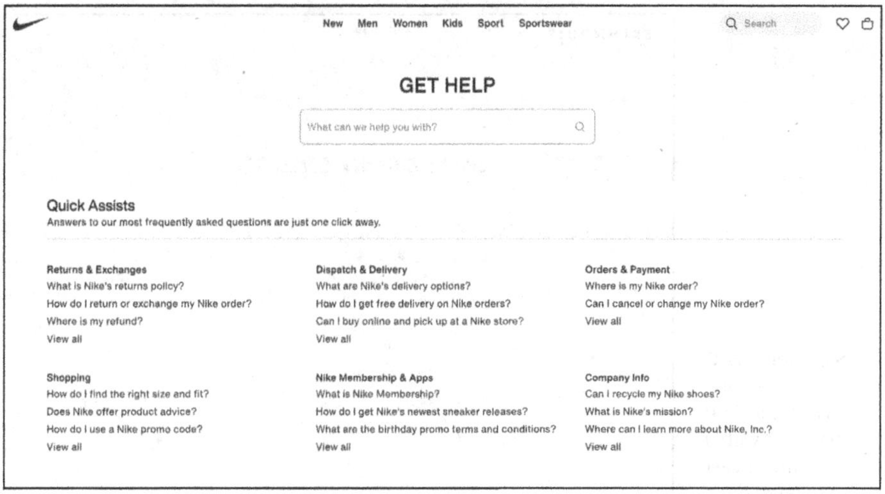

FIGURE 12-2: Nike's Returns & Exchanges and Orders & Payment links appear first, guiding users to common actions.

Source: Screenshot of `nike.com`*, used under fair use for commentary.*

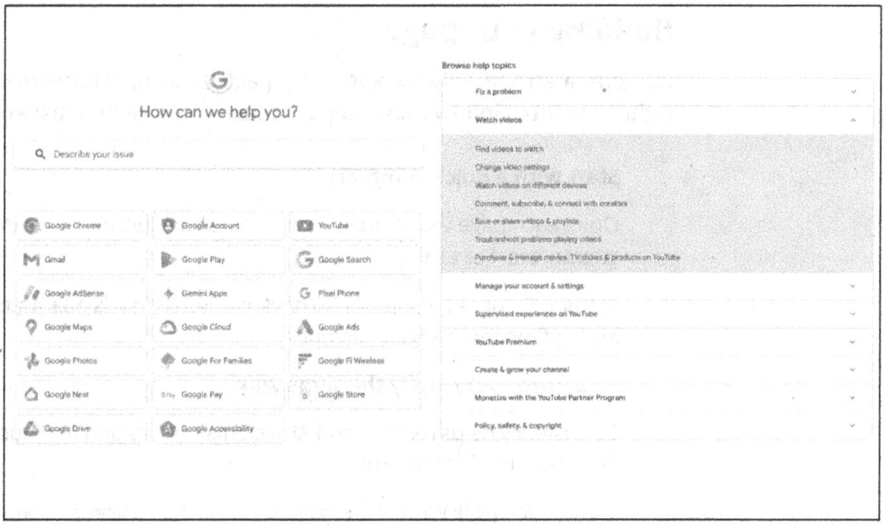

FIGURE 12-3: Google Support's product-chooser step improves accuracy for both humans and AI.

Source: Screenshot of `google.com`*, used under fair use for commentary.*

- Skinnydip uses one question per URL with Last Updated dates, reinforcing authority and freshness.

  Figure 12-4 shows a Skinnydip FAQ example that uses one question per page and clearly displays the Last Updated date for freshness.

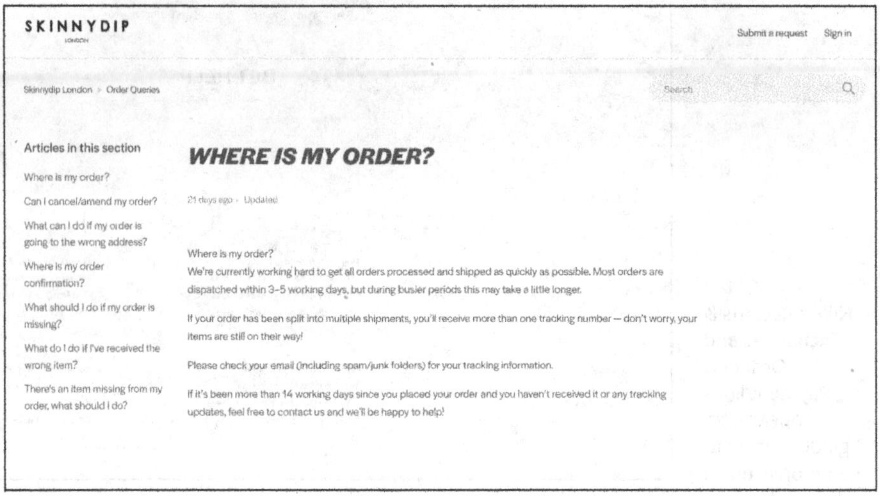

FIGURE 12-4: Skinnydip's FAQ layout shows one clear question per page with a visible Last Updated date.

Source: Screenshot of `skinnydiplondon.com`*, used under fair use for commentary.*

Building your page

Building a strong Policies and FAQs page is straightforward when you have the right structure. Follow these steps to make yours clear, trustworthy, and quotable:

1. **Start with a quick summary.**

   Open each page with a one-sentence "In short" promise that defines your core guarantees. For example:

   In short: Returns are free for 30 days, workmanship is guaranteed for one year, and uptime targets 99.9 percent.

2. **Structure every entry the same way.**

   Consistency helps readers and AI systems understand and quote your answers. Use this pattern:

   - *Question (H3):* Write it literally and from the customer's perspective.
   - *Answer:* Keep it short — two to five sentences or as many as three concise bullets in plain English.
   - *Next step:* End with an action such as Start a Return, Read Our Warranty, or Contact Support.

3. **Group by theme.**

   Organize related questions under headings that reflect buyer intent, such as Pricing, Delivery & Returns, Contracts, Setup, Support, Security, Policies, and Implementation.

4. **Show your process.**

   Add a short What Happens Next section that walks buyers through what to expect. A step-by-step checklist works well:

   - *Order confirmed*
   - *Preparation and scheduling*
   - *Delivery or kickoff*
   - *Review and sign-off*

5. **Include key specs or standards.**

   Support your promises with facts. Add technical details, compatibility notes, and service boundaries. If you have many specifics, include a small table for quick reference and a downloadable PDF that mirrors the page. Always include a version number and a clear Last Updated date.

6. **Prove recency and ownership.**

   At the bottom of each page, list Last Updated and Owner so that readers and AI systems know your information is current and reliable.

7. **Add schema and smart links.**

   Apply FAQ Page schema to improve visibility in search and AI results. Link each FAQ page to your Pricing, Policies, Process, and Specs or Security pages for full context.

TIP

If you do not manage your site code directly, do not get stuck here. Ask your developer, CMS support team, or SEO plugin to add FAQPage schema that matches the questions and answers visible on the page. The visible answer and the schema answer should say the same thing.

Sample statements

Here are some examples of BoF-ready statements that various types of businesses use to create lines that are easy to scan and quote:

- **Local business:** Workmanship guaranteed for one year; installs scheduled within seven days; parts per manufacturer warranty; refunds not available for diagnostic fees.
- **E-commerce store:** Returns free for 30 days; shipping in two to five business days; exchanges free while stock lasts; final sale items excluded.
- **SaaS company:** Kickoff within two days; 99.9 percent uptime target; data encrypted in transit and at rest; 10 percent credit if uptime drops below the target.

REMEMBER

The clearer and more consistent your answers and policies, the less your team has to explain them and the less likely AI is to invent its own version.

News and Roadmap

Your News and Roadmap page is the public record of your progress. It shows buyers and AI that your brand is active, transparent, and improving. When you publish updates consistently, you control how your story is told and prevent others from defining it for you.

Taking notes from other brands

Here are some examples of what other brands have done to keep their names in the news:

- Apple uses its Newsroom to announce launches, partnerships, and milestones with dated headlines and quotes from leadership.

  Figure 12-5 shows Apple's Newsroom layout, which organizes company updates with clear dates and executive quotes that build authority.

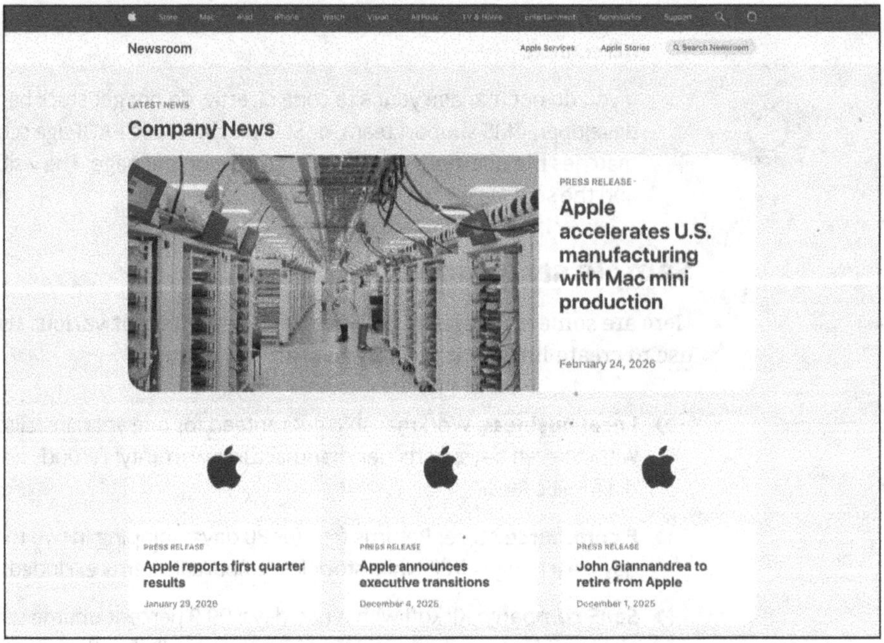

FIGURE 12-5: Apple's Newsroom page highlights new launches and milestones with dated posts and leadership quotes.

Source: Screenshot of `apple.com`*, used under fair use for commentary.*

- Microsoft 365 keeps a public roadmap with clear Launched, Rolling Out, and In Development labels so that users always know what's next.

  Figure 12-6 shows the Microsoft 365 Roadmap, where updates are grouped by release stage so that users can see progress at a glance.
- Stripe posts a plain-English change log that summarizes what changed and links to details for developers or customers.

  Figure 12-7 shows Stripe's change log format, which lists each release with a short summary and links to technical notes.

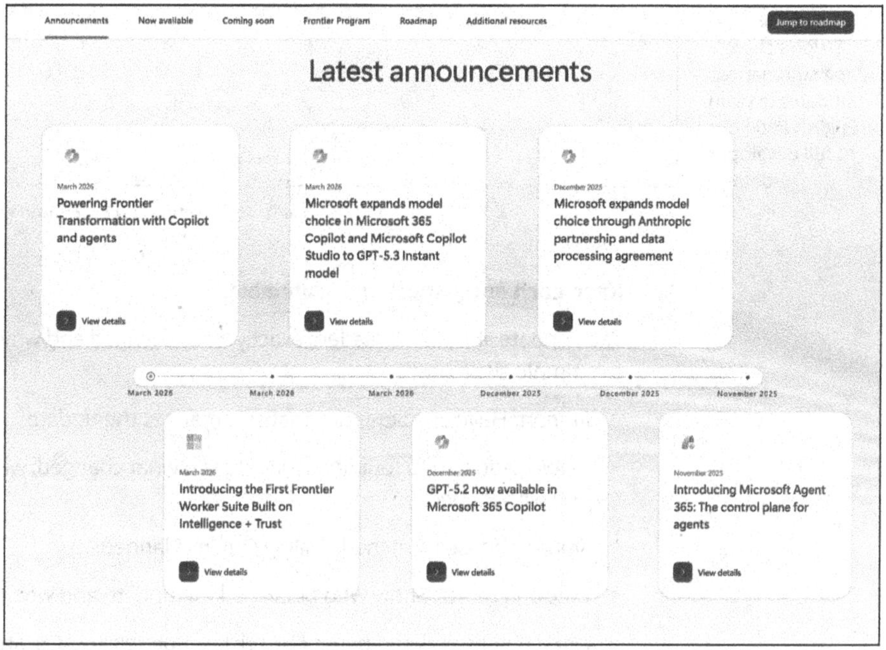

FIGURE 12-6: Microsoft 365's public roadmap displays features by Status, Launched, Rolling Out, and In Development, for full transparency.

Source: Screenshot of `microsoft.com`*, used under fair use for commentary.*

Building your page

A clear News and Roadmap page shows that your brand is active and accountable. Follow these steps to create one that people and AI can trust:

1. **Start with a single hub.**

   Build one central page that lists all launches, improvements, and upcoming releases in order. Make it easy to sort with filters such as Launched, Rolling Out, and Planned.

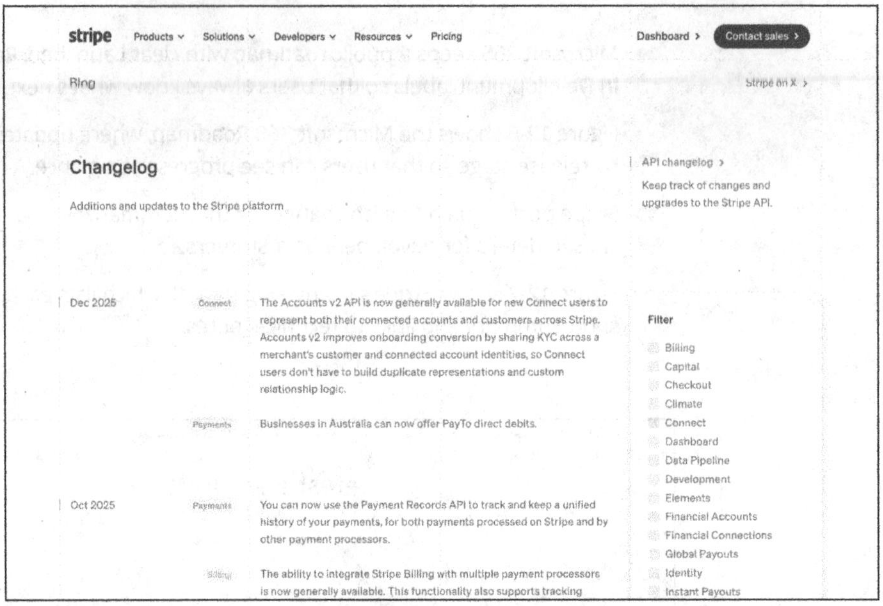

FIGURE 12-7: Stripe's change log summarizes updates in plain English and links to full developer details.

Source: Screenshot of `stripe.com`, used under fair use for commentary.

2. **Keep each entry short and scannable.**

   Each update should tell readers exactly what changed and why it matters. Use this simple structure:

   - *In short:* Have one sentence that summarizes the update.
   - *Details:* Add two to four lines that explain what changed, why it matters, and who it affects.
   - *Status:* Choose Launched, Rolling Out, or Planned.
   - *Date and owner:* Show who published the update and when.
   - *Links:* Point to related pages like Pricing, Policies & FAQs, and Documentation.

3. **Add transparency.**

   Include a change log that highlights what has shipped recently, along with a Roadmap block that previews what is coming next quarter. This item gives readers and AI a clear sense of progress.

4. **Make it quotable.**

   Start every launch entry with an "In short" line that states the benefit directly. Keep the language factual, clear, and easy to quote.

Example:

In short: We launched Content Optimizer 2.0 to help teams produce higher-quality drafts in half the time.

Released April 2025, Owner: Product Team
Status: Launched

- Added multilanguage support
- Introduced clear scoring for content quality
- Updated our Help Center with new training guides

Links: Pricing; Policies & FAQs; Documentation

5. **Keep it current.**

   Review your News and Roadmap page every month. Archive older entries but keep them accessible. A page that shows regular updates signals reliability and freshness to both people and AI systems.

Sample statements

This section highlights some examples of how various types of businesses can utilize the News and Roadmap page:

- **Local business:** Announce new service areas or seasonal offers with launch dates and photos.
- **E-commerce store:** List new product drops, shipping updates, and major restocks.
- **SaaS company:** Share new features, integrations, and performance improvements with release notes and roadmap previews.

REMEMBER

Your News and Roadmap page is proof that your brand delivers on its promises. When you document progress in clear, dated updates, you earn trust from both customers and AI.

Quick wins

Your pages tell your story. They also can move people from deciding to finalizing. Use these quick wins to keep the momentum going:

- Publish a clear Pricing page with an "In short" summary near the top and honest ranges or starting points. Include plan anchors, a chooser, and links to Policies and FAQs.

- Build your Policies and FAQs hub that covers refunds, warranties, delivery timelines, setup steps, specs, and security. Use one question per page, each with a Last Updated date and an Owner line.
- Add a News and Roadmap page to share launches, change log updates, and plans in progress. Begin every post with a one-sentence "In short" summary and tag it as Launched, Rolling Out, or Planned.
- Cross-link everything. Each canonical page should link to the other two and appear in your site navigation and footer under an Official Answers block.
- Keep it current. Review and refresh your Pricing, Policies, and News pages at least once per quarter to keep buyers and AI working from the same source of truth.

REMEMBER

When your official answers are clear, linked, and current, you control the story, not random reviews or AI guesswork.

Creating Comparison and Review Content

When someone is close to buying, they do not search like a student. They search like a shopper. That is why pages built around "best," "alternatives," "vs," and "review" queries punch above their weight in AI answers. These pages help buyers compare options, and they give AI systems clean material to use when they generate shortlists and recommendations. The sections that follow explain how to build the content, expand it into a scalable asset library, and make each page useful for both human buyers and AI-generated recommendations.

Start with a category listicle

The fastest path is to publish one pillar listicle that anchors the category, then build supporting pages around the commercial questions buyers and AI systems naturally ask next. Such as:

- Best [solution] for [year]. Example: "22 Best AI search Tracking Tools for 2025."
- Best [solution] for [use case]. Example: "Best AI search Tracking Tools for Agencies."
- Best [solution] for [location] if the offer is local. Example: "Best Emergency Plumbers in Chesterfield, Missouri."

The pillar page defines the category, explains how you evaluated options, and links to deeper pages for each brand, use case, or service area. Think of it as the buyer's shortlist and the AI system's easiest source to quote.

Build satellite pages from fan-out queries

AI systems often break one commercial question into several smaller questions before assembling an answer. You can support that behavior by building pages that match common fan-out patterns. For example:

- [Competitor] alternatives
- [Your brand] alternatives
- [Your brand] vs [Competitor]
- [Competitor] vs [Competitor] vs [Your brand]
- [Competitor] review
- [Your brand] review

This approach turns a single pillar into a scalable content roadmap. If you cover 30 relevant competitors and create three page types per competitor — alternatives, comparisons, and reviews — you already have 90 assets. Add the pillar page and a few "best for" use-case pages, and you can build roughly 100 assets around one decision topic without needing 100 separate ideas.

Make each page answer-ready

A strong BoF page does more than mention products. It helps the reader choose. Use repeatable blocks so every page presents the same kind of decision support. Incorporate:

- **Verdict box:** Say who the option is best for, who it is not ideal for, and the quick takeaway.
- **Comparison table:** Show pricing range, primary use case, strengths, limits, and key buying factors.
- **Proof:** Add screenshots, case studies, reviews, benchmarks, or examples near the claim they support.
- **Pick based on your situation:** Give practical guidance such as "Choose this if . . ." or "Choose that if . . .".

» **BoF FAQs:** Answer pricing, onboarding, integrations, support, limits, and "Is it worth it?" questions.

These blocks make the page useful to humans and easier for AI systems to summarize accurately. The goal is not to attack competitors. The goal is to help the buyer understand fit.

Handling competitor concerns

Some companies do not want to talk about competitors. That is understandable, but avoiding comparison content does not make the comparison disappear. Buyers still ask, competitors still publish, and AI systems still assemble answers from whatever sources they can find.

If you or your client is strongly against competitor pages on the main site, use a softer detour. Publish broader "best [solution] for [year]" or "best [solution] for [use case]" content on relevant industry blogs, association sites, or partner publications. This approach is slower, but it lets you participate in the same decision space without hosting direct competitor pages on your own domain.

REMEMBER

If you do not define the comparison, someone else will. BoF comparison content is how you keep the buyer's decision grounded in accurate, current information.

Building Depth with Commercial Clusters

Go a mile deep before you go a mile wide. The biggest mistake with commercial content is topic hopping. A team publishes one "best tools" list, jumps to a different category, and then chases the next idea. The result is a site full of isolated pages that never stack authority.

Instead, build depth around one commercial topic until the pages reinforce one another and behave like a connected asset. The following sections show you how to fully develop a commercial cluster, connect the pages through internal links, structure the cluster for growth, and determine when it is complete enough to move on.

Build one cluster until it is exhausted

Treat every commercial topic like a cluster you fully build before moving on. Use these guidelines:

- Pick one pillar keyword, such as "best AI search tracking tools."
- Build every BoF page that naturally fans out from that pillar.
- Only move to an adjacent cluster after the current cluster is tapped out.

For example, after you have wrung everything out of "AI search tracking tools," you can move to an adjacent cluster such as "best SEO content optimization tools," especially if that next cluster supports a different product or offer. This is how you build depth instead of noise.

Make internal links do the work

The real power of a cluster is that the pages support one another. Internal links help crawlers, AI bots, and human readers move through the whole decision set without guessing where to go next. Be sure to:

- **Link every secondary page back to the pillar.** Use a contextual link near the top, such as "See our Best [Solution] Tools for [Year] guide."
- **Cross-link each competitor group.** A review page, alternatives page, and "your brand vs competitor" page should point to one another.
- **Link laterally when it helps the reader.** A competitor alternatives page can point to another competitor alternatives page when the user wants more options.
- **Use consistent anchor text.** Repeat patterns such as "best [solution] tools," "[competitor] alternatives," "[brand] vs [competitor]," and "[competitor] review."

This structure helps bots travel through the cluster quickly and helps AI systems understand how the pages relate. It also creates a compounding effect. If one page in the cluster earns a backlink, smart internal links help some of that authority flow to the pillar and to related pages. A rising tide lifts all ships.

Use a simple cluster architecture

A commercial cluster does not need to be complicated. Use a hub-and-spoke structure, then create mini-clusters inside it. Set it up like this:

- **Pillar:** Best [solution] tools for [year].
- **Use-case pages:** Best [solution] for [audience], [industry], or [location].
- **Competitor pages:** [competitor] alternatives, [brand] vs [competitor], and [competitor] review.

- **Mini-cluster:** Each competitor group cross-links among its review, alternatives, and comparison pages.

You can also add a small "related decision pages" module near the bottom of each BoF page. Link back to the pillar, the relevant competitor review, and one or two closely related pages. Keep the module useful, not spammy.

Check the cluster before moving on

Before you start the next commercial cluster, make sure the current one is complete enough to behave like one ranking asset. Be sure:

- Every satellite links to the pillar.
- Every competitor group cross-links to itself.
- Every page has a clear next step for the buyer.
- The pillar links to the most important satellites.
- Product, pricing, and proof pages are linked where relevant.

TIP

Do not start a new commercial cluster just because you are bored with the old one. Move on only when the current cluster has enough depth, links, and proof to stand on its own.

Bringing It All Together

BoF pages are where AI visibility can turn into revenue. Your official pages give buyers and AI systems the facts. Your comparisons, alternatives, and reviews help them choose. Your commercial clusters and internal links turn those pages into a connected system instead of a pile of isolated URLs.

Your next move is simple: choose one decision-stage topic, build the official answer set, publish the comparison assets, and link the whole cluster together. Then keep it current. When your BoF content is clear, honest, and easy to quote, you make it easier for buyers to trust you and easier for AI systems to represent you accurately.

IN THIS CHAPTER

» Finding content gaps and planning depth without bloating your site

» Recognizing what topical authority means in an AI answer world

» Aligning entities so that search engines (and the AI layers on top) can connect the dots

» Building an update cadence and consolidating content without losing rankings

Chapter 13
Earning Topical Authority

Topical authority used to mean one thing: You had lots of pages about a topic, and Google could see that you were active in that space.

That old world is fading. In the new world, *topical authority* requires a sharper definition: Systems trust you as a source of truth and recommend you consistently. (Picture search engines plus the AI layers that summarize, cite, and recommend.) It's not just "Can you rank?" — it's "Can an AI pull from you confidently and get it right?" Some AI systems show citations, while others use sources behind the scenes; in either case, the systems retrieve and summarize based on confidence and relevance signals.

That's why you're chasing two outcomes at the same time:

- **Traditional SEO:** Stable rankings for the *topic clusters* (groups of related content built around a core subject) that you want to own

» **AI answers:** Repeatable brand mentions and citations for commercial prompts people enter before they're ready to buy

When topical authority clicks, you feel it. Your content begins ranking for related searches you didn't target directly — the *shoulder* queries that sit just beyond your main keywords. Your best pages become common citation sources. And competitors stop leapfrogging you with their thin Best Of lists because now you've built something they can't fake: depth and clarity. This happens because search systems expand queries semantically and match your content to related intents, even when exact keywords aren't present.

To build that kind of authority, in this chapter you stack these four elements:

» **Coverage:** Address the full decision space, not just the obvious questions.

» **Gaps and depth:** Find the holes and answer the hard follow-up questions buyers ask next.

» **Entity alignment:** Machines connect your brand, products, people, and claims without guessing.

» **Freshness and consolidation:** Your source of truth stays current, clean, and consolidated.

REMEMBER

Keep this list in mind as you work through this chapter: Topical authority doesn't mean more pages. It means more confidence in what you publish.

Expanding Coverage: Gap Analysis and Depth Planning

Before you write a single new page, you need a map. Not a list of keywords — a map of the topic the way a buyer experiences it, from initial curiosity to final decision. This map defines your coverage: what you include, what you're missing, and how comprehensive your content on the subject is. By way of gap analysis and depth planning, you show where the holes are and how thoroughly you need to cover each topic. When you have that map, your content plan stops being guesswork. This section covers how to map your entire topic and how to run a gap analysis and add depth to your pages.

Mapping your topic universe

Think of your topic universe as a full set of concepts, questions, and subtopics that AI associates with your subject. To map your topic universe, start by defining the topic boundary. This is how you prevent your content from drifting into "everything about everything" and losing focus. First, clarify the scope:

- **What's in scope** includes the core problem you solve, the most common use cases, the audiences who need it, and the constraints that shape the decision. Constraints are the reality checks people care about, like budget, tools, time, compliance, team skill, or risk. When you're clear on scope, you stop writing for imaginary readers and start writing for real ones.
- **What's out of scope** is just as important. These adjacent topics might be interesting, but they dilute your message and steal attention from the pages that should be doing the heavy lifting. If a topic doesn't support the user's decision or your business goal, it doesn't belong in your universe. Park it for later or build it as a separate cluster.

Once the boundary is clear, divide your universe into four buckets; they help you build authority in a balanced way rather than overproduce a single content type:

- **Core explanations:** Definitions, how it works, and the concepts people need to know to understand the space
- **Decision content:** Comparisons, alternatives, and Best Of pages that help people choose
- **Implementation content:** Steps, checklists, templates, and workflows that turn theory into action
- **Proof content:** Case studies, benchmarks, original data, and evidence that backs up your claims

When these buckets exist, you're no longer guessing what to create next. You can see your coverage, see your gaps, and prioritize the work that significantly moves rankings and revenue.

Running a gap analysis and adding depth

Most gap analyses fail because they start with the question "What keywords are missing?" rather than "What decisions are buyers trying to make?" You're not building a thesaurus. You're building confidence.

A *keyword tool* is software that estimates what people search for and how often, helping you identify potential topics. But this tool doesn't give the full scope of real demand. Don't ignore a topic just because a tool says that no one searches for it (as in zero-volume keywords): People may still be asking those questions, and they're often easier opportunities to win. You'll find those in Google Search Console (queries earning impressions even when tools show low or no volume) and via keyword gap tools (competitors ranking for terms you didn't realize mattered yet).

TIP

For clarity, use *keyword* for an exact phrase you find in a search tool, *query* for the words a person actually types or speaks, and *topic* for the broader subject or cluster those keywords and queries map to. Keywords help you map a topic, but they aren't the topic by themselves.

To find out where holes may exist and make your page the authority on a topic with layers of depth (stacking information so that readers can go deeper if needed), follow these steps:

1. **Build your seed list.**

   Your seed list is a starting set of commercial queries, prompts, and shorthand phrases that point to one buyer decision area. You use it to decide which topics deserve pages or deeper sections.

   Start with the queries that signal intent, not curiosity:

   - *Write 10 to* commercial prompts buyers enter*20* when they're evaluating options, trying to solve the problem faster, or comparing approaches.
   - *Add category shorthand terms* that people use when they don't want to explain themselves, like *best tool, alternative, template, checklist, pricing, for agencies*, or *for beginners.*
   - *Pull Search Console clues,* especially low-volume queries that still earn impressions and clicks. If you're seeing impressions, the demand is real, even if the tool says zero.
   - *Use zero-volume keywords* consistently to mean phrases that third-party tools report as zero searches. If Search Console shows impressions for one of those phrases, treat it as real demand.

   This seed list becomes your reality anchor. It keeps your universe tied to money and outcomes.

2. **Compare what you have versus what you need.**

   Build a simple matrix so that you can spot gaps quickly without overcomplicating it:

- *Rows:* Topic subareas such as features, pricing, use cases, objections, integrations, and risks
- *Columns:* Your pages, top competitors, and third-party sources that keep showing up

Mark each cell:

- *Owned:* You have a strong page that fully answers the intent.
- *Thin:* You mention it, but you don't actually answer it.
- *Missing:* You don't cover it in any meaningful way.

This is where you usually see the truth. You don't need more content. You need coverage in the areas that keep surfacing across competitors and third-party sources.

3. **Add depth layers so that your pages win retrieval.**

   Here's the key shift: You're planning pages to be recommendable, not just optimized.

   For each page, plan these three depth layers:

   - *Primary answer:* Two or three sentences that solve the query without rambling
   - *Follow-up answers:* Between five and ten subquestions that people ask next, the ones that show up in actual conversations and evaluations
   - *Decision support:* Who it's for, who it's not for, the tradeoffs, and proof that your recommendation holds up

   This structure is what makes content survive both traditional ranking and AI summarization. It's how you turn a page from informative into trusted.

Aligning Your Entities

AI-driven search systems don't just match keywords. They try to understand entities and then decide which ones they trust enough to recommend. An *entity* is basically an item or element that a system can identify and track, like your brand, product, founder, category, location, credentials, or competitors. This section shows you the importance of entities in getting your site recommended, building a trustworthy entity home page, setting up an entity alignment checklist, using sameAs signals (see the upcoming section "Examining the use of sameAs signals (and what they're for)") to match other profiles to your entity to enhance your credibility, and creating a quick entity alignment sheet to use for guidance (see the upcoming section, "Creating an entity alignment sheet").

I cover several entity types in this book, including brand, product, person, location, category, and competitor entities. This section focuses on your owned Entity Home because it gives search systems one official place to verify who you are. You audit broader entity and profile pages in Chapter 17.

Knowing why entities decide who gets recommended

In traditional SEO, you could win many battles by matching keywords and covering topics. In AI-driven search and answer systems, that's not enough. These systems don't just look for pages that "mention the phrase," for example. They try to understand who is being discussed, what they are, and how they connect to everything else.

That's where entities come in. AI systems build relationship maps between entities. When your signals — like naming processes, wording methods, and internal links — are clear, consistent, and well-linked, the system can confidently connect the dots:

- This is the same company across multiple pages.
- This product belongs to that brand.
- These claims match what's known about them.

When your signals are inconsistent, the opposite happens. Mentions don't consolidate. Citations split across variations of your name. Your product gets confused with a category. And after the system hesitates, it usually recommends someone else.

Topical authority isn't just "We know a lot." It's "Machines can confidently understand who we are."

Building your entity home and linking everything back to it

You need one main page, sometimes called a canonical hub that acts as your entity's home address. This page makes it easy for humans and machines to confirm the basics and trace everything back to a single source.

For most brands, your About page works. If you want to be more explicit, create a dedicated Brand page or Company page that's built to be the main source of truth. Your entity home should include this information:

- **Exact brand name plus category descriptor:** Example: "Rankability is an SEO content optimization platform for agencies."
- **What you do (one-sentence limit):** Tight, consistent, and repeatable across your site. For example: "We help agencies plan, optimize, and monitor SEO content."
- **Who it's for:** The audience that matters most, stated clearly. For example: "Built for SEO agencies managing multiple clients."
- **Proof markers:** Awards, certifications, notable customers, trusted data points, or third-party validation. For example: "Trusted by 500 agencies," "G2 leader," or "10,000 audits completed."
- **Links to key profiles:** Official social accounts, major listings, and other profiles you control. For example: LinkedIn, Google Business Profile, Crunchbase, G2, or another official category profile.

TIP

Treat this page as the root of a tree. Everything important should connect back to it, directly or indirectly.

Applying an entity alignment checklist across your site

Entity alignment is mostly consistency work, and it pays off like compounding interest. The following sections show which signals to check to make sure your entity is aligning.

Naming consistency

Lock down the exact way you write your brand name, product names, feature names, and plan names.

The goal is to prevent accidental fragmentation. If you call it Content Optimizer in one place and Optimizer in another, systems may treat them as different items.

Same claim, same wording, where it matters

Some phrases shouldn't be reinvented on every page. If your core language changes too often, systems can't reliably attach the claim to your entity.

Create a simple language lock for your positioning statement, key differentiators, and service areas (for local businesses).

This doesn't mean every page reads like a template. It means your identity statements stay stable so that machines recognize them instantly.

Internal linking

Make sure your entity home is easy to reach from your most important pages:

- Every major page should link back to the entity home (directly or indirectly).
- Keep anchor text clean and consistent (usually, your brand name).

Internal links are one of the simplest ways to reinforce the statement "This belongs to the same entity."

Examining the use of sameAs signals (and what they're for)

In structured data, *sameAs* is a way of telling systems, "These URLs all refer to the same person, company, or organization." It's essentially an identity alignment signal. Think of it like identity links that help systems see that "these profiles refer to the same thing."

TECHNICAL STUFF

More precisely, sameAs is a structured data signal from `Schema.org` that suggests multiple URLs refer to the same entity. It reinforces identity, but it doesn't create identity on its own.

Think of it this way. A profile is the public page that represents you on another site, such as LinkedIn or a directory listing. The URL is the web address for that profile, and that URL is what you include in sameAs.

You use sameAs whenever you have a clearly defined entity and you want to help systems confidently connect that entity across different places on the web. Here's where you typically point sameAs:

- Major social profiles
- Credible directory profiles
- Wikipedia or Wikidata (when applicable)
- Knowledge base references (when applicable)

REMEMBER

Don't treat sameAs like a magic button. It reinforces only what's already consistent. If your offsite profiles disagree with your site, you're not fixing the problem — you're amplifying confusion.

REMEMBER

Include only the profiles you actually control or that clearly represent you. Don't point to random mentions and hope it helps.

Creating an entity alignment sheet

To make sure your entity is operational (and scalable across a team), build a simple entity alignment sheet.

Use this list as a quick reference to align your entity — one row per entity:

- **Entity name:** Obvious, right?
- **Entity type:** Brand, Product, Person, or Location, for example
- **Canonical URL:** Your entity home
- **Key attributes:** The identity facts you want to remain consistent
- **sameAs URLs:** Official profiles and references
- **Where referenced:** Which pages mention or depend on this entity

Add a short language lock for your core descriptors so that your team repeats the same phrasing across pages, bios, schema, and profiles.

When you do this well, you reduce ambiguity. And when you reduce ambiguity, you get recommended more often.

Keeping It Fresh and Consolidated

Freshness and consolidation are how you keep topical authority from decaying as your site grows. One keeps your content trustworthy; the other keeps your site from turning into a confusing pile of duplicates.

Why freshness is an authority signal

Freshness used to feel optional. You could publish a helpful guide, earn links, and ride it for years. That still happens sometimes, but AI answers and modern SERPs (Search Engine Results Pages) put more pressure on one question: Is this source still current enough to trust?

Old but accurate content can still win. A timeless explanation or a stable process can rank for a long time. The problem is that most pages don't age like fine wine — they age like milk. Pricing changes. Features shift. Screenshots go stale. Recommendations become outdated. Then your content becomes old and vague, and vague is the fastest way to lose trust.

Freshness isn't about chasing dates. It's about removing uncertainty. When a system sees that you maintain your key pages, it has fewer reasons to doubt you. That's what authority looks like in practice.

How to keep it fresh

You need to create a schedule for maintaining freshness, but it needs to make sense. The biggest mistake is creating an update plan you never follow. The goal is a cadence that fits your team, your site size, and your business model.

Start by setting your rhythm by content type:

- **Money pages:** Monthly light review, quarterly deep review
- **Light review:** Accuracy check, internal links, calls to action (CTAs), and obvious gaps
- **Deep review:** Major additions, restructuring, proof updates, and consolidation decisions
- **Comparisons and alternatives:** Quarterly review (or whenever pricing or features change); pages that decay fast because they depend on third-party details you don't control
- **Stats and facts:** Quarterly review and whenever new data is published; pages that should include timestamps and source notes so that every number is easy to verify and update
- **Evergreen guides:** Semiannual review; usually stable, but still in need of clarity, examples, and refreshes as the ecosystem changes

TIP

To make freshness visible, add a simple freshness box (a short update note on the page) on key pages, including this information:

- Last updated
- What changed (one to three bullets)
- Link to supporting sources or your own fact hub

The Freshness box does two jobs at one time: It signals care to readers and reduces doubt for systems that evaluate reliability.

Where consolidation matters

As you publish more, your biggest enemy stops being not having enough content — it becomes having too much overlapping content. You want to consolidate your content smartly without losing traction.

Consolidation is how you protect topical authority as you scale. It's how you keep your site clean, decisive, and easy to trust.

Consolidation triggers

You know it's time to consolidate when:

- Two pages target the same intent
- One page cannibalizes the other
- Multiple pages exist only because of keyword variants
- A weaker page keeps getting cited or ranking for the wrong intent

If you fail to address these triggers, you end up splitting relevance, links, and trust.

Consolidation playbook

A consolidation playbook gives you a controlled way to combine overlapping content so that you strengthen a single source of truth instead of diluting it. Use a consistent process so that consolidation is safe and repeatable:

1. **Pick the winning URL.**

   Start with a main page you can build on and consolidate everything into it. Choose the page with the best history, strongest links, and clearest intent match.

2. **Move the best sections into the winner.**

   Avoid merging everything. Merge whatever improves clarity and decision value.

3. **Add internal anchors so that the merged page stays skimmable.**

   Consolidation fails when the page becomes a wall of text. Anchors keep it navigable.

4. **Use a 301 redirect to send retired pages to the main page when appropriate.**

   This step consolidates signals and prevents dead ends.

5. **Update internal links to point to the winner.**

   Resist leaving your own site reinforcing the old structure.

6. **Update your sitemap and indexation signals.**

   Make it easy for crawlers to understand the new source of truth. In practice, this means updating your XML sitemap, resubmitting it in Google Search Console, checking that retired pages use the right 301 redirects, and confirming that canonical tags point to the winning URL.

TIP

Consolidation should improve the user's path to a decision. If it makes the page more difficult to use, you're not consolidating — you're cluttering.

When authority needs an update log

When visibility changes, most teams guess. An update log turns guessing into diagnosis.

Use this log for both freshness updates and consolidation work. Freshness entries show when you changed facts, examples, screenshots, or source notes. Consolidation entries show when you merged pages, redirected URLs, or changed internal links.

Keep one shared log that records the date, the URL, what changed, why you changed it, and what you expect to improve.

Later, when rankings shift, traffic drops, or AI visibility changes, you have an evidence trail. It's one of the simplest ways to learn what truly works.

IN THIS CHAPTER

» Identifying pages with weak performance before making random changes

» Improving on-page basics

» Comparing your page to true competitors

» Spotting the most common reasons that pages underperform

» Measuring whether your fixes produced verifiable lift

Chapter 14

Fixing Underperformers

A page may draw impressions but few clicks. It may rank but never convert. It may attract traffic from Google but rarely appear in AI answers. When that happens, don't start rewriting blindly. Some pages simply underperform.

A weak page is a page that matters to your business but is not doing its job. It may fail to earn clicks, conversions, rankings, AI mentions, citations, or another outcome the page was created to support.

In this chapter, I show you how to diagnose why a page is weak, improve the on-page elements that help search engines and AI systems understand it, measure your page against your competitors, spot the most common failure patterns, and determine whether your fixes worked.

Diagnosing Pages before Making Changes

One major SEO mistake is trying to fix a page before you know what's broken. You can waste lots of time rewriting copy when the true problem is unclear intent, aimless structure, weak topic coverage, or missing support from the rest of the site.

This section explains which pages to choose and helps you identify what the page is supposed to do before determining which changes to make.

REMEMBER

Start with diagnosis, not edits.

Choosing pages worth fixing

Not every weak page deserves your time. Start with pages that matter to the business or already show signs of life.

Look first at pages that:

- Attract high impressions but a low number of clicks
- Rank anywhere on Page 2 of the search results or low on Page 1
- Bring in traffic but don't convert
- Target valuable topics but keep losing to competitors
- Are rarely cited or mentioned in AI answers

These pages are usually the best opportunities because they already have some signal. You're not starting from zero — you're just looking to improve what's already working.

Clarifying the job of the page

Before you edit anything, ask yourself this simple question: What is this page supposed to win?

That means identifying:

- The primary keyword
- The main prompt or question

- The searcher's stage of awareness
- The action you want the reader to take next

If you can't clearly explain the page's job, the page probably isn't clear yet.

Evaluating intent and page type

The fastest way to assess intent is to look at what's already ranking. Start by examining the search results to see what's authentically winning.

Check search results for:

- What page type appears most often?
- How quickly do top pages answer the main question?
- What angle or promise appears in the title tags?
- What subtopics, FAQs, or proof elements keep repeating?
- Are AI answers citing brand pages, review sites, directories, or informational guides?

You may find that Google and AI systems prefer pages with these types of information:

- Comparisons
- Services
- Products
- Local landings
- Deep guides
- FAQ-style answers

If the winning pages are mostly comparisons and your page is a broad educational article, you may have the wrong format for the query.

REMEMBER

A page can be well written and still fail if it doesn't match the true intent behind the search.

Tightening the On-Page Basics

Sometimes, the page isn't failing because of some mysterious algorithm problem. Sometimes, the basics just aren't strong enough. *On-page basics* are the elements that ensure a page is clear, relevant, and easy to navigate. This section spells out three main on-page basics — keywords, headings, and scannability — to scrutinize before making page changes.

Placing the primary keyword in the right spots

For page-level optimization, make sure the primary keyword appears in the places that send the clearest topic signals.

Check these locations:

- URL
- Title tag
- Meta description
- H1
- First couple of sentences
- One close variant in the first H2

You don't need to force the keyword everywhere. You do need to make the topic obvious.

TIP

If the exact keyword is missing from one of these places, add it when you can do so naturally. If the phrase sounds forced, use a close variation instead. The point is not to stuff the keyword into the page. The point is to make the page's main topic clear in the places readers, search engines, and AI systems check first.

Making headings pull their weight

Weak headings often create weak pages. A vague H1 or generic H2 structure makes it harder for readers and machines to absorb the content of the page.

A stronger page usually has these elements:

- A single, clear H1
- H2s that reflect actual questions or subtopics

- H3s only when needed
- Headings that reveal what content comes next

For more on retrieval-friendly structure, see Chapters 10 and 11.

Improving scannability

A page that looks dense usually performs worse than a page that feels easy to navigate.

To improve scannability, use these elements:

- Short paragraphs
- Bulleted lists
- Numbered steps where order matters
- Tables where comparison helps with comprehension
- Direct answers near the top of sections

This strategy helps humans read faster and helps AI systems extract clear passages.

Comparing Your Page to True Competitors

Strong page diagnosis doesn't happen in a vacuum. You need to compare your page with what's already winning. You don't need to reinvent the wheel: By checking on what competitors have done and searching for recurring topics and coverage, you can give yourself a solid outline of how to improve your page.

Pulling competitors from Google and AI answers

You build a competitor set from these two places:

- Traditional Google results
- AI platforms such as AI Mode, ChatGPT, Gemini, and Perplexity

For Google, search the target query and review the top five to ten organic results. Record the URLs, page types, title angles, and recurring sections that appear across those pages.

For AI platforms, run the same query or a natural-language version of it. Record the cited URLs, mentioned brands, answer format, and page types that show up in the response.

Combine the results into one list and remove duplicates.

This list gives you a more realistic view of the competitive landscape because you're not looking only at classic rankings — you're also looking at the sources AI systems trust enough to cite.

Looking for recurring patterns in top-ranked pages

With your competitor list handy (see the previous section), review the top-ranked pages from your search results and identify the topics they consistently cover.

Look for these recurring page elements:

- Entities
- Subtopics
- Questions
- Features
- Benefits
- Objections
- Decision factors

The recurrence of these items matters because search engines and large language models use natural language processing, or NLP, to understand what a page is about. They don't just look for one keyword — they look for related concepts that help define the full topic.

When the same ideas show up across multiple top pages, that's a signal they're essential. Use those patterns to shape your page so that it fully covers what the query requires.

Turning competitor coverage into a better outline

Review the top-ranked pages of your competitor and ask yourself this blunt question:

> Does my page adequately cover the important ideas this topic requires?

REMEMBER

If the strongest competitor pages all mention key themes that your page skips, that's a strong clue your page may feel incomplete to readers and AI systems.

TIP

You can skim competitor pages manually and use ChatGPT or a similar AI tool to identify recurring entities, topics, and gaps.

For example, using a tool such as Rankability or Surfer SEO pulls competitors from Google and major AI platforms, dedupes them (the deduplication process eliminates redundant records), and extracts topics and entities based on frequency and relevance. Any solid content optimization workflow can help here, but the main goal stays the same: Build a stronger outline from the full competitive set, not from a single keyword alone.

A strong outline should cover:

- A direct answer near the top of the page
- H2s that match recurring subtopics and questions
- Key entities and terminology competitors consistently use
- Proof points, examples, and decision criteria
- FAQs that answer natural follow-up questions
- A clear next step for the reader

TIP

If you're revising a weak page, compare your page outline side-by-side with the recurring topics from the competitive set. Gaps then become obvious fast.

Looking at Additional Places Pages Break Down

After you check intent, on-page basics, and topical coverage, keep looking for problems that are less obvious but still important. The following sections cover patterns that explain why a page still struggles after the obvious fixes are handled.

Burying the answer too deep

Some pages take too long to become useful.

Watch for pages that:

- Open with unnecessary introductory content
- Delay the main answer
- Hide the useful material halfway down
- Use long, dense paragraphs instead of clean sections

Readers want quick confirmation that they are in the right place. AI systems also prefer pages that make extraction easy. Strong pages answer early, frame the topic clearly, and move fast.

Sending weak trust signals

A page can be technically sound and still feel generic.

Pages often lose trust when they lack:

- Clear proof
- Specific examples
- Credible authorship
- Consistent brand signals
- Evidence supporting major claims

AI systems are more likely to cite content that is specific, structured, and supported by credible signals.

Lacking support from the rest of the site

Some pages do not need a rewrite. They need backup.

Support often comes from:

- Internal links
- Hub pages

- FAQ pages
- Comparison pages
- Proof pages
- Related cluster content

A decent page can still stall if it sits alone. Stronger surrounding content helps search engines and AI systems understand the page's role and importance.

Failing after the click

Some pages get traffic but still underperform because they do not move the reader forward.

That usually means:

- The offer is not clear
- The next step is weak
- The page does not reduce hesitation
- The proof is not strong enough to support a decision

Rankings matter, but they do not mean much if the page never helps the visitor take action.

Fixing the Page and Measuring the Fix

Making changes feels productive. Measuring your fixes tells you whether the change authentically helped. This section gives you guidance on applying a fix, tracking changes, and scrutinizing results.

Turning diagnosis into fixes

Before measuring anything, you need to turn your diagnosis into a clear set of page-level changes. Every issue you identify should connect to a specific fix.

Look to:

- **Fix intent** by changing the page type, angle, or target query so it matches what searchers and AI answers already reward.
- **Fix on-page basics** by placing the primary keyword and close variations in the right spots and making the page structure clearer.
- **Fix topical gaps** by adding missing subtopics, entities, questions, examples, and decision factors.
- **Fix weak trust signals** by adding proof, examples, sources, author details, reviews, screenshots, or other credibility markers.
- **Fix weak site support** by adding internal links from hubs, FAQs, comparisons, and related cluster pages.
- **Fix conversion gaps** by clarifying the offer, answering objections, strengthening the call to action, and making the next step obvious.

After your fixes are in place and you run the changes, you can evaluate your progress.

Logging the change

Each time you change, or update, a page, record the following basic information so that you can learn from the result later:

- The page URL
- The date
- What changed
- Why you changed it
- What result you expected

Define success before making the update. Without it, you can't evaluate whether the change worked.

Tracking the proper metrics

Different pages have different jobs, so don't judge every page by the same numbers. Before making changes, decide what success looks like for that page and choose the metrics that best measure whether it's doing its job.

Match the metric to the page's job:

- **Awareness or guide pages:** impressions, clicks, rankings, engaged visits, and internal clicks to next-step pages
- **Comparison and BoF pages (bottom of funnel; see Chapter 12):** click-through rate, rankings, leads, demos, sales, and assisted conversions
- **Local or service pages:** calls, contact form submissions, actions from map listings (such as directions requests or clicks), local rankings, and booked appointments
- **AI visibility pages:** mentions, citations, first mention, and share of voice across tracked prompts

The question is not just whether traffic went up — the question is whether the page improved at doing the job it exists to do.

Giving the change sufficient time

Avoid judging a page too early. Search results fluctuate, AI answers vary, and internal links take time to be processed.

Before you decide whether the fix worked or failed, make sure you aren't reacting to short-term noise, such as:

- A brief ranking spike
- A short dip after publishing
- Normal search volatility
- Inconsistent AI answers from one prompt to the next

Give the page enough time to show a true trend before you make the next move.

TIP

As a general rule, review small title or meta updates after two to four weeks. Review larger content rewrites, consolidations, or internal-link changes after four to eight weeks. For AI visibility, test weekly but look for a trend across at least four weeks instead of reacting to one answer.

Avoiding change overload

If you rewrite everything at one time, you may improve the page, but you won't be able to pinpoint why.

Whenever possible, follow this order:

1. **Diagnose the main bottleneck first.**
2. **Make the most important fix.**
3. **Measure the outcome.**
4. **Escalate (only if needed).**

For example, suppose a comparison page has a weak title tag, missing proof, and a vague call to action. If you change all three at once, you may improve the page, but you won't know which fix helped. Instead, start with the issue most likely to hold the page back. Update the title if clicks are weak. Add proof if readers hesitate. Strengthen the call to action if traffic arrives but no one takes the next step.

REMEMBER

The goal isn't to make a page look busier. The goal is to remove the main bottleneck that's holding it back.

Wrapping up the fix

Fixing underperformers isn't about endlessly rewriting pages. It's about diagnosing clearly, tightening basic on-page elements, filling the right gaps, and measuring results.

When you do that, weak pages stop feeling mysterious. You can see what's wrong, choose the right fix, and learn from the outcome.

IN THIS CHAPTER

» Making visual media easier for people and AI systems to digest

» Using captions, transcripts, alt text, and schema to add clarity

» Turning data into reusable assets that support visibility and trust

» Building FAQ and dataset pages that keep working across your site

Chapter 15

Making Images, Video, and Data Work for You

Media — such as images, video, and data — can do more than dress up a page. Used well, media helps people comprehend your point faster, helps search engines interpret your content more accurately, and gives AI systems stronger material to retrieve and cite.

The issue is that most media gets published without sufficient context. For example, a team uploads a chart with no explanation. A video goes live without a transcript. A screenshot appears on a page with no useful caption; no meaningful *alt* text (*alternative* text is a short sentence that explains an image in words); and no structured support. The asset may look helpful, but it doesn't do much for accessibility, search visibility, or AI retrieval.

In this chapter, I show you how to make media assets work harder. I show you how to write captions, transcripts, and alt text that add clarity, how to apply schema without overcomplicating the process, and how to turn datasets and FAQs (Frequently Asked Questions) into reusable assets that strengthen your entire site.

Using Words to Explain Visual Content

Media doesn't explain itself. A human can often look at a chart or screenshot and infer the point. A search engine or AI system, however, needs clearer signals. That means your media needs supporting text that explains what it is, what it shows, and why it matters. This section describes three important types of supporting text: captions, transcripts, and alt text.

Creating helpful captions

A *caption* is the text paired with an image to help people and AI understand what they're looking at. A weak caption labels the asset. A strong caption explains the *takeaway* — the main point a viewer should gain from an image.

Compare these two captions:

- Weak caption: "Google Search Console dashboard."
- Better caption: "Google Search Console shows branded impressions increasing after the company added a clear product-comparison page."

The second version turns the image into evidence.

A useful caption usually accomplishes at least one of these results:

- Explains the main takeaway
- Tells the reader what content to notice
- Connects the visual element to the point of the page
- Adds context that isn't obvious from the image alone

Here's a simple caption formula:

What this is + What it shows + Why it matters

Take a look at these examples:

- "This heat map shows where users stop scrolling, which helps explain why the call to action underperformed."

- "This chart compares citation visibility before and after the team added FAQ blocks."
- "This screenshot shows a service-page FAQ section reinforcing the same claim in plain language."

REMEMBER

A good caption doesn't merely name the image; it explains what the reader is supposed to learn from it.

Different assets need different kinds of captions, and the caption must match the specific media type being used. This list explains various matchups:

- **Screenshot:** The feature, issue, or pattern that's visible onscreen
- **Chart:** The trend, comparison, or takeaway
- **Diagram:** The process or relationship
- **Product or service image:** What matters to the buyer or user

TIP

Place captions directly under the image, chart, diagram, or screenshot they explain. That placement makes the connection obvious for readers and gives search engines and AI systems nearby context to interpret the visual correctly.

Unlocking video value with transcripts

Video content often underperforms because the useful information stays trapped inside the player. A *transcript,* which is the written version of a video, turns spoken content into indexable, reusable text.

Including transcripts of uploaded video helps you:

- Improve accessibility
- Give search engines more readable content
- Create reusable copy for summaries, FAQs, and articles
- Preserve language that AI systems can quote or paraphrase

If a video supports education, conversion, or visibility on your site, a transcript should usually be part of the asset because AI may not watch the video — though it will read the text so that it can interpret the content.

CHOOSING THE CORRECT TRANSCRIPT FORMAT

You don't always need a raw, word-for-word transcript. In many cases, a cleaned transcript works better because it removes filler words, rambling phrases, and minor grammar issues, and it makes the content easier to read.

Use a full transcript whenever precision matters most. Use a cleaned transcript whenever readability and reuse matter more.

For example, use a full transcript for webinars, interviews, compliance-sensitive explanations, or any asset where exact wording matters. Use a cleaned transcript for demos, educational videos, and thought-leadership content where readability and reuse matter more than preserving every filler word.

REMEMBER

As a practical rule, include a transcript for any video embedded on a page that supports search visibility, education, or conversions. You can usually skip a full transcript for purely decorative clips, quick brand montages, or short social snippets that are not meant to rank, teach, or answer a question.

You can make transcripts more useful by adding:

- » A short summary at the top
- » Timestamps for longer videos
- » Section headers
- » Pull quotes or highlighted takeaways

Figure 15-1 shows a sample video page layout.

Exercising caution with AI-generated transcripts

Many platforms now generate transcripts automatically, including sites like YouTube and LinkedIn. This autogenerated text helps algorithms, search systems, and AI tools more easily comprehend video content, because it gives them readable language to work with rather than just audio.

The problem is that automatic transcripts are often inaccurate. They may misspell your brand name, confuse product names, misinterpret technical terms, or convert an important point into a misleading one. If the transcript is wrong, the machine-readable version of your content is wrong, too.

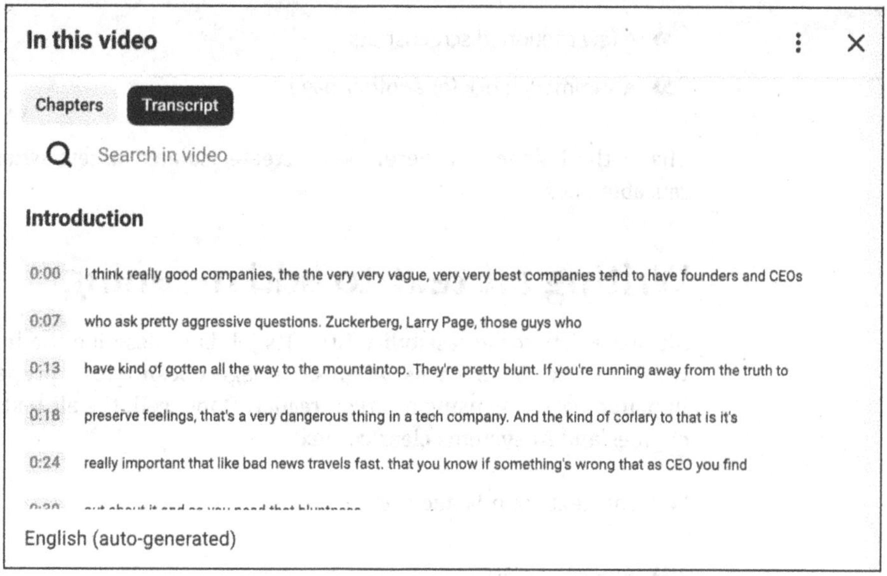

FIGURE 15-1: Sample video page with a video player, short summary, timestamped transcript, and highlighted takeaway.

TIP

Never assume that an autogenerated transcript is good enough as is. As soon as you publish an important video, review the transcript manually and correct obvious errors. Pay special attention to your brand name, product names, people's names, industry terminology, and numbers.

This strategy matters even more on platforms where transcripts may be visible, crawlable, or used to understand the context of the post. On LinkedIn in particular, treat the transcript as part of the published asset. Review it right away so that the machine-readable version of the post reflects what you meant to say.

TIP

When reviewing an AI-generated transcript, evaluate these five items first: brand names, product names, proper nouns, numbers, and industry terms. Those are often the errors that create the most confusion.

Turning one video into multiple assets

A single video can support much more than one embedded player. Once you have the recording and transcript, you can reuse that material in multiple formats.

- A transcript
- A recap article
- A short checklist
- Several FAQs

» A few captioned screenshots

» A summary block for another page

That's the bigger idea here: Don't create isolated assets when you can create reusable ones.

Writing alt text to add meaning

Alt text exists for accessibility first. Its job is to describe the image for someone who can't see it, such as when an image doesn't load properly or a visually impaired person is using a screen reader. Done well, the alt text also gives search engines and AI systems clear context.

Weak alt text sounds like this:

» "Image of graph"

» "Screenshot"

» "SEO chart"

Better alt text sounds like this:

» "Line chart showing citation coverage increasing after FAQ sections were added"

» "Screenshot of a product comparison table with pricing and feature columns"

» "Bar chart comparing branded and nonbranded AI answer mentions by month"

Notice the difference: The useful examples describe the meaningful content, not just the file type.

Alt text should match the image type:

» **Decorative image:** Use empty alt text.

TECHNICAL STUFF

Empty alt text means leaving the alt attribute blank, so screen readers skip a decorative image instead of reading a useless description. In HTML, that usually appears as alt="". Use it only when the image adds no meaning and the surrounding text already gives the reader everything they need.

» **Photo:** Describe the relevant subject.

- **Screenshot:** Describe the visible feature or key point.
- **Chart:** Summarize the trend or comparison.
- **Diagram:** Describe the flow or relationship.

Here's a useful question to ask: If someone can't see this image, what do they need to know to understand the page?

WARNING

Avoid the temptation to stuff keywords into alt text. For example, if the image is a person working at a computer, state it this way: Person working on computer at home. *Don't* say it this way: Person freelance remote work computer home office. The jumble of words hurts accessibility and usually makes the description less useful.

Running a quick media check

Before publishing an important page, make a quick pass to ask these questions:

- Does each image, chart, and video clarify, prove, or simplify something?
- Does each asset have a useful caption?
- Does each meaningful image have proper alt text?
- Does each important video have a transcript or summary?
- Can any asset be reused elsewhere on the site?

This simple check catches lots of missed opportunities.

Sizing Up Media Schemas

Structured data can help search engines understand what a page contains, what media appears on it, and how the parts fit together. Schema connects media to meaning. But schema isn't a shortcut. It works best when the visible page is already clear.

This section helps you start off with a strong page and then apply the proper schema to reinforce your page content. (See Chapter 4 for more details on how schema is used with AI systems.)

Starting with the page itself

Before adding schema markup, make sure the page clearly answers these questions:

- » What is this page about?
- » What media appears on it?
- » What does that media show?
- » What is the main task, claim, or takeaway?

If the page is vague, fix the visible content first. Add better headings, labels, captions, and summaries. Then add schema. This order matters because search engines compare markup with what users can see.

Choosing the proper schema

You don't need every schema type. You need only the ones that match the page. Schema should describe the function of your content — not just its existence. The examples in this list of media schemas show which parts of a page they can connect with:

- » **VideoObject:** Embedded video
- » **ImageObject:** A specific image that has stand-alone value
- » **FAQPage:** Visible question-and-answer sections
- » **Article or BlogPosting:** Editorial content
- » **Relevant page-level schema:** Schema, such as Product, Service, or Organization, when it supports the page purpose

For example, a tutorial page with an embedded video and visible FAQs might use Article, VideoObject, and FAQPage together.

Marking up media cleanly

Markup is the practical step where you add schema fields that describe the media and connect it to the page. In other words, you are labeling the video, image, or FAQ so search engines can understand what it is, what it contains, and how it supports the page.

For videos, keep the basic elements accurate:

- Name
- Description
- Thumbnail
- Upload date
- Duration
- Canonical page location

REMEMBER

For images, schema usually works best when the image itself plays an important role, such as an infographic (a visual representation of information or data), a product image set, or an original diagram. In many cases, strong captions and surrounding copy matter more than complex image markup.

TIP

Schema works best when the title, heading, caption, and markup all point to the same meaning.

Avoiding common schema mistakes

The most common problems are simple:

- Marking up content users can't see
- Leaving outdated titles or descriptions in place
- Applying FAQ schema to low-value or hidden content
- Piling on too many schema types without a purpose

Keep schema aligned with what users actually see on the page so that search engines and AI systems interpret the content consistently and reliably.

Using Public Datasets and Reusable FAQs

Public datasets and well-written FAQs are high-leverage assets. They help people make decisions, give other sites facts and visuals to cite, and give AI systems clear information to retrieve. When you pair those assets with charts, screenshots, and answer blocks, they become even easier to understand and reuse.

This section shows you how to build dataset pages that explain technical information clearly and FAQ blocks that point to helpful media when readers need visual proof, examples, or next steps.

Publishing a clear dataset

A *dataset* is a collection of original data that others can reference, analyze, or build on. You don't need a massive industry report. A small, focused dataset can be valuable if it's clear and useful.

Because numbers may be hard to understand on their own, align datasets with visual elements to help explain what the data means.

These are some examples of datasets:

- Pricing benchmarks
- Customer surveys
- Product usage trends
- Service timelines
- Local market comparisons
- Before-and-after performance changes

A strong dataset page usually includes these elements:

- A clear title
- A short summary near the top
- The date range
- The source or sample size
- A plain-English methodology note
- Charts or tables
- A written explanation of the findings

TIP

Help readers interpret raw numbers — don't make them do it on their own. If using charts or tables, explain the point in one or two sentences.

Here's an example:

"Smaller agencies adopted transcript publishing faster than enterprise teams, likely because they could update pages without long approval cycles."

This kind of sentence helps both humans and machines.

A good dataset should not live in isolation. Reuse the dataset across the entire site. Pull its findings into elements like these:

- Blog posts
- Service pages
- Comparison pages
- Fact hubs
- Outreach pitches
- Webinar decks
- FAQ sections

That's how a single source starts compounding in value.

REMEMBER

A dataset becomes stronger when the rest of your site links back to it as the source of truth.

Writing strong FAQs

FAQs and media work together by linking questions with visual proof, turning explanations into content that users can both read and see. However, having too many FAQ sections feels like they're an afterthought. The questions are generic, the answers ramble, and the language changes from page to page.

A strong FAQ section does three things:

- Answers a real buyer question
- Uses plain language
- Gives an answer you can reuse elsewhere

That last point matters because repeated inconsistency creates confusion. If five pages answer the same question in five different ways, AI systems may retrieve any one of them, and your stronger answer may be lost.

Building an FAQ bank

Rather than write fresh answers every time, create a small bank of approved, reusable answers for key questions about your brand, products, services, and niche.

This bank works even better when each answer can point to supporting media such as a chart, screenshot, video clip, or dataset. In that setup, the FAQ gives the direct answer while the media provides proof, context, or a quick visual explanation.

Check out these examples:

- What does this product do?
- Who does it serve best?
- How long does setup take?
- What makes it different?
- Does it replace another tool or complement it?

After those answers are approved, place them across product pages, service pages, pricing pages, comparison pages, and support content.

Putting an FAQ formula into play

When you pair FAQ answers with media, use the text to deliver the direct answer and use the image, video, chart, or screenshot to reinforce the point visually. A strong FAQ answer usually follows this pattern:

Direct answer + Qualifier + Next step or context

For example:

Question: Do I need a transcript for every video?

Answer: No. You don't need a transcript for every video, but you should add one for videos that support search visibility, education, or conversions. Start with videos embedded on product, service, and blog pages.

That answer is short, clear, and reusable.

4

Building Credibility across the Web

IN THIS PART . . .

Discover what AI signals are and how to improve the signals that shape your visibility.

Make sure your content is clear and consistent across all platforms.

Strengthen your topical authority by building trust across your own content and various third-party platforms.

Earn reviews that count.

Get links and mentions to strengthen your reputation and increase your chances of being cited.

Avoid risk by checking on privacy and accuracy and using caution with sensitive topics.

IN THIS CHAPTER

» Evaluating which signals help AI systems trust your brand

» Improving brand accuracy and consistency across the web

» Strengthening visibility using reviews, sentiment, and mentions

» Seeing why links still matter in AI SEO

Chapter 16

Identifying Signals That Move AI Systems

AI systems don't invent answers from nowhere. They look for patterns, consistency, and supporting evidence across the web. When your brand shows up clearly and accurately in multiple places, you make it easier for AI systems to mention you with confidence. When your information is messy, outdated, or contradictory, you make their job harder, and that usually means less visibility for you.

That doesn't mean you need to chase every shiny AI theory or obsess over some mysterious ranking factor. In most cases, the signals that help AI systems are the same ones that help humans trust you: accurate brand details, strong reviews, relevant mentions, and authoritative links. The difference is that AI systems often compare those signals across many sources at one time. They're looking for agreement — consistency and consensus across the web.

In this chapter, I show you what makes up an AI signal and how to improve the signals that shape AI visibility. Then I spell out how to tighten up your brand information, strengthen third-party proof, and make your authority easier for both machines and people to verify. Then I explain why links are an important part of solving the signal puzzle.

REMEMBER

AI systems trust consensus more than claims. You can say you're the best all day long. It matters far more when other trusted sources support that story.

Examining AI Signals in Depth

An *AI signal* is any clue that helps a system understand who you are, what you do, whether you're credible, and when it should mention you.

Some signals come from your own website. Others come from the rest of the web. Together, they help answer questions like these:

- Is this business real?
- Is its name, location, and offer clear?
- Do other sources describe it the same way?
- Do customers seem satisfied?
- Do trustworthy websites mention it or link to it?
- Does the brand appear established in its category?

You can't control every signal directly, but you can influence many of them.

A simple way to think about AI signals is to split them into these three buckets:

- **Identity signals:** Your brand name, business details, category, descriptions, profiles, and entity information
- **Reputation signals:** Reviews, sentiment, third-party mentions, citations, and community discussion
- **Authority signals:** Links, expert mentions, digital PR, and references from strong websites

If these three buckets line up, your brand becomes much easier to retrieve, cite, and recommend.

If they don't line up, you create doubt.

Suppose that your website says you're an AI SEO platform for agencies, your LinkedIn page says you're a content marketing tool, a review site lists you under blogging software, and a directory still shows your old brand description. That mismatch creates noise. AI systems may still mention you, but they're more likely to get the details wrong or choose a competitor who's clear instead.

The following sections help you break through the noise to create clear and consistent signals so that you can be a source of truth for AI systems to reference.

Tightening Up Brand Accuracy and Consistency

Brand accuracy allows search engines to describe a company's products, positioning, and reputation correctly and consistently. This concept may sound boring, but it's one of the highest-leverage aspects you can fix. If AI systems can't confidently identify your business and match your core facts across the web, your visibility suffers before the contest even starts.

Your goal is simple: Make your brand easy to recognize everywhere it appears. The next three sections help you kick up your consistency.

Clarifying your core brand facts

Your core *brand facts*, the information that defines the brand, should always be accurate, no matter who is referencing it. To form a clear idea of how your facts are being presented across the web, follow these steps:

1. **Create a list of the core facts you want every platform to reinforce. The list should include these elements of yours:**
   - Exact brand name
   - Website URL
   - Category or primary offer
   - Short description
   - Long description
   - Logo and brand visuals
   - Phone number, address, and service area if you're local

- Current pricing or plan structure, if it's public
- Top products, services, or modules

2. **Write down your core facts in a master reference document that becomes your signal source of truth.**
3. **Compare your signal source of truth against your public footprint. Check to see how your facts appear in various locations, such as**
   - Your website home page
   - About page
   - Contact page
   - Google Business Profile
   - LinkedIn company page
   - Crunchbase
   - G2, Capterra, and software directories
   - Local directories and citations
   - Social bios
   - Press mentions and contributor bios
4. **Look for drift. *Drift* happens when your core brand facts are presented differently across sources. Look for**
   - Inconsistent descriptions
   - Outdated information
   - Conflicting details

REMEMBER

The goal is consistency. If two sources describe you differently, AI systems won't know which version to trust.

Aligning your positioning

Positioning is how AI describes your brand so that people understand where you fit and why you matter. To align your positioning, you don't need every profile to use the exact same statement, but they should all tell the same story.

Here are some examples of poor positioning statements:

» **Site home page:** "AI SEO software for agencies"

» **LinkedIn:** "Content marketing and blogging solution"

- **Review sites:** "Marketing analytics tool"
- **Press bio:** "SEO training company"

Each description may be partly true, but together they muddy the waters.

Now compare these examples to cleaner versions:

- **Site home page:** "AI search visibility platform for agencies"
- **LinkedIn:** "AI SEO software that helps agencies plan, optimize, and improve content"
- **Review sites:** "SEO and content optimization software for agencies"
- **Press bio:** "Nathan Gotch, the founder of Rankability, an AI SEO platform for agencies"

The cleaner versions give AI systems far less room to guess.

TIP

Pick a single primary category and a core positioning message. Use them consistently across your homepage, LinkedIn page, review profiles, and press bio. The wording doesn't have to be identical, but the story should remain the same.

Fixing outdated and conflicting information

Conflicting brand information spreads faster than most people realize. Old directories linger. Review platforms retain stale screenshots. Someone writes a post about your business and never updates it. An old service description keeps getting quoted long after you've moved on.

To clean up outdated and conflicting information about you, fix the highest-impact issues first. You should:

- **Correct your owned properties.** Update the places you fully control, such as your website, social bios, and official profiles, so they accurately reflect your core facts. Fix one-line descriptions, product descriptions, stats, claims, screenshots, and calls to action that no longer match your current business.
- **Fix major third-party platforms.** Update Google Business Profile, LinkedIn, review sites, and top directories so they use your current brand name, category, description, logo, website URL, contact information, and service area.
- **Prioritize pages that already rank or get cited.** If an outdated page appears in branded searches or AI citations, correct the facts that can mislead buyers, including pricing, product names, availability, guarantees, and feature details.

» **Standardize your business details.** For local brands, align your name, address, phone number, hours, service areas, and categories. For non-local brands, standardize your product names, company description, support links, and official URLs.

» **Update old media kits and bios.** Refresh founder bios, press kits, speaker profiles, podcast bios, and partner pages so they use current positioning, credentials, links, and proof points.

You're not trying to make the whole Internet perfect. You're trying to reduce ambiguity in the places that matter most.

Building Better Review, Sentiment, and Mention Signals

AI systems pay attention to what other people say about your brand. Reviews, discussion, and mentions help shape whether you look trusted, controversial, loved, ignored, or simply unclear.

That's why your job isn't just to get mentioned. Your job is to get mentioned positively, accurately, and often enough to create a pattern.

Earning reviews that strengthen your signal

Review signals can add a significant level of trust to your brand. To create review signals that work for you, you need to be deliberate about three aspects: the kinds of reviews you earn, where those reviews live, and how consistently you generate them. The next three sections break down how to shape stronger review content, focus your efforts on the platforms that matter, and build a simple system to keep those signals growing over time.

For a deeper review-management workflow, see Chapter 19. Here, the focus is how reviews work as trust signals that AI systems can observe and compare across sources.

Shaping review content

A handful of five-star reviews from three years ago don't carry much weight. Your review profile page should look alive and be believable. Your goal isn't just to collect reviews — it's to create a review profile that's active, detailed, and consistent enough to be trusted.

Focus on building these signals:

- **Volume:** It's more useful than just one or two glowing reviews.
- **Freshness:** Recent reviews signal relevance.
- **Specificity:** Detailed reviews beat vague praise.
- **Spread:** Reviews across multiple respected platforms help more than all reviews living in one place.
- **Consistency:** A steady flow looks healthier than one giant burst.

Your review profile should show recent, detailed, platform-relevant reviews that mention the service, product, or outcome the customer experienced (see the later section "Building a review acquisition system" for details on getting the reviews you want). A strong review doesn't just say, "Great service." It says what happened.

REMEMBER

A review profile is the full public record of reviews tied to your business on a platform. It includes your star rating, total review count, review dates, review text, owner responses, photos, and recurring themes. A strong profile looks active, specific, and believable instead of thin, stale, or suspicious.

For example:

- "They improved our local visibility in Ballwin and helped us show up for emergency dental searches."
- "The software helped our agency speed up optimization without losing quality."
- "Their communication was fast, clear, and honest about scope."

These details create stronger signals because they connect your brand with outcomes, use cases, and categories, which are exactly the signals that AI systems use to cite you.

Concentrating your review effort

Not all review platforms carry the same weight.

If your business is local, your Google Business Profile should usually draw the majority of your attention when it comes to building review signals. In many cases, that means spending about 80 to 90 percent of your review acquisition effort there (see the later section "Building a review acquisition system," for info on gathering reviews). The remaining 10 to 20 percent should go toward the most important third-party directories and review platforms in your niche.

REMEMBER

Why put so much emphasis on Google Business Profile? Because, for local businesses, it's often the most visible review asset tied directly to your brand. It influences how you appear in local search, Maps, and branded searches. It also acts as one of the clearest public trust signals connected to your business.

After you're established in Google Business Profile, you want to earn reviews on the platforms that truly matter in your category.

For example, here are some third-party categories to consider for various industries:

- **Home services:** Angi, Thumbtack, Yelp, and similar service directories
- **Legal:** Avvo, FindLaw, Justia, and other legal directories
- **Healthcare:** Healthgrades, Vitals, Zocdoc, and relevant physician directories
- **Software:** Capterra, G2, TrustRadius, and related software review sites
- **Restaurants and hospitality:** OpenTable, TripAdvisor, Yelp, and similar platforms

The key is relevance. A random review on a low-value platform doesn't help as much as a smaller number of reviews on the platforms that people and machines in your category authentically trust.

TIP

Don't spread your review requests too thin (see the next section). Dominate the platform that matters most first and then layer in niche-relevant directories.

Building a review acquisition system

Don't leave reviews to chance. If you do, you may end up with gaps, outdated feedback, and missed opportunities to shape how your brand is perceived. A structured system gives you control over when, where, and how reviews are generated. Follow this approach to garner strong reviews:

1. **Pick the right moment.** Ask for a review immediately after a win, milestone, or positive interaction.
2. **Send a direct link.** Make the review as easy as possible.
3. **Give gentle guidance to secure details.** Ask customers to mention what service they used, what problem you solved, and what stood out.
4. **Direct most requests to your primary review platform.** For local businesses, that's usually Google Business Profile.

5. **Rotate secondary platforms when appropriate.** Send a smaller percentage of happy customers to the niche directories that matter in your market.
6. **Make it ongoing.** A steady review system beats a desperate review sprint.

For example, if you're a local roofing company, you might send most review requests to Google Business Profile while occasionally directing customers to Angi or Yelp. If you're a law firm, you may still prioritize Google heavily for local trust, but you also want a review footprint on Avvo and Justia because those sites are important in legal circles.

The big idea is simple: Don't chase reviews everywhere. Chase them where they're most visible and most trusted.

WARNING

Don't bribe people for reviews or pressure them to leave only positive feedback. Manipulated reviews can damage trust faster than no reviews at all.

Managing sentiment, not just star ratings

Sentiment is the emotional tone around your brand. It shows up in reviews, comments, forums, social posts, and articles.

You can improve sentiment by improving the customer experience, of course, but you also need to manage the public trail.

Pay attention if you're attracting feedback with recurring patterns like these:

- Confusion about pricing
- Complaints about onboarding
- Praise for one feature you rarely promote
- Negative assumptions based on outdated information
- Mismatch between what people expected and what you offer

These patterns tell you where your public messaging is off.

If multiple reviews say, "Great product, but setup took longer than expected," that's not just a support issue. It's a signal issue. Your onboarding content, FAQs, and sales messaging may need work.

To improve sentiment, fix the source of the repeated complaint and then make the fix visible. If people mention pricing confusion, create or update a clearer pricing table. If people complain about onboarding, add step-by-step setup instructions, expectations, and timelines. If reviews praise a feature you rarely promote, bring that proof into your sales pages and FAQs. For related fixes, see Chapter 12 on bottom of funnel pages, Chapter 14 on improving underperforming pages, and Chapter 19 on reviews.

Turning mentions into stronger signals

Mentions are any references to your brand across the web that aren't formal reviews but still communicate opinions, experiences, or context about your business or brand. Mentions can be found across the web, and although not every mention includes a specific link, unlinked mentions still matter. They can reinforce your brand name, category, expertise, and reputation.

Look for mentions in places like these:

- Listicles
- Review roundups
- Industry blogs
- Podcasts
- News articles
- Forums
- Reddit threads
- YouTube descriptions and transcripts
- Event speaker pages
- Local sponsorship pages

When you find a mention, ask these questions:

- Is the brand name correct?
- Is the description accurate?
- Is the context positive, neutral, or negative?
- Does the mention align with how you want to be known?
- Could this mention become a link or a profile opportunity later?

Sometimes, the best next move is simply to improve the accuracy of the mention. A correct mention without a link can still help more than a linked mention with the wrong description.

TIP

To improve a mention, give the publisher a clear, easy-to-verify source. That source can be an updated About page, a current media kit, a product page, or a short correction note that includes your official brand name, category, URL, and one-sentence description. The easier you make the correction, the more likely the source is to update it.

Understanding Links, Mentions, and Citations

Every few years, someone announces that links are dead.

They aren't. Links still matter because AI systems are influenced by brand mentions, citations, and links. When your brand appears across trusted third-party sources, it becomes easier for AI systems to see you as part of the landscape. What matters most is whether your brand is present on the kinds of sources AI systems repeatedly retrieve, summarize, and cite.

That's a major shift in thinking.

REMEMBER

In traditional SEO, people often built giant prospecting lists and chased almost any site that looked powerful enough to pass authority. In AI SEO, a smarter approach is to identify the websites that already shape answers in your market and prioritize those first.

In other words, it's no longer just about whether a site links to you — it's about whether your brand is consistently cited.

Differentiating links, citations, and mentions

Links, citations, and mentions often get lumped together, but they're not identical. Here's an examplc of how each one is used:

- **Link:** A clickable URL points to your site.
- **Citation:** A source refers to your business or information, sometimes with supporting details.
- **Mention:** Your brand name appears somewhere.

All three can help. For example, a local news article naming your dental practice is a mention. A chamber of commerce listing with your name, address, and URL is a citation plus a link. An industry publication referencing your original study and linking to it is a strong authority signal.

REMEMBER

To understand your authority, AI systems seem to be influenced by the full footprint — links, citations, and mentions — not just one narrow type of signal.

Replacing old-school prospecting with retrieval-driven prospecting

Old-school prospecting means building a broad list of sites because they look authoritative. *Retrieval-driven prospecting* means starting with the sources AI systems already cite, then working to get your brand included there. This is where the playbook changes.

Rather than build a giant random list of websites that might be good link and citation prospects, start by studying the websites AI systems are already using.

Here's the process for gathering websites to build a strong prospecting list:

1. Run lots of relevant prompts across AI platforms. Use the kinds of questions your customers actually ask.
2. Collect the citations and repeated sources. Note which domains show up over and over again.
3. Build a large master list of sources. Over time, that may mean gathering anywhere from 500 to 1,000 citations in your industry.
4. Identify actual citation opportunities on those sites. Ask how your brand could realistically get mentioned, listed, cited, quoted, reviewed, or linked.
5. Prioritize the sites that appear most often. If a source repeatedly influences answers, it deserves your attention.

This approach is much smarter than old-school prospecting because you're not guessing which sources might matter. You're reverse-engineering the sources that already do matter.

REMEMBER

If AI systems keep citing a source in your niche, that source matters whether or not it fits someone's old definition of the perfect SEO link prospect.

Going after citation opportunities, not just link opportunities

After you build your prospecting list (see the previous section), the next step is to look for ways to earn a presence on those domains. A citation opportunity can shape AI answers even when it does not produce a classic link, because it places your brand on a source that AI systems already use as evidence.

To gain presence on specific sites, try these strategies:

- Getting listed in relevant directories
- Contributing expert commentary
- Earning inclusion in listicles and roundups
- Sponsoring organizations or events that lead to mentions
- Publishing original data that journalists or bloggers cite
- Building resources worth referencing
- Appearing on podcasts, interviews, or expert panels
- Securing review profiles or marketplace listings
- Getting mentioned in local news or industry publications

The exact tactic matters less than the placement.

TIP

For each target source, choose the most natural path to inclusion. If it is a directory, claim or submit a profile. If it is a roundup, pitch a specific update with proof. If it is a podcast or expert article, offer a quotable point of view. The goal is to earn a brand mention, listing, quote, review profile, or link on from sources AI systems already use.

If you know that a website is part of the retrieval layer in your industry, earning visibility there should be a priority.

Focusing on presence over link purity

Prioritizing whether your brand shows up on important, trusted sources should be your focus, even if the link isn't perfect in a technical SEO sense. Focusing on *link purity*, which refers to the strength of the link directing to a website, doesn't mean technical SEO principles should disappear completely. Relevance still matters. Context still matters. Spam is still spam.

If you obsess too much over whether a link is follow, nofollow, or sponsored, you may miss the bigger opportunity. (In this context, a *follow link* is a standard link that search engines may use as an authority signal. A *nofollow link* is tagged to tell search engines not to pass traditional ranking credit. A *sponsored link* is tagged as paid or promotional.)

For AI visibility, it often seems more important that:

- Your brand is present on important retrieval sources.
- Your brand is described accurately.
- Your category and expertise are clear.
- Your mentions appear on sites that repeatedly influence answers.

That's why a nofollow mention on a highly cited industry source may do more for your AI visibility than a follow link on an irrelevant site that nobody trusts and no AI system seems to retrieve.

Avoiding outdated link habits

Some link tactics create noise instead of trust. Avoid shortcuts that put your brand on irrelevant, low-quality, or misleading pages, because those placements can weaken the signal you're trying to build.

Avoid tactics like these:

- Buying garbage links at scale
- Spamming guest posts with no editorial value
- Stuffing exact-match anchor text everywhere
- Using fake personas for outreach
- Submitting to junk directories
- Chasing irrelevant links just because the site looks powerful

Those tactics can create a messy footprint that weakens trust instead of building it.

Aim for link-building that looks like reputation-building because, in the long run, that's what it is.

IN THIS CHAPTER

» Auditing the pages and profiles that shape how your brand appears online

» Prioritizing the platforms that matter most for trust, discovery, and AI visibility

» Fixing inconsistent, incomplete, and outdated brand information

» Building a simple system to keep your profiles accurate over time

Chapter 17 Looking Good Wherever You're Found

When people look up your business, they rarely see only your website.

They also see your LinkedIn page, your Google Business Profile, your review profiles, your directory listings, your social bios, and sometimes a random old page you forgot existed. AI systems pull from that same mix of sources when forming an understanding of your business.

So do customers.

That means your brand doesn't live in one place. It lives everywhere that people and machines can find it.

If those pages tell the same clear story, you look trustworthy. If they conflict, look abandoned, or say almost nothing, you create confusion. In this chapter, you audit the pages that represent your business across the web, decide which ones deserve attention first, and fix the issues that make your brand look fragmented or outdated.

Auditing the Profiles That Shape Your Entity

Before you can fix your online presence, you need to see it clearly. That starts with an audit.

An audit sounds formal, but here it simply means making a list of the pages that define your business online and checking to see whether they help or hurt you.

Some of these pages are *profile pages* — the listings you create or manage on review sites, business directories, social networks, and other third-party platforms. Others are broader *entity pages* — any page that helps define who you are across the web. It's important to look at both, because together they shape how your business is understood.

Looking at entity and profile pages

Profile pages are a type of page: They're created on platforms and represent an account or presence you control (or at least manage). Entity pages are a broader concept. An entity is how AI systems understand your business as a distinct object. An entity page is any page that helps define or confirm that entity (see Chapter 4 for details on building your entity).

These pages generally fall into two groups:

Common entity pages include:

- Your About page
- Your Contact page
- Your founder or author bio
- Business database entries such as Crunchbase
- Industry directories
- Chamber or association listings

Common profile pages include:

- Your Google Business Profile
- Your LinkedIn company page
- Your social media bios
- Review platform profiles such as G2, Capterra, Yelp, or Clutch
- Marketplace pages

Follow this simple rule: If a customer or AI assistant might use the page to understand your business, include it in the audit (see the later section "Running a practical profile audit").

REMEMBER

Your website matters, but it isn't the whole story. People and machines often build their understanding of your brand from multiple sources.

Seeing how profile pages support your entity

The practical work in this section focuses mostly on profile pages because those are the pages you can usually claim, edit, and maintain. But every profile-page fix also improves your broader entity because it confirms the same core facts about your brand in another public place.

Each profile sends signals, whether you intended that or not. Together, those signals shape how your business is understood as an entity across the web.

These pages often communicate:

- Your official brand name
- Your category or business type
- Your products or services
- Your location or service area
- Your website URL
- Your phone number and address
- Your logo and images
- Your reviews and ratings

- Your expertise or specialty
- Whether the business looks active or neglected

If one profile says you're a software company, another says you're a consultant, and a third says almost nothing, you're forcing the web to guess. That's a bad bet.

Running a practical profile audit

The practical profile audit focuses on your profile pages because they set the baseline for how your business appears across the web. You don't need special software to do this. A spreadsheet is sufficient.

Create columns for these elements:

- Platform
- URL
- Claimed or unclaimed
- Brand name accuracy
- Description accuracy
- Category accuracy
- Contact info accuracy
- Logo and imagery
- Reviews present
- Last updated
- Priority
- Notes

Then run a search for these:

- Your brand name
- Your brand name plus city
- Your brand name plus founder name
- Your brand name plus product name
- Your brand name plus reviews
- Your brand name plus category

Start with the most visible results and then move into the major platforms for your business type.

TIP

After you run a search, log every meaningful result in your spreadsheet. Paste the URL, note the platform, mark whether you control the page, and give it a green, yellow, or red score. Use the Notes column to capture the fix, such as old logo, wrong category, duplicate listing, or missing website link. If a page appears high in branded search or gets cited by AI systems, mark it as high priority.

You're trying to answer this question: Which profile pages shape how my brand appears when someone goes looking?

Focusing on the details that matter most

When reviewing each profile, focus on the fields that create the most confusion when they're wrong:

- **Brand name:** Does the page use your official business name?
- **Website URL:** Does it link to the proper site?
- **Category:** Does it reflect what you actually do?
- **Description:** Does it explain your business clearly?
- **NAP information:** For local businesses, is your name, address, and phone number consistent?
- **Images and branding:** Does the profile use your current logo and visuals?
- **Reviews:** Are they present, recent, and relevant?
- **Freshness:** Does the page look current or abandoned?

TIP

If you examine only three items on every profile, check the brand name, website URL, and description first.

Spotting the usual problems

Most audits reveal the same issues:

- Duplicate profiles
- Outdated phone numbers or addresses
- Broken links

- Weak descriptions
- Wrong categories
- Inconsistent brand names
- Empty profiles
- Old logos
- Unclaimed listings
- Unclear founder bios
- Review pages with no responses

None of these problems feel huge on their own. Together, they make your brand look messy.

Using a simple scoring system

To keep the audit manageable, score each profile with a traffic light system:

- **Green:** Accurate, complete, and current
- **Yellow:** Mostly okay, but needs cleanup
- **Red:** Inaccurate, thin, outdated, or unclaimed

That's enough to make smart decisions without overengineering the process.

Prioritizing Your Pages

Not every page that mentions your business deserves equal attention. Some pages carry far more weight in how people and AI systems understand and trust your business. The key is knowing which ones to fix first.

Fixing high-impact pages

Some pages influence trust and visibility far more than others — these are your high-impact pages.

A tiny directory that no one sees usually doesn't matter much. A weak Google Business Profile, incomplete LinkedIn page, or outdated review profile can matter a great deal.

High-impact pages are the ones that:

- Show up in search results
- Shape buyer perception
- Get referenced by AI systems
- Support your authority
- Reinforce your category and positioning

Using these criteria, most businesses will find that their top priority list includes:

- Your home page
- Your About page
- Your Contact page
- Your founder or bio page
- Your Google Business Profile, if you're local
- Your LinkedIn company page
- Your main review platform profiles
- Your strongest third-party category pages

These pages usually have the most visibility and influence.

REMEMBER

Fix your most trusted and visible pages first. They do the most work.

Matching priorities to your business type

Not every business should prioritize the same types of profile pages. Different businesses surface in different places, which means different pages carry more weight.

The following practical breakdown shows where each type of business should focus first:

- **Local businesses:** Consistency in name, address, and phone number matters. Focus on these sites:
  - Google Business Profile
  - Apple Maps and Bing Places, if relevant
  - Yelp
  - Local directories
  - Chamber listings
  - Local review platforms
- **SaaS companies:** The main problem is usually weak positioning or missing category alignment, not map data. Prioritize these items:
  - Home page and product pages
  - About page
  - LinkedIn company page
  - Founder profiles
  - G2
  - Capterra
  - TrustRadius
  - Crunchbase
  - Product hunt
- **Agencies and professional services:** These businesses often win by combining strong company profiles with visible personal authority. Focus on:
  - Service pages
  - About page
  - Founder bio
  - LinkedIn company page
  - Google Business Profile
  - Clutch
  - Industry directories
  - Review profiles

- **E-commerce brands:** Clarity, trust, and product consistency matter most. Pay attention to:
  - Your brand site
  - Product pages
  - Marketplace storefronts
  - Social commerce profiles
  - Review platforms
  - Retail partner profiles

Building a quick priority framework

If you're deciding between pages to prioritize for fixing, ask these five questions:

- Does it rank for branded searches?
- Could a buyer see it before choosing me?
- Could an AI system use it as evidence about my brand?
- Does it support my positioning?
- Can I realistically fix it this week?

Then sort your pages into these three tiers:

- **Tier 1:** High visibility, high trust, important to fix now
- **Tier 2:** Useful support pages
- **Tier 3:** Low-visibility listings you can clean up later

This keeps you from wasting time polishing obscure profiles while your main pages stay inaccurate.

WARNING

Don't confuse activity with impact. Updating ten obscure profiles can feel productive while your most important pages stay broken.

Executing the Fixes

Now comes the fun part: cleaning things up. Noting how your brand appears across the web and finding the most important pages to fix first are the keys to strengthening your brand (see the earlier sections in this chapter). In this section, I show you how to make the fixes that improve your visibility.

TIP

Start with a consistent set of core brand facts. Check out Chapter 16 to see just how to keep this source-of-truth document up-to-date and consistent.

Rewriting weak descriptions

A *profile description* is a short summary text on a profile page that explains what your business does. Many profile descriptions fail because they try to sound impressive rather than clear.

Here's an example of a poor description:

> "We provide innovative, customer-centric solutions that empower brands to maximize outcomes."

It says almost nothing.

Here's a better example:

> "We help SEO agencies create content that performs better in traditional and AI-driven search."

This description is better because it clearly states who the business serves, what it does, and the specific outcome it delivers.

TIP

Use this simple formula to keep your profile descriptions clear and strong:

> We help [audience] do [job] through [category or solution].

Plain language works better than vague marketing copy.

Updating for consistency, not sameness

Consistency doesn't mean that every page must use the exact same wording. It means that the core facts stay aligned across the web.

Make sure these items stay consistent:

- Official name
- Main category
- Website URL
- Core offer
- Positioning
- Geography, if relevant
- Brand visuals

You can adjust wording for the page, but the story should stay the same.

Cleaning up duplicate pages

Duplicate profiles split trust and create conflicting signals.

When you find them, follow these steps:

1. **Claim the correct profile.**
2. **Save the duplicate URL.**
3. **Request a merge, removal, or closure.**
4. **Strengthen the surviving profile.**

If you can't remove a duplicate immediately, make sure the correct version is fuller, clearer, and easier to trust.

For more help correcting conflicting brand details across the web, see Chapter 16. For duplicate local or directory listings, start with the platform's own claim, merge, or report-a-duplicate process because each platform handles cleanup a little differently.

Correcting review profile weaknesses

Review pages are also brand profiles, so they deserve attention. They carry weight because they publicize consumer feedback.

Review each profile and make fixes as needed:

- **Is the profile complete?** If not, fill in the description, category, website link, images, services or products, and contact fields.
- **Are the categories correct?** If not, choose the closest primary category and remove categories that make your business look like something it is not.
- **Do you have recent reviews?** If reviews are stale, ask recent happy customers for honest reviews on the platform that matters most for your category.
- **Have you responded to important reviews?** If not, reply with a short, specific note that shows you are active and paying attention.
- **Do the reviews support the positioning you want?** If not, update your profile description and FAQs so the page reinforces the same promise your website makes.

You don't need a perfect review profile. You need one that looks credible, active, and relevant. See Chapters 16 and 19 for more on creating strong review profiles.

Connecting profiles back to your website

Your profiles should reinforce your main brand entity, not sit around like disconnected islands.

Wherever possible, link profiles back to the correct page on your website. Also make sure your site connects back to key profiles when appropriate.

Strengthen those connections by checking these items:

- Point each profile to the most relevant page, not automatically to the homepage.
- Link from your About, Contact, or footer pages to major profiles when those links help users verify your business.
- Add important profile URLs to Organization, LocalBusiness, or Person schema sameAs (see Chapter 4) fields when appropriate.
- Use the same brand name, logo, and category language on both sides of the link.
- Update or remove links that point to old domains, old locations, retired social accounts, or abandoned profiles.

You're making it easier for people and machines to connect the dots.

REMEMBER

After these connections are in place, your profiles stop competing with each other and start reinforcing the same signal.

Building a practical workflow

Rather than fix everything randomly, follow this sequence:

1. **Finalize your source-of-truth document.**
2. **Fix your website's core identity pages.**
3. **Update Tier 1 profiles.**
4. **Clean up duplicates and broken links.**
5. **Strengthen review pages and third-party profiles.**
6. **Log whatever you changed.**

A repeatable checklist works better than a one-time cleanup sprint.

Creating a lightweight maintenance routine

After you clean up your *footprint* — the collection of profile pages that represent your business online — keep it clean.

A practical cadence looks like this:

- Review Tier 1: Check high-impact profiles quarterly.
- Review Tier 2: Check secondary profiles twice a year.
- Update profiles after major business changes.

ASSIGNING OWNERSHIP

Profiles grow messy when no one owns them.

Give one person clear responsibility for profile upkeep. In a small business, that may be you. In a larger one, it may be a marketing manager, SEO lead, or brand operations owner.

If everyone owns it, no one owns it.

» Log new accounts as soon as they're created.

» Store credentials and ownership information securely.

TIP

Major changes include a rebrand, address change, new product launch, pricing shift, or new target market. All those should trigger a profile update sprint.

WARNING

An outdated profile rarely announces itself. It just quietly becomes the wrong version of your brand.

IN THIS CHAPTER

» **Blanketing answer surfaces and search results**

» **Controlling the story with your own assets**

» **Borrowing reach from other people's audiences**

» **Building trust in communities that shape recommendations**

» **Planning and measuring ownership, and avoiding mistakes**

Chapter 18
Owning the Topic

Showing up once is nice. Owning the topic is better.

That's the shift this chapter is all about. In AI SEO, you don't win by publishing one decent article and hoping a chatbot then falls in love with it. You win by creating so much useful, trustworthy, consistent presence around a topic that your brand becomes the obvious answer. You show up in classic search results, AI-generated answers, videos, profiles, interviews, roundups, and conversations that people are already having.

In other words, I want you to stop treating visibility like a single ranking and start treating it like territory.

In this chapter, I show you how to do exactly that. I show you how to blanket the search engine results page, or SERP — the page a search engine displays after a user submits a query — with helpful assets, use channels you own to shape the message, tap into other people's audiences to expand your reach, and earn trust in communities without acting like the person everyone hopes will soon leave the group chat. From there, I spell out how to strengthen your ownership with consistency, measure your progress, and avoid common mistakes — as well as complete a topic ownership plan.

Exploring the True Meaning of Topic Ownership

Having topic ownership doesn't mean that you literally own a topic. You can't file paperwork and declare yourself the official ruler of "commercial roof repair" or "AI SEO software." Nice try.

What you can do is build enough relevance and trust around a topic that search engines, AI answer surfaces, and humans start associating that topic with your brand.

Think about what happens when someone searches or asks a question: They might:

- See a traditional search result
- See an AI overview
- Watch a YouTube video
- Skim Reddit
- Peruse reviews
- Ask ChatGPT, Gemini, or Perplexity
- Click a podcast, roundup, or comparison article

If your brand appears in only one of those places, you have a visibility win.

If your brand appears across many of them, with a clear and consistent message, you're starting to own the topic.

TIP

When you think about topic ownership, stop asking, "Do I rank?" and start asking, "Where does my brand appear when someone tries to learn, compare, validate, or decide on a topic?"

Owning a topic usually includes these four factors:

- **Coverage:** You have content for the major questions, use cases, objections, and comparisons.
- **Consistency:** Your message stays aligned across channels.
- **Credibility:** Other people mention, cite, review, or discuss you.
- **Community trust:** People recognize your brand and connect it to a specific problem you solve.

That's the big idea behind this chapter. You're not building one page — you're building a footprint.

Blanketing Answer Surfaces and SERPs

If you want to own a topic, you need to appear in more than one format and more than one position. That's what I mean by blanketing.

You're not trying to cram duplicate content everywhere. You're trying to cover a topic from multiple useful angles so that no matter how someone searches, asks, compares, or validates, they keep bumping into your brand — across both SERPs (lists of results) and answer surfaces (interfaces that generate direct answers, like AI assistants, such as ChatGPT).

Answer surfaces come into play when content assets, such as comparison pages and review profiles, get condensed into a direct response. For example, an AI assistant may use your comparison page, review profile, and support article to build one answer, even when the user never sees a traditional results page.

Covering the main query types

Most topics break into a predictable set of query types. Covering the main query types means creating content that directly addresses each type of search intent people use when they explore a topic. This ensures you show up at different stages of the user journey and increases your chances of being surfaced in both SERPs and answer surfaces. Here's a list of common query types:

- Definition
- Problem-aware
- Solution-aware
- Comparison

- Best Of
- Cost or pricing
- Review and alternative
- Local or service
- FAQ and objection

Let's say you sell bookkeeping software for freelancers. Topic ownership wouldn't come from one page labeled Best Bookkeeping Software. It would come from covering topics like these:

- Definition query: What bookkeeping software does for freelancers
- Problem-aware query: Why freelancers struggle to track expenses
- Solution-aware query: How bookkeeping software helps freelancers track expenses
- Comparison query: QuickBooks versus FreshBooks for freelancers
- Best Of query: Best bookkeeping tools for freelancers
- Cost or pricing query: How much bookkeeping software costs for freelancers
- Review and alternative query: QuickBooks alternatives for freelancers
- Local or service query: Bookkeeping services for freelancers near me
- FAQ and objection query: Do freelancers need bookkeeping software, or is a spreadsheet enough?

That coverage helps traditional SEO. It also helps AI systems retrieve the right passages when users ask related questions in different ways. On answer surfaces, that same coverage gives AI systems more clean passages to summarize, cite, and use when forming direct recommendations.

Creating more than one result type

You need more than one asset type on the SERP or answer journey. For example:

- A core landing page
- A supporting blog post
- A YouTube video
- A comparison page

- A downloadable checklist
- A founder interview
- A review profile
- A guest article
- A podcast appearance

Individually, each of these assets serves a specific role. But in an answer surface, they don't remain isolated. They can be combined as supporting evidence in a single synthesized response — even if none is the top organic result on its own.

This is where familiarity starts to matter. The goal isn't just visibility in one position. It's repeated presence across formats so that when someone explores the topic, your brand feels consistent and recognizable rather than occasional or incidental.

REMEMBER

Topic ownership happens when your brand becomes easy to retrieve, easy to verify, and easy to remember.

Building a SERP blanket

You want to expand from a single topic into a full visibility footprint. To do that, you need a process that increases your chances of appearing across various formats and in AI-generated answers. Use this process for any topic cluster:

1. **Pick a single priority topic.** Don't start with 20. Choose one that matters to revenue, authority, or strategic positioning.
2. **List the top search intents around the topic.** Consider awareness, comparison, validation, and conversion.
3. **Map one asset to each intent.** Match the format to the question. A pricing question may need a landing page. A how-to question may need a blog post or video. A credibility question may need case studies or reviews.
4. **Look at the live SERP.** Search the core topic and the top supporting terms. Note the types of pages and platforms showing up.

   TECHNICAL STUFF

   Top supporting terms are closely related phrases and prompts that help define the larger topic, such as pricing, alternatives, reviews, use cases, and who-it-is-for queries. Look for them in autocomplete, People Also Ask, related searches, AI follow-up questions, and the pages that repeatedly rank or get cited.

5. **Fill the obvious gaps.** If the SERP favors videos and you have none, that's a gap. If alternative searches, meaning queries that ask for substitutes or other options, show only competitor pages, that's a gap. If third-party mentions dominate, that's a clue you need earned visibility, too.

Avoiding content cannibalization while blanketing

Many marketers hear "Cover the topic from multiple angles" and immediately publish several articles targeting the same keyword with slightly different outfits.

Don't do that.

Instead, assign a distinct job to each asset:

- Your pillar page covers the main commercial or educational intent.
- Your supporting articles answer subquestions.
- Your comparison pages handle decision-stage queries.
- Your videos explain, demonstrate, or summarize.
- Your downloadable assets turn complex info into reusable tools.

TIP

If two pages are trying to do the exact same thing, merge them, redirect one, or reposition one.

Controlling the Narrative with Owned Assets

Owned assets are the channels you control directly. Your website, email list, YouTube channel, podcast, LinkedIn newsletter, and downloadable resources all fall into this category. These are where you define and reinforce your viewpoint on a topic so that you can make it easy for both people and systems to understand what you stand for. These assets matter because rented platforms change. Algorithms change. Search layouts change. AI products change. Your owned assets give you a stable home base.

The following three sections help you turn a topic into a focal point, repurpose a topic source to gain further coverage, and align owned assets via consistency.

Turning your site into a topic hub

Your website should function like mission control for a topic.

That doesn't mean every page has to be long. It means the site should make your expertise easy to understand. A good topic hub usually includes:

- A main pillar or service page
- Supporting educational content
- Trust-building proof, like reviews, case studies, or testimonials
- Clear internal links
- A consistent point of view
- Up-to-date facts and claims

If someone lands on your site after seeing your brand mentioned elsewhere, they should quickly understand these three concepts:

- What you do
- Who it's for
- Why they should trust you

Repurposing without becoming repetitive

Many people take a topic, create one good article about it, and then move on like they just completed a heroic act for the Internet. Why put that hard work to waste by assigning it to only one asset?

A better move is to repurpose strategically.

A single core topic can become

- A pillar page
- A blog post
- A short video
- A long-form YouTube video
- A podcast segment

- An email
- A LinkedIn post
- A checklist
- A webinar
- An FAQ page

The key is to adapt the angle, not just copy and paste the same wording everywhere. Different channels need different packaging, but the underlying message should remain consistent.

For example, a pillar page may explain the full framework. A YouTube video may show examples. A LinkedIn post may spotlight one mistake. A checklist may simplify implementation.

Keeping owned assets aligned

If your site says one thing, your YouTube channel says another, and your founder interviews say something else, you're making retrieval and trust harder than it needs to be.

Pick a clear message for the topic, such as:

- What you want to be known for
- What makes your approach different
- What outcomes you help create
- What language you want associated with your brand

Then reinforce that message across your owned properties.

TIP

Create a simple messaging sheet for every core topic. Include your main positioning line, top claims, proof points, preferred terminology, and the three to five phrases you want strongly associated with your brand. Use this sheet as a reference when creating, reviewing, or repurposing content so that your message stays consistent across every channel.

Benefiting from Other People's Audiences

You don't have to build every audience from scratch. In fact, if you're trying to own a topic quickly, that's usually a bad idea.

Other people's audiences, or OPAs, help you borrow trust and distribution from platforms, publishers, creators, experts, and communities that already have attention. In this section, I help you pick the right OPAs, contribute to places where audiences are looking to learn about a topic, and expand your content to appear in multiple places.

Choosing the right OPAs

Not all reach is good reach. The goal isn't to be everywhere — it's to show up in the places that reinforce your authority on a specific topic.

You want OPAs that strengthen your association with the topic you're trying to own, including:

- Industry podcasts
- Niche newsletters
- Trusted trade publications
- YouTube channels in your space
- Expert roundups
- Webinars with strategic partners
- Conference talks
- Guest articles on relevant sites

The best OPAs usually meet these three tests:

- The audience overlaps with your ideal audience.
- The host or platform has credibility.
- The topic fit is obvious.

TIP

A simple way to choose the right OPA for your topic is to score each opportunity against three factors: audience fit, topical fit, and trust fit. If an opportunity does not clearly reach your buyer, reinforce your topic, and come from a credible source, skip it.

A generic large audience can attract attention. A relevant audience can build authority.

Supplying useful content

The easiest way to get ignored is to pitch yourself like this:

> "Hi, I'm amazing. Please feature me."

Nobody is opening their calendar for that strategy.

To earn attention, you need to contribute in places where people are actively looking to learn, evaluate, or improve on a topic.

To gain that attention, you need a contribution angle. Bring useful content to the format you're looking to get into, such as:

- Original data
- A tested framework
- A bold but defensible point of view
- A case study
- A process breakdown
- A tactical checklist
- Lessons from real-world implementation

You're far more likely to get invited, cited, or published when you make the audience smarter.

Turning one appearance into many signals

As I discuss in the earlier section "Repurposing without becoming repetitive," you want to make good use of your content — not just in one place, but in multiple places. Let's say you appear on a podcast. Don't let it be just a one-day event.

Instead, turn it into one of these:

- A quote on your site
- A social clip

- A blog recap
- An email to your list
- A transcript excerpt
- A link on your press page
- A reference in future pitches

Now, one borrowed audience becomes multiple trust signals.

That matters because topic ownership grows by way of repetition across surfaces. One mention rarely changes the game. Compounding mentions does.

WARNING

Don't chase OPAs that have no topical relevance just because they look impressive. Being featured in the wrong room can inflate your ego but not strengthen your position.

Building Trust in Communities

Communities give people a place to validate — or challenge — marketing claims based on firsthand experience. Unlike SERPs or answer surfaces, where visibility is driven by ranking systems or generated responses, communities are driven by conversation, experience, and peer validation.

That's why they matter — they are where topic ownership is confirmed by humans.

Forums, subreddits, Slack groups, Discord communities, Facebook groups, industry comment sections, and niche communities often shape what people believe before they ever buy. They also influence what gets repeated, referenced, and surfaced later. This section describes how to be active in communities and gain their trust so that you become a source of truth.

Showing up like a human, not a billboard

If you want positive human response, you need to act like an actual human. This statement should be obvious, but the Internet keeps proving otherwise.

If you enter a community just to drop links and talk about yourself, people will notice. Then they'll ignore you, roast you, or remove you — and sometimes all three.

A better approach is to earn trust by carrying out these tasks:

- Answer questions clearly.
- Share examples.
- Explain tradeoffs honestly.
- Mention your own brand only when relevant.
- Link out only when it truly helps.
- Participate consistently.

If your contributions are genuinely useful, your brand becomes associated with expertise without your forcing it.

Listening for the issues people are talking about

Communities are research gold mines. They show you what people are talking about, what words they're using in discussions, and what solutions people are looking for.

When on a community platform, look for these problems:

- What confuses people
- What words they use
- What objections keep coming up
- Which competitors get mentioned
- Which pain points are most emotional
- Which myths won't die, no matter how badly they should

TIP

Use this information to improve your content and positioning. Rewrite key explanations in the language your audience uses, resolve recurring objections, and adjust your positioning so that it reflects how people already think about the problem.

For example, if your audience never says the term *entity optimization* but constantly asks, "How do I get AI systems to mention my brand?" that's a signal. Start with their phrasing in your content and then translate it into the underlying concept after the idea is clear.

Contributing to build durable trust

Community trust tends to be slower than traffic spikes, but it lasts longer.

A helpful comment, useful answer, or smart thread can lead to these benefits:

- Direct traffic
- Brand searches
- Private recommendations
- Mentions in newsletters or blogs
- Invitations to speak or collaborate
- A better understanding of audience needs

That's why communities are a part of topic ownership — they create the human layer that reinforces your published assets.

REMEMBER

Many community platforms are partially visible to search engines and AI systems, but even when they aren't, they still influence brand perception, language patterns, and what people repeat elsewhere. That indirectly affects matters.

Building Topic Ownership via Consistent Signals

With the goal of showing up in more places, consistency matters even more.

If every appearance makes a different claim, uses different language, or targets a different audience, your visibility fragments. You may gain impressions, but you won't build a strong association — or topic ownership. This section focuses on getting people to mentally connect your brand to a topic by repeatedly choosing associations that hype your brand and on knowing which items bear repeating.

Determining what you want to own

Owning a topic is about consistently reinforcing a specific association within that topic until your brand becomes the main reference point for it. If a topic is the subject area you're operating in, the association is the specific angle or position you want to be known for within that topic. You want to pick the association deliberately.

Ask yourself these questions:

- What problem do we want to be known for solving?
- Which topic cluster matters most to our business?
- What angle or philosophy makes us different?
- What proof supports that position?

For example, maybe you want to own a topic such as one of these:

- "AI SEO for agencies"
- "Emergency plumbing in West County"
- "Fractional CFO services for SaaS"
- "Natural skin care for sensitive skin"

Owning that topic doesn't mean you ignore other topics forever. It means that you lead with one clear association.

Repeating the right content

Yes, repetition can feel boring to the person creating the content. That's fine. You're not creating for yourself. You're creating for the market.

Repetition is how topic ownership is built. The more consistently you reinforce the same signals, the more you become the default association for that topic.

Repeat the following elements to help people remember and retrieve you:

- Your category
- Your audience
- Your point of view
- Your proof
- Your terminology
- Your signature frameworks

This type of repetition helps humans remember you and helps machines "connect the dots."

Measuring Your Ownership of the Topic

You can't just "vibe" your way into topic ownership. You need evidence.

Look for signs across these three signals:

- **Visibility:** Track where you appear:
  - Organic rankings
  - AI answers and citations
  - Video search presence
  - Branded search growth
  - Third-party mentions
  - Review site visibility
- **Coverage:** Track the completeness of your footprint:
  - How many key subtopics you cover
  - How many search intents have dedicated assets
  - How many relevant formats you've published
  - How many third-party placements support the topic
- **Trust:** Track whether the market is validating your position:
  - Reviews
  - Testimonials
  - Community mentions
  - Podcast invitations
  - Partnership requests
  - Backlinks and unlinked brand mentions

TIP

Create a simple topic ownership scorecard. Pick one topic cluster and review it monthly. Grade yourself on coverage, consistency, credibility, and community presence. Don't overcomplicate it. A simple tracking sheet beats a perfect dashboard you never open.

Avoiding the Most Common Topic Ownership Mistakes

Everyone makes mistakes. But I want to help you hurdle some common obstacles that may get in the way of your topic ownership. Here are a few issues that may sabotage your progress and ways to combat them:

- **Publishing random content:** If your content calendar looks like it was assembled by a caffeinated raccoon, your authority will feel scattered, too.

  Choose related topics that reinforce the same association.

- **Overvaluing your website and ignoring everywhere else:** Your site matters. It just isn't the whole game. If all your proof lives on your own domain and nowhere else, trust will grow more slowly.

  Balance owned and earned visibility. Keep your site as the source of truth, but build supporting mentions on review platforms, directories, podcasts, industry publications, and community threads where buyers already look for proof.

- **Chasing every platform:** You don't need to be everywhere. You need to be in the places that shape discovery and trust for your market.

  Choose platforms where your audience goes to discover information about your topic. For one niche, that may be YouTube, Google, and industry podcasts. For another, it may be Reddit, local directories, and review platforms.

- **Being inconsistent:** If your offers, claims, bios, and positioning keep changing, your authority signal weakens.

  Stable messaging wins. (Wait — have I said that before?) Use your core topic messaging sheet (see the earlier section "Keeping owned assets aligned") to remain consistent across the web.

Creating a Practical Topic Ownership Plan

You don't need a giant empire on day one. Start with one topic and build a repeatable system.

Here's a practical plan:

1. **Choose one commercially relevant topic cluster.**

   Pick one that matters to leads, sales, or strategic brand position.

2. **List the core intents around it.**

   Include awareness, comparison, validation, and decision-stage queries.

3. **Build your owned asset hub.**

   Create or improve the pillar page, supporting content, internal links, and proof assets.

4. **Add supporting formats.**

   Turn the topic into video, email, social posts, FAQs, checklists, or webinars.

5. **Pursue three to five relevant OPAs.**

   Pitch a useful idea, not your ego.

6. **Join and contribute to two to three communities.**

   Help first. Mention yourself second.

7. **Review your footprint monthly.**

   Track what's live, what's ranking, what's being cited, and where credibility gaps remain.

Following these steps allows you to move from "We published some content" to "We're becoming the brand this topic points to."

When you're reviewing your progress, look for these ten signs that show you're becoming a topic owner master:

- People search for your brand plus the topic.
- You rank for multiple related queries.
- AI tools mention or cite your brand more often.
- Third-party sites reference your ideas.
- You appear in roundups and comparisons.
- Communities mention your brand organically.

» Prospects say, "I keep seeing you everywhere."

» Your positioning becomes easier to explain.

» Partnerships and speaking invitations increase.

» Competitors start reacting to your messaging.

Owning the topic doesn't happen because you declared it on LinkedIn with a heroic thread and a dramatic hook. It happens because you built a network of useful, consistent, trustworthy assets on and off the SERP. Do that well, and your brand becomes much harder to ignore and much easier to recommend.

IN THIS CHAPTER

- » Choosing the review platforms that matter most
- » Building a steady system for earning reviews
- » Responding well to strengthen trust
- » Keeping review quality high over time

Chapter 19

Garnering Reviews That Count

Reviews do more than make your business look good. They help potential customers decide whether to trust you, and they give search engines and AI systems more confidence in mentioning your brand. In other words, reviews can influence both conversions and visibility.

The problem is that many businesses handle reviews poorly. They ask inconsistently, send customers to the wrong platforms, ignore negative feedback, or chase review volume without paying attention to quality. That approach creates a weak reputation footprint.

In this chapter, you discover how to focus on the right review platforms, build a repeatable review process, and respond in a way that strengthens trust. You also see how to improve the quality of your reviews so that they carry more weight with both people and machines.

Picking the Right Platforms

Not all review platforms matter equally. If you try to push reviews everywhere, you spread your effort too thin. Instead, focus on the places your buyers already trust and the places most likely to influence search and AI visibility.

This section gives you some platform know-how by showing you how your platform choice affects results, noting which platforms will perform best for your business, reviewing what your current review presence looks like on certain platforms, and setting up a platform priority list.

Knowing why platform choice matters

People rarely rely on one source when looking for information about a business. They compare platforms, scan for patterns, and look for consistency. Search engines and AI systems do something similar: They look for outside signals that support your credibility.

Different platforms signal different priorities. A broad platform like Google shows whether your business looks active, local, and trusted at a glance, and industry-specific sites highlight category credibility, peer comparisons, and proof that buyers in your niche often weigh before they choose.

For example, a software buyer may trust a detailed G2 review more than a Google review, while a local customer may check Google Maps first. Platform choice matters because each site answers a different trust question.

That means a scattered or neglected review footprint can work against you. A strong Google profile paired with an empty industry profile sends mixed signals. Fresh reviews on one site and three-year-old reviews everywhere else can make your brand look stale.

You don't need to dominate every review site. You do need to look active and trustworthy in the right places.

REMEMBER

A good review strategy is about relevance, not about being everywhere.

Matching platforms to your business type

Finding the right platforms for your business depends on what you sell. Here are some examples based on business type (also check out Chapter 16 for a list of where to focus your review efforts):

- **For local businesses,** Google Business Profile is usually the top priority. Yelp may matter too, along with local and niche directories.
- **For SaaS companies,** platforms like G2, Capterra, Trustpilot, and app marketplaces are important.

- **For e-commerce brands,** Google, Amazon, and retailer-specific review systems can carry the most weight.
- **For professional services,** the best mix often includes Google plus category-specific sites such as Avvo, Clutch, Healthgrades, Houzz, or similar directories.

TIP

You want to identify one to three platforms that actually influence buying decisions in your space. Search your service like a customer, and note which platforms consistently show up and feature active reviews. Those platforms are the ones shaping decisions in your market.

Auditing your current review footprint

You don't need to try to garner as many reviews as possible. You first want to evaluate how your business appears at a glance to both customers and systems. If your presence is inconsistent and outdated, adding more reviews can *amplify* those issues rather than improve perception. So, before asking for more reviews, look at what you already have. Think of this as a baseline check, and review each of your important profiles for these elements:

- Review count
- Average rating
- Recency
- Level of detail
- Profile completeness
- Brand consistency
- Response activity

This audit helps you spot weak links. Maybe one profile has positive reviews but no recent activity. Maybe another has an outdated business description. Maybe your business name, address, or positioning differs from one platform to another.

These gaps create friction. Clean them up before driving more people to those profiles.

Creating your priority list

When you have a list of platforms where your business is mentioned (see the earlier section "Matching platforms to your business type"), create a priority list so that you know where to focus first. Sort your platforms into these three groups:

- **Primary:** The top one to three platforms that matter most
- **Secondary:** Platforms worth maintaining
- **Low priority:** Platforms you keep accurate but don't actively push

This makes your review strategy easier to manage. It also prevents confusion when you ask customers to leave feedback. How so? The priority list gives customers one clear destination instead of a confusing menu of choices. Send most happy customers to your primary platform, and rotate secondary platforms only when you have a specific reason to build those profiles.

TIP

If you're unsure where to focus, start with the platform most visible in branded searches and most trusted by buyers in your category.

Building a Steady Review System

A few bursts of review activity don't help as much as a steady flow over time. A healthy review profile looks active, recent, and natural. That requires a system.

The good news is that your system doesn't need to be fancy. It just needs to happen consistently. The next six sections help you build a strong, repeatable system.

Moving from random requests to a repeatable process

Many businesses ask for reviews only when someone remembers to do it. That leads to inconsistent results. You end up with long gaps followed by sudden spikes, which isn't ideal.

A better approach is to tie review requests to specific moments in the customer journey. Consider coordinating after one of these moments takes place:

- A successful appointment
- Delivery of a product

- Onboarding completed
- Resolution of a support issue
- Positive feedback shared privately by a client

These moments work because the customer has already experienced value.

Asking at the right time

Timing matters. Ask for a review too early, and the customer has nothing meaningful to say. Ask too late, and the momentum is gone.

REMEMBER

The best time to ask is shortly after a clear win.

For a dentist, that might be after a smooth appointment. For a SaaS company, it might be after a user receives their first strong result. For an agency, it might be after a successful launch or reporting milestone.

Think of it this way: Earn the ask before you make the ask.

Creating a simple workflow

Your review workflow should answer these four questions:

- Who asks?
- When do they ask?
- Where do customers go?
- How do you follow up?

Answering these questions naturally maps to the steps in your workflow. A simple process looks like this:

1. Choose the trigger point.
2. Assign responsibility.
3. Send the request via email or text or in person or in an app.
4. Link directly to the correct review page.
5. Send one polite follow-up if needed.
6. Track requests and results.

REMEMBER

This workflow narrows the broader review-acquisition guidance from Chapter 16 into a single request cycle. Chapter 16 explains why reviews matter as a reputation signal; this list shows how to make one review request happen, from trigger to follow-up to tracking.

Writing better review requests

Make it your goal to gather reviews that mean something. Reviews should work for you by giving others a clear sense of what it's like to work with you to drive business back to your site. Here's the difference between weak and strong review requests:

- **Weak requests usually sound self-serving.** They focus on getting star ratings rather than on helping the customer share a true experience — for example, "Please leave us a five-star review."
- **Strong requests invite honesty and give a little direction without scripting the response.** For example, "Thanks again for trusting us. If you're open to it, we'd appreciate a review. Sharing a few details about your experience can help others make a good decision."

The wording in the strong request works because it feels natural and encourages useful detail.

Prompting for specifics without scripting

Never tell customers exactly what to write. But you can suggest the kinds of details that are helpful.

You can encourage them to mention:

- The problem they wanted solved
- What stood out about the experience
- The result they got
- Who they'd recommend you to

This strategy leads to richer, more believable reviews.

A "Great service" response is fine. "The team explained everything clearly, made the process easy, and finished faster than expected" is much more useful.

That kind of review helps future customers and creates stronger trust signals around your brand.

Building review requests into operations

A review workflow works only if it's part of how your business runs. If your review process depends on memory or good intentions, it will break. Build your workflow steps into your daily processes.

Add your review requests to your day-to-day operations, like tracking customers via customer relationship management (CRM) software, the onboarding process, support follow-up, the appointment completion sequence, or client milestone checklist.

You can also train your team on a few simple rules:

- Ask for a review after a positive outcome.
- Never pressure the customer.
- Send customers to the right platform, usually your primary review platform unless you are intentionally rotating a secondary platform.
- Thank them whether they leave a review or not.

WARNING

Avoid shortcuts like fake reviews, review gating, and platform rule violations. They may create a short-term lift, but they can damage trust fast.

Review gating means screening customers first and inviting only the happy ones to leave public reviews while routing unhappy customers somewhere private. That creates a misleading review profile and can violate platform rules.

Managing Reviews for Long-Term Trust

Attracting reviews is only half the job. Your responses matter, too.

A thoughtful response shows that your business is active, professional, and trustworthy. A bad response, or no response, can weaken the value of even a strong review profile.

Responding to positive reviews

When replying to positive reviews, keep it short, warm, and human. Thank the reviewer, and mention specific feedback, if possible.

For example, don't say:

> "Thank you for your five-star review."

Instead, say this:

> "Thanks so much, Jenna. We're glad the team made your first visit comfortable and easy. We truly appreciate you taking the time to share your experience."

The latter response feels more real, especially by mentioning the customer by name, and it reinforces the value the customer cited.

Handling negative reviews professionally

Negative reviews are never fun, but they're part of the game. The key is to stay calm and avoid turning one complaint into a public argument.

A strong, negative review response usually does these four things:

- Acknowledges the concern
- Remains professional
- Avoids debating details publicly
- Offers a next step

A response might say:

> "Thanks for sharing this feedback. We're sorry to hear your experience didn't meet expectations. We take concerns like these seriously and would like the chance to learn more. Please contact our office so that we can look into this directly."

This response signals responsibility without escalating the matter.

TIP

Write review responses for future readers, not just for the original reviewer.

Dealing with fake or misleading reviews

Sometimes, a review isn't legitimate. In that case, report it on the platform and respond professionally, if needed.

For example:

> "We take feedback seriously, but we can't identify this experience in our records. We'd be glad to investigate if you contact us directly."

Stay calm. Don't accuse. Don't overreact.

Improving review quality over time

Not all reviews carry the same value. A detailed review with context is more useful than a vague one-liner.

High-quality reviews usually mention some combination of the problem, the experience, and the outcome. They're more persuasive, more believable, and more helpful for visibility.

You improve review quality by:

- Asking at better times
- Encouraging specifics
- Delivering a better customer experience

That last one matters most. The best review strategy is ensuring that you're doing great work. Over time, these small improvements compound into reviews that are more consistent and more valuable.

Using reviews as feedback

Reviews aren't just trust signals. They're feedback you can learn from.

Look for patterns in what customers praise and what they complain about. If people repeatedly mention friendliness, clarity, speed, or expertise, those are strengths you should highlight in your messaging.

If they repeatedly mention poor communication, delays, or confusion, those are operational issues you should fix.

REMEMBER Reviews tell you how the market describes your business when you're not in the room.

Avoiding Common Review Mistakes

A few common mistakes can weaken your review strategy fast. Watch out for these problems:

- **Chasing quantity rather than relevance:** Ten strong reviews on the right platform can help more than 50 on the wrong one.
- **Letting reviews go stale:** Freshness matters because it shows that your business is still active.
- **Giving customers too many options for where to leave a review:** Too much choice creates friction and confusion.
- **Replying like a robot:** Template responses may save time, but they can make your business sound cold and generic.

Keep your system focused, human, and consistent.

IN THIS CHAPTER

» Targeting decision-making pages that influence buyers

» Using expertise and digital PR to earn better citations and mentions

» Creating assets that people want to cite and link to

» Avoiding tactics that weaken trust

Chapter 20
Earning Links, Mentions, and Citations

As search evolves, *links* (clickable references to your site) and *mentions* (unlinked references to your brand) still matter, but the goal has changed. Here you're moving beyond collecting *backlinks* (links from other websites pointing to your site; see Chapter 4) like trophies. You're trying to earn the kinds of third-party signals that strengthen your reputation, support traditional rankings, and increase the odds of being cited or recommended in AI-driven search.

In this chapter, links, citations, and mentions work together as evidence signals: links point back to your site, citations identify sources that support an answer, and mentions reinforce that your brand belongs in the category.

That means relevance matters more than volume. A few strong mentions and citations on the right sites can do far more than dozens of weak links from places nobody trusts.

In this chapter, I show you how to target the right external sites, lead with expertise rather than generic outreach, and create assets people *want* to reference.

Targeting Decision-Making Pages

One fast way to improve visibility is to get included on pages that already shape buying decisions. These pages are high-impact *off-site opportunities* — external pages where people compare options and decide which brands to trust.

These include:

- Best Of lists
- Top-tools roundups
- Alternatives pages
- Niche directories
- Local best-in-city pages
- Expertly curated resource pages

These pages are important because they influence both people and machines. Buyers use them to compare options. Search engines and AI systems use them as repeated third-party signals to prove that your brand belongs in a certain category. If your brand keeps appearing on credible decision-making pages, that helps reinforce your relevance.

Finding the right opportunities

Not all offsite opportunities are worth pursuing. The goal is to show up on the pages that influence decisions and define your category.

Your job is to find the pages where your brand needs to be mentioned.

Start with search queries like these:

- best [category]
- top [category]
- [category] alternatives
- best [category] for [audience]
- best [service] in [city]
- top [industry] companies

- [category] tools
- [category] roundup

TIP

If your business is local, include location modifiers, such as "best plumber in St. Louis," "family dentist in Dallas," or "HVAC company near Denver." If you're a SaaS company, include competitor and alternative terms like "Surfer SEO alternatives," "HubSpot AEO alternatives," or best "CRM for agencies." If you're a service business, look for evaluator-style pages and niche directories and include "best accounting firm for startups," "top fractional CMO agencies," or "business litigation attorney directory."

Prioritizing pages that matter

After you identify potential opportunities (see the preceding section), the next step is deciding which ones are worth pursuing. Focus on pages that are:

- Highly relevant to your category
- Clearly written for buyers
- Editorially credible
- Updated and maintained
- Aligned with your positioning

Skip pages that feel thin, off-topic, or built only to sell placements.

Here's a simple way to test whether a page is worth your efforts: If there were no SEO value, would you still want your brand featured there? If not, move on.

Making your brand easy to include

The easier you are to understand, the easier you are to include — and the more consistently you show up across the pages that define your category. The people creating the pages you're targeting, such as editors and writers, have no time to figure out what your company does or where it fits. Make it obvious.

To make it easy to include you, prepare these items:

- A one-sentence description of your company
- A short explanation of who you're for

- Key proof points
- Accurate pricing or pricing ranges, if relevant
- Visuals or screenshots, if relevant
- A clean page explaining your offer

Tracking your target pages

Tracking your target pages is where your efforts turn into actual visibility. By creating a tracking system, you can ensure that you know what you've targeted, what's in progress, and where your brand is starting to show up across the pages that matter to you.

Use a simple spreadsheet with these columns:

- Target page
- Site
- Contact
- Page type
- Why you belong
- Outreach angle
- Priority
- Status
- Live link or mention
- Notes

You don't need fancy software. You need consistency (see the section "Building a Simple Weekly System," later in this chapter, to see how to keep your tracking on track).

Using Expertise to Drive Digital PR

Weak outreach asks for a link. Strong outreach contributes something useful.

Outreach is the act of asking for visibility. Expertise and digital PR (public relations) are what make that visibility possible. *Expertise* is the knowledge or experience your business has that others don't. *Digital PR* is the process of turning that expertise into useful assets that others will want to include.

Content creators look for sources to strengthen their content. If you can provide that, you become easy to include. The best links, citations, and mentions often come from offering:

- » Expert commentary
- » Original data
- » A practical framework
- » A strong point of view
- » A real example
- » A clear explanation of a trend or mistake

The next three sections walk you through identifying your expertise, working on your pitch angles to get you included, and creating a PR kit so that your information is ready and reusable for content creators to cite.

Using what you already know

You don't need to be famous to lead with expertise. You just need real-life, first-hand experience that gives you credibility others might not have and makes you a more desirable source.

Expertise can come from these activities:

- » Serving clients
- » Running campaigns
- » Building a product
- » Seeing trends in your market
- » Solving the same problem repeatedly

Your job is to package that experience into content, commentary, or data a writer can quote or cite.

For example, rather than say, "Can you add us to your article?" say, "We've seen this pattern across 100 campaigns, and here are the three biggest takeaways."

TIP

You use this line in the actual outreach request, such as an email to an editor, a reply to a journalist request, a website contact form, or a LinkedIn message to a creator.

That's much more valuable.

Creating better pitch angles

In digital PR, you're not just pitching your business — you're packaging your expertise in a way that makes it easy for creators to use.

That's where pitch angles come in. A *pitch angle* is simply the way you frame your know-how so that it feels useful to someone creating content.

Strong pitch angles usually include one of these:

- A surprising insight
- A contrarian opinion
- A simple framework
- A timely reaction
- A repeated mistake
- A practical checklist
- A short case-based lesson

The pitch doesn't need to be long. It just needs to be useful.

Here's a basic structure for creating a strong pitch. State:

- Why the topic matters now
- What insight you can offer
- Why you're qualified
- What you can provide quickly

Keep it short, specific, and easy to quote. For example, a short pitch might look like this:

Hi [Name], I saw your recent roundup on [topic]. We have been seeing [specific trend] across [number or type of campaigns], and one takeaway may help your readers: [one-sentence insight]. If useful, I can send a short quote, the supporting data point, or a quick example you can include.

Building a simple PR kit

To make outreach easier, create a PR kit that content creators can turn to for information. A PR kit gives writers and editors the details they need to easily include you as a source, so no guesswork is involved, making it more likely that they'll want to include you.

Prepare a reusable PR kit with the following information:

- Founder or company bio
- Company boilerplate
- Headshot or logo
- Topic areas you can speak on
- Approved proof points or stats
- A few prewritten quotes

A reusable PR kit helps you respond faster and makes you easier to cite. The value is speed. The kit lets a writer pull accurate details, quotes, and proof points without chasing you for basic information. That makes you a lower-friction source.

Creating Link-Worthy Assets

A goal you want to strive for is creating assets designed to attract links from other websites. The best ones aren't gimmicks — they're genuinely useful, original, or interesting enough that people naturally want to reference them.

These are some examples of assets that can garner links:

- A study
- A statistics page
- A free tool

- A calculator
- A checklist
- A framework
- A local resource
- A benchmark report
- A practical template

Read on to find out which asset type is the right one to use for your type of business, how to create an asset that's easy to reference, and how to get that asset noticed by the people you want to see it.

Choosing the right asset type

The best asset to use depends on your business.

For local businesses, choose:

- Local guides
- Local statistics pages
- Neighborhood resources
- Seasonal homeowner checklists

For SaaS companies, pick these:

- Original studies
- Benchmark reports
- Calculators
- Free tools
- Templates

For agencies and consultants, select:

- Audit templates
- Frameworks

- Scorecards
- Implementation checklists

The point is to create content that helps people do their job better. A stronger way to think about it is this: Create assets that people can use as reference tools when they need evidence, examples, or a shortcut to a better decision.

Making the asset easy to cite

Even strong ideas get ignored if the presentation is weak. You want to ensure that your asset is straightforward and functional.

Make your asset easy to use by including:

- Clear title
- Main takeaway near the top
- Summary bullets
- Strong visuals or tables
- Quotable findings
- A short methodology if data is involved

Think about the writer, editor, or creator who may reference it. Help them find the value fast.

Promoting the asset

Publishing the asset on your own website or resource hub isn't enough. You need to distribute it intentionally to create visibility.

Promote it by these means:

- **Targeted outreach:** Email writers who have covered the same topic and point to one specific statistic, finding, or tool they can cite.
- **Industry communities:** Share the asset in relevant groups with a short takeaway and a question that invites discussion.
- **Newsletters:** Send the asset to newsletter editors who curate useful resources in your niche.

- **Social posts:** Pull one chart, quote, or insight from the asset and turn it into a post that links back to the full resource.
- **Guest appearances:** Mention the asset on podcasts, webinars, and interviews as supporting evidence for your point.
- **Existing relationships:** Send the asset to partners, customers, vendors, or industry contacts who may find it useful enough to reference.

One asset can support multiple outreach angles if you package it correctly.

Avoiding the Wrong Kinds of Links, Mentions, and Citations

Not all links, mentions, and citations carry value. Some can create the appearance of visibility without building any real trust. Shortcuts are tempting, but risky. They may increase the occurrence of links, mentions, or citations, but they rarely improve how your brand is understood or trusted.

Avoid trying to manufacture links, mentions, or citations via tactics like these:

- Paid link schemes without disclosure
- Mass link exchanges
- Private blog networks
- Spammy guest posting
- Irrelevant directory submissions
- Low-quality AI filler built only for links or references

These tactics may increase numbers, but they rarely build the trust you truly want.

Even though it's tempting to try to get your brand linked, mentioned, or cited in as many places as possible, it's important to know when to walk away. Skip an opportunity whenever:

- The site is off topic.
- The page feels low-quality.
- The audience doesn't fit.

- The placement creates brand confusion.
- The site obviously sells links or placements.
- You would be embarrassed to show it to a prospect.

If the link, mention, or citation weakens your credibility, it isn't worth it.

Building a Simple Weekly System

Your goal is to steadily build visibility by consistently creating, promoting, and tracking assets that earn links and mentions over time. To make this happen, use this simple weekly process:

1. **Find five opportunities.** Look for two decision-making pages, two expert commentary or digital PR opportunities, and one asset-promotion opportunity.
2. **Choose one angle for each one.** Decide why you belong on that page or what useful expertise, data, or asset you can offer.
3. **Send focused outreach.** Keep the message short, personal, and tied to the specific page, article, or creator you're contacting.
4. **Follow up once or twice.** Send one polite reminder three to five business days later, and one final follow-up about a week after that if the opportunity is valuable.
5. **Track results.** Record who you contacted, what you pitched, when you followed up, and whether you earned a link, citation, mention, or reply.
6. **Double down on what works.** Repeat the page types, pitch angles, and assets that generate real responses instead of starting from scratch every week.

This process keeps your effort steady without turning it into a full-time project.

After a few weeks, patterns start to appear. You'll see which pages accept updates, which pitches get replies, and which assets earn real citations or mentions. Use those patterns to make the next round easier, more focused, and more likely to create trustworthy visibility.

IN THIS CHAPTER

» **Avoiding privacy, consent, and defamation mistakes**

» **Treating YMYL topics, accessibility, and bias with extra care**

» **Sending clearer signals to crawlers and AI systems**

» **Protecting your content through better rights and licensing habits**

Chapter 21
Playing It Safe: Governance, Risk, and Compliance

The more visible your content becomes, the more careful you need to be about what you publish.

That's especially true in AI SEO. A sloppy claim on a comparison page can get repeated in an AI summary. A customer quote used without permission can show up in more places than you expected. A health- or finance-related page with weak sourcing can create trust problems fast. And if your crawler rules, rights, and content policies are a mess, you'll confuse both humans and machines.

The good news is that you don't need an overstaffed legal team or a 20-page policy manual to protect yourself. You just need a few practical guardrails.

In this chapter, I show you how to publish with more confidence by reducing avoidable risk. Then I show you how to handle privacy, consent, YMYL content (Your Money or Your Life advice, such as health or financial information), accessibility, bias, crawler guidance, provenance, and content rights without turning your workflow into a bureaucratic nightmare.

Avoiding Privacy, Consent, and Defamation Mistakes

In AI SEO, the result of bad decision-making can spread further than the original page.

A risky testimonial, an unverified accusation, or a screenshot with private data no longer simply lives on your website: It can be indexed, summarized, cited, quoted, and reused by platforms you don't control. That means content teams need better judgment before they press Publish.

In the following six sections, I guide you through how to keep private information private and use permissions accurately as well as watch out for derogatory information and note the difference between fact, opinion, and allegation. I also include a review process to keep items in check.

Keeping private information off public pages

Just because you have access to information doesn't mean it belongs in your content. Good content should be useful and trustworthy without exposing personal, confidential, or unnecessary information.

Be careful with the following information, and double-check to see whether it's necessary to include:

- Personal phone numbers or email addresses
- Customer account details
- Medical or financial information
- Internal documents
- Screenshots that expose sensitive data
- Any detail that might identify or embarrass someone unfairly

Private information can accidentally appear in many types of content, such as testimonials, videos, and blog posts. In particular, case studies are a common problem area. Teams often believe that adding detail automatically makes the story stronger. It doesn't. Usually, readers need only a few essentials, like these:

- Which kind of client
- What problem they had
- What you changed
- What result happened
- What lesson the reader should take away

The reader usually doesn't need full names, account screenshots, or sensitive numbers, unless you were clearly authorized to share them, to gain the benefit of the case study's purpose.

WARNING

If a detail can expose someone, embarrass someone, or create legal trouble, leave it out — unless you have verifiable permission (see the next section).

Acquiring permission for personal and company content

Even when you're careful about keeping private information off your pages, sometimes you want to include identifiable people or company proof (such as logos, branded images, or an About Us page) to strengthen your content. In those cases, the key difference is simple: You need permission before you publish anything that identifies someone or represents their involvement.

If your content includes identifiable people or company proof, don't wing it. Be sure to get approval before using any of these:

- Testimonials
- Logos
- Headshots
- Photos or videos
- Screenshots
- Quotes from calls, emails, or messages
- Case study details that identify the client

TIP

Written permission is best. It doesn't need to be fancy. An approval email is much better than just saying, "I'm pretty sure they said yes."

Before you publish, make sure you know:

- Exactly what they approved
- Where you can use it
- Whether you can edit it
- Whether you can use it in ads, social posts, or sales pages
- Whether there's an end date on the permission

Securing permissions matters even more in AI SEO because brand mentions and proof points can travel well beyond the original page.

Avoiding defamatory opinions

You can publish strong opinions without publishing reckless claims.

That line matters significantly on:

- Competitor comparison pages
- Alternative pages
- Review pages
- Articles that allege misconduct or criticize a company, product, or person
- Posts about scams, fraud, or wrongdoing

WARNING

Be especially careful when your content moves from describing facts to implying misconduct.

For example, this statement is appropriate to describe a hard-to-use platform:

> "Some users may find this platform hard to use because the reporting workflow takes too many steps."

This statement takes the point and makes it defamatory:

> "This platform is deceptive and designed to trap users."

One describes an experience; the other makes a damaging accusation.

Separating fact, opinion, and allegation

When creating content, especially content tied to people or companies, clearly separate what's verifiable from what's interpretive. If you don't, you make your content less trustworthy to both readers and AI systems. Clarifying the difference between fact, opinion, and allegations is one of the easiest ways to reduce risk.

TIP

Use this filter when deciding how to present your content:

- **Fact:** Something you can verify
- **Opinion:** Your interpretation or judgment
- **Allegation:** A claim someone made that may or may not be true

Don't blur them.

For example:

- **Fact:** The company changed its pricing page in January.
- **Opinion:** The new pricing page is harder to understand.
- **Allegation:** Some users have claimed the billing flow was confusing.

When those categories get mixed together, your content gets riskier fast. Clearly labeling facts, opinions, and allegations helps AI systems interpret your content more accurately and reduces the chance of misinformation appearing in AI-generated answers.

Creating a simple review trigger

You don't need a formal committee to keep your content clean and verifiable. You do need a review step for risky content.

A *trigger* is a simple rule that tells your workflow, "This page needs an extra review before it goes live." To set one, add the categories in the following list to your content checklist, brief template, or project-management task.

Set a trigger for any page that includes this type of information:

- Health, legal, or financial advice
- Claims about competitors
- Identifiable customer details

- Sensitive screenshots
- Regulated topics
- Bold guarantees
- Accusations or misconduct language

When a page hits one of those triggers, run this quick check:

1. **Verify names, dates, screenshots, and factual claims.**
2. **Confirm written permission where needed.**
3. **Remove loaded wording and unsupported accusations.**
4. **Save source material and approvals.**
5. **Get a second reviewer if the stakes are high.**

Your next move

TIP

To keep your content legal and accurate, audit your top pages for risk, especially:

- Comparison pages
- Review pages
- Case studies
- Testimonial-heavy pages
- YMYL pages
- Downloadable PDFs with extractable, accessible text, ideally supported by an HTML landing page or summary, that may be cited by AI systems

If anything feels slightly questionable, correct it now instead of cleaning up a bigger mess later.

Raising Standards for YMYL, Accessibility, and Bias

Some content deserves a higher editorial standard because the stakes are higher.

If your content affects a person's health, money, safety, legal decisions, or broader trust in your brand, "good enough" isn't good enough.

That's where YMYL, accessibility, and bias review come in, as explained next.

Introducing YMYL

Putting YMYL — Your Money or Your Life — at the forefront of your thinking means you understand that some types of content carry more responsibility than others. You recognize that people may use that information to make important real-world decisions.

YMYL covers topics where weak information can do true harm, such as in these areas:

- Medical advice
- Legal guidance
- Financial decisions
- Safety information
- Mental health topics
- Major life planning

A casual blog post and a high-stakes guidance page should not be held to the same standard. If a page might influence an important decision, it needs stronger sourcing, more careful wording, and better review.

Raising the evidence bar

For YMYL content, don't settle for "This sounds about right."

You want content that is:

- Based on trustworthy sources
- Current
- Clear about limitations
- Reviewed by someone qualified when needed
- Updated when facts change

In practice, you should link to credible sources and date-sensitive information and remove weak claims that can't be supported.

If a statement feels shaky, cut it or qualify it.

REMEMBER

The higher the stakes, the less room you have for vague sourcing and marketing hype.

Removing false certainty

Certainty sells. It also creates problems.

Be cautious with words like these:

- Always
- Never
- Guaranteed
- Risk-free
- Proven
- Cure
- Prevent

These words often overstate what the content can honestly support.

Instead, use wording like this:

- May help
- Can reduce
- Often improves
- In many cases
- Depending on the situation

This kind of phrasing sounds more precise because it is more precise.

Using accessibility to make content easier to use

Accessibility means designing content so that people with different abilities, devices, and ways of consuming information can still digest and use it effectively. It also improves how easily search engines and AI systems can interpret your content. Accessibility isn't just about compliance — it's about clarity, usability, and discoverability.

Provide the following items for more accessible content:

- » Add alt text to meaningful images.
- » Use captions for videos.
- » Provide transcripts for audio and video.
- » Structure headings in logical order.
- » Use descriptive link text.
- » Break up giant text walls.
- » Explain charts and diagrams in surrounding copy.

REMEMBER

If someone can't see the image, hear the audio, or skim the page easily, your content is weaker. Period. Accessibility helps AI systems comprehend your content more clearly, especially when transcripts, image descriptions, and structure are in place.

Reviewing content for bias

In AI SEO, *bias* refers to unbalanced or misleading framing that favors certain viewpoints, assumptions, or groups of people while overlooking others. Bias isn't always intentional. It often shows up in subtle ways by way of wording, examples, omissions, or patterns in how information is presented.

Bias can appear as:

- » Lazy assumptions about the reader
- » One-sided examples
- » Stereotypes in examples or language
- » Broad generalizations
- » AI-generated phrasing that sounds polished but unfair

Avoiding bias matters because AI systems can amplify flawed framing just as easily as they amplify good content.

Before publishing content, ask yourself these questions:

- » Who is missing from these examples?
- » What assumptions am I making?
- » Does this language sound fair and respectful?
- » Would this advice still make sense for people in different situations?

Reviewing AI-assisted drafts with a human brain

Whenever you use AI to help create content, you also need a human review process that checks for accuracy, fairness, clarity, and context. AI can produce fast drafts, but it often smooths over nuance and sounds more confident than it should. It doesn't reliably understand real-world consequences or accessibility needs or whether advice is appropriate for different audiences and situations.

When reviewing AI-assisted content, watch for these problems:

- » Unsupported claims
- » Overconfident phrasing
- » Stereotypes
- » Weird generalizations
- » Missing caveats
- » Advice that sounds universal when it isn't

Don't just edit for grammar — edit for judgment.

Your next move

For any page that touches health, money, law, safety, or major decision-making, follow these steps:

1. **Review the sourcing.**
2. **Remove exaggerated claims.**

3. **Check accessibility basics.**
4. **Read for bias and fairness.**
5. **Add a second reviewer if the topic is high-stakes.**

Sending Clear Signals to Crawlers and AI Systems

You can't control every crawler, bot, or AI platform.

You can control whether your own signals make sense.

That means deciding which content you want discovered, which content you want limited, and which rules or clues you're sending through your site settings and public policies.

Providing provenance without overthinking it

Provenance simply means being able to show where something came from.

For content, that can include:

- Who created it
- Where it was published
- Whether it was edited
- Whether it can be traced back to an original source

This is especially important when provenance and authenticity are critical, such as with original research, media assets, brand statements, and public-facing evidence.

Most businesses have no need to obsess over provenance on every page. However, for important claims, research, media assets, and public-facing evidence, you should maintain documentation showing where information came from and how it was created or verified.

Using robots.txt the right way

The robots.txt file is a guidance document that helps tell compliant crawlers what they should and shouldn't access. The file can reduce wasted crawl and help keep low-value sections out of the way.

TIP

To create one, make a plain-text file named robots.txt and place it at the root of your domain, such as `example.com/robots.txt`. Most CMS platforms, SEO plugins, or developers can help you add and test it.

A simple starter file might look like this:

```
User-agent: *
Disallow: /internal-search/
Disallow: /staging/
Sitemap: https://www.example.com/sitemap.xml
```

For AI SEO, the goal is to keep crawlers focused on useful public pages while keeping low-value or internal areas out of the way. Don't block pages you want search engines or AI systems to discover, summarize, or cite.

The robots.txt file is useful for elements such as these:

- Internal search pages
- Messy parameter URLs
- Thin utility pages
- Staging environments
- Low-value crawl traps

But if content truly should not be public, don't rely on robots.txt to protect it.

Creating a crawler policy

Most companies have no need for a huge technical crawler policy. You just need one clear internal reference that your team can easily use.

Your crawler policy should answer these questions:

- Which bots are allowed, limited, or blocked?
- Which sections of the site should stay open?

- Which sections should be restricted or deprioritized?
- How do you handle staging sites?
- Who approves rule changes?
- How often do you review them?

This is where lots of drift happens. Marketing wants visibility. Development blocks access. A subdomain launches. PDFs go public. Nobody notices that the signals are now inconsistent. Establishing an easy-to-follow crawler policy helps solve that problem.

Matching your signals to your true intentions

Many websites say one thing and do another. In AI SEO, your *signals* are the instructions you give to search engines and AI systems. Your *intentions* are what you want to happen with your content: what should be found, ignored, or prioritized. Problems happen when signals and intentions don't match.

For example:

- You say a section should be discoverable, but it's blocked.
- You say a file is restricted, but it's still publicly accessible.
- You want AI systems to interpret your best material, but your important resources aren't linked or included in your site map.

To ensure that your signals match your intentions, run this quick audit:

1. **List your major content types.**
2. **Decide whether each one should be open, limited, or blocked.**
3. **Check your actual settings.**
4. **Look for contradictions.**
5. **Assign one owner to maintain the policy.**

Your next move

Look at places where inconsistencies tend to build up over time, especially when different teams or tools have managed them separately.

Audit these first:

- PDF files
- Support docs
- Gated assets
- Staging areas
- Comparison pages
- Research pages
- Subdomains
- Utility folders

These are some of the easiest places for crawler-policy confusion to pile up.

Checking Your Content Rights

The AI era makes one age-old question more important than ever:

Do you have the right to use the content you're publishing?

That question applies to not only the final page but also all the ingredients that comprise it.

Knowing what you own

For the content you use, you need to know what rights you actually have over each asset you publish. Not all assets are equal. Different parts of your content may come with very different legal and usage permissions, and those differences affect how safely you can reuse, distribute, or rely on them across channels and platforms.

Your content stack may include these content types:

- Employee-created articles
- Freelancer-created content
- Stock photos

- Screenshots
- Embedded videos
- Customer reviews
- Data from third-party studies
- User-generated content
- Contractor-produced graphics or video

Some of these assets you may own outright. Some of them you may be licensed to use only in certain ways.

Don't assume "We paid for it" means "We fully own it."

For example, if you use outside creators, check the contracts.

Your agreement should make clear:

- Who owns the final deliverable
- Whether you can edit it
- Whether you can reuse it across channels
- Whether the creator used third-party material
- Whether AI tools were used in creating it
- Whether the creator is confirming that the work doesn't infringe on others' rights

If those points are fuzzy, fix the agreement before you need it.

Contracts are a starting point, but rights are often defined across multiple layers. You need to look at all of them to be confident you can reuse content safely.

Being careful with third-party content

When it comes to third-party content, such as screenshots, quotes, and borrowed material, it's easy for teams to copy, reuse, or embed material without fully thinking through where it came from or whether it's allowed to be used.

These are some common examples of third-party content:

- Competitor screenshots on comparison pages
- Charts pulled from reports

- Platform UI screenshots in tutorials
- Article excerpts in thought leadership
- Public reviews reused in sales materials

Sometimes, the use may be okay. Sometimes, it may not. The point is never to guess.

Before using third-party material, ask yourself these questions:

- Do we have permission?
- Is this use allowed by the license or platform terms?
- Are we using only what's necessary?
- Do we need attribution?
- Should someone else review this before it goes live?

WARNING

Don't build pages around third-party screenshots, charts, quotes, reviews, or images unless you have permission, a license, or a clear fair-use rationale. Otherwise, you may have to remove key assets later, which can weaken the page and create rights problems.

Setting internal rules for AI-assisted work

When teams start using AI tools for content generation and assistance, the biggest risk isn't the output — it's what gets put into the tool in the first place. Without clear rules, employees may accidentally expose sensitive data or publish content that hasn't been properly reviewed.

Create an internal policy that sets rules for using AI tools. In the policy, answer questions like these:

- Can employees paste private client information into a tool?
- Can they upload contracts or internal documents?
- Can they publish AI-generated content without review?
- Which tools are approved?
- Which facts must always be verified by a human?

A short internal policy can prevent lots of bad decisions.

Reviewing your site terms

Your *site terms* (often called *terms of use* or *terms and conditions*) are the legal rules that explain how people are allowed to use your website and its content. These terms set expectations between you and anyone who visits, downloads, shares, or interacts with your material.

Your site terms won't stop every misuse, but they can definitely help.

The terms can clarify these issues:

- Who owns your content
- How visitors may use it
- What commercial reuse is prohibited
- How trademarks and user submissions are handled
- What disclaimers apply

This review is especially useful if your site contains original research, templates, data, or media assets that others may want to reuse.

Keeping a simple permissions log

You don't need fancy software to keep your content rights documented. A spreadsheet works well to record what you have permission to use. This also gives you a quick place to reference when questions arise on what you have the right to use.

For assets that contain permission-necessary content, identify these elements:

- Asset name
- Source
- Creator
- Permission status
- Allowed uses
- Date approved
- Expiration date, if any
- Link to the agreement or approval

This simple habit makes it easier to decide later whether you can reuse, update, retire, or expand an asset.

Your next move

Review the assets used across your top marketing and SEO pages, especially these:

- Screenshots
- Customer proof
- Contractor-created visuals
- Licensed photos
- Third-party charts
- AI-assisted drafts created from private materials

If ownership or permission is unclear, treat that as a fix-it-now issue.

5
The Part of Tens

IN THIS PART . . .

Bust common AI SEO myths that can waste your time or misdirect your priorities.

Gain creative strategies to help verify your content, make you a trusted source, and allow you to be easy to cite.

IN THIS CHAPTER

» **Debunking dramatic claims about the future of search**

» **Keeping what still works from traditional SEO**

» **Avoiding bad decisions based on AI hype**

» **Adjusting your strategy for how different platforms really work**

Chapter 22
Ten Common AI SEO Myths

AI SEO gets plenty of attention, which means it also attracts plenty of bad advice. Some people are declaring the end of Google. Others insist nothing has changed at all. And plenty of marketers treat every AI platform like it works the same way.

None of that helps you make better decisions for ranking in traditional search, earning visibility in AI answers, and becoming a trusted source.

The truth is less dramatic and far more useful. Search is changing, but it hasn't disappeared. Traditional SEO still matters, but it's no longer the whole picture. AI SEO introduces new surfaces, new behaviors, and new ways for your brand to get discovered, cited, included, or ignored.

This chapter clears away ten myths that can waste your time, distort your priorities, or push you into extreme decisions. As with many marketing situations, the winning move usually isn't panic. It's perspective.

Google Is Dead

The myth: Google is on its way out, so you can stop worrying about traditional search.

The reality: Google is changing, but it's still one of the most widely used discovery engines on the web.

This myth usually appears right after someone tries an AI chatbot, receives a decent answer, and decides that search engines are finished. That's a fun headline, but it's a terrible strategy.

Google isn't dead. It's evolving.

People still use Google to search for products, services, comparisons, reviews, pricing, locations, tutorials, and answers, especially when Google shows AI Overviews or AI Mode results alongside the traditional results. Even when AI answers appear in Google, they're still connected to search behavior. Users still type queries. Pages can still be surfaced. Brands can still earn visibility. And many AI-driven experiences still depend on web content, structured information, and authority signals that look much like traditional SEO inputs. For more about how AI answers sit on top of traditional search behavior, see Chapter 2.

If you treat Google like old news, you may stop investing in the content, authority, and technical foundations that help your brand appear across both classic and AI-driven search surfaces.

TIP

Think in terms of expansion, not replacement: Keep investing in high-intent search content and watch where AI changes the click path. Also, treat Google as part of your AI SEO ecosystem.

REMEMBER

AI SEO adds new doors to discovery; it doesn't eliminate the old ones.

Traditional SEO Is Dead

The myth: AI SEO has replaced traditional SEO, so the old fundamentals no longer matter.

The reality: Traditional SEO still matters. What's dying is lazy, outdated SEO.

If your idea of SEO is stuffing keywords, spinning articles, and buying junk links, that version deserves to fade away. But real SEO foundations still matter.

AI systems still need something to retrieve, interpret, summarize, and trust. That "something" often starts with the same strong foundation SEO has always required, including these structural pillars:

- Clear site architecture
- Crawlable pages
- Indexable content
- Useful internal links
- Strong titles and headings
- Helpful content
- Relevant authority signals
- Fast, accessible pages
- Consistent brand information

AI didn't make these fundamentals irrelevant. It made them more important because machines need clean signals to understand what your business does, who it helps, and why it deserves to be included.

For more on technical and LLM-readiness details, see Chapters 10 and 11.

AI SEO Is Just SEO

The myth: AI SEO is nothing new. Just keep doing regular SEO and you're covered.

The reality: AI SEO overlaps with traditional SEO, but it also adds new visibility work.

This myth makes sense because it contains a sliver of truth. Yes, AI SEO depends on many traditional SEO fundamentals. But saying it's "just SEO" causes people to miss the visibility work AI SEO requires.

Traditional SEO often focuses on helping your own pages rank and earn clicks. AI SEO builds on traditional SEO and helps your brand get mentioned, cited, included, compared, or excluded inside generated answers.

For more about Share of Voice, entities, and AI visibility language, see Chapter 4. For off-site authority signals, see Chapter 16.

Blocking AI Crawlers Is a Good Idea

The myth: Blocking AI crawlers, meaning preventing AI companies' automated bots from accessing or copying content from your website, protects your content and is always the smart move.

The reality: Blocking may protect certain business interests, but it can also reduce discoverability.

Some site owners hear that AI systems crawl content and immediately want to slam every digital door shut. That reaction is understandable, especially if you publish valuable content. But it's not always strategic.

Sometimes, blocking certain crawlers makes sense. A publisher may want licensing leverage. A paid research company may want to protect proprietary content. A business may have legal, privacy, or competitive reasons to restrict certain bots.

But broad blocking isn't automatically smart. If you block AI crawlers without understanding the tradeoff, you may reduce the chances of your content being discovered, cited, summarized, or used as a source. In some cases, you're protecting your content. In other cases, you're making yourself invisible.

For example, a public product guide, service page, FAQ page, or educational article may benefit from being discoverable. A paid database, gated research report, members-only lesson, or private documentation area may deserve more restriction.

For more on crawl controls and technical access checks, see Chapter 10.

You Can Rank in ChatGPT

The myth: You can rank in ChatGPT the same way you rank in Google.

The reality: ChatGPT Search may rank sources behind the scenes, but AI visibility is more about source selection, inclusion, context, and citation than a fixed page position.

ChatGPT isn't a standard search engine results page with ten blue links (the traditional list of webpage results) and stable positions, so you don't really "rank" in ChatGPT the way you rank in classic Google search.

Can your brand appear in ChatGPT responses? Yes. Can it be cited, mentioned, included, compared, or ignored? Absolutely. But that's not the same as ranking number three for a keyword.

AI systems assemble answers dynamically. The output can vary based on prompt wording, source availability, retrieval settings, geography, personalization, memory, product updates, and the way the platform decides to generate an answer.

That makes the idea of a single fixed rank much less useful.

A better question is this: How often does your brand appear, in what context, and for which prompts?

For more on prompt tracking and AI visibility measurement, see Chapters 5 and 6.

Long Content Is Good for AI

The myth: AI systems prefer long content, so longer pages are always better.

The reality: Clear, complete, well-structured content beats bloated content.

You've probably seen one in the wild: a 4,000-word article that says what a 900-word article could've said better. That's not depth. That's padding.

Long content isn't automatically better for AI systems. Useful content is better.

Some long pages perform well because they cover a topic thoroughly, clearly, and in a well-organized way. But many long pages are padded, repetitive, vague, and exhausting. That kind of content can make it harder, not easier, for systems and humans to find the best information.

AI systems often benefit from content that is:

- Well organized
- Easy to scan
- Broken into clear sections

- Rich in facts and examples
- Concise where possible
- Deep where necessary
- Written with descriptive headings
- Supported by evidence or experience

Length should be the result, not the goal, of covering the topic well.

For more on improving page structure and underperforming content, see Chapters 14 and 15.

AI Content Gets Penalized

The myth: If you use AI to create content, search engines and AI systems will automatically penalize it.

The reality: Low-quality content is the problem, not AI assistance by itself.

This myth causes two opposite mistakes: One group avoids AI tools completely out of fear; the other group uses AI recklessly and assumes that no one will notice.

Both groups miss the real issue.

AI-assisted content can be useful when it's planned, reviewed, edited, and improved by a responsible human. It can also be risky when it's published with no fact-checking, no experience, no originality, and no editorial judgment.

The issue isn't whether AI helped create the draft. The issue is whether anyone took responsibility for the final content.

For more on planning accurate, useful pages and maintaining decision-stage content, see Chapters 9 and 12.

Here's an example of poor AI use and an improved version:

- **Poor AI use:** You ask AI to write "a 2,000-word article about the best CRM software," paste the output into your CMS, and publish it without testing products, checking facts, reviewing pricing, or adding anything from real-life experience.

- **Improved AI use:** You use AI to create a draft and then add product testing notes, screenshots, pricing checks, expert commentary, examples, and editorial review before publishing.

Your Website Is the Only Asset That Matters

The myth: Your website is all that matters for AI SEO.

The reality: Your website is your home base, but AI systems also retrieve, reference, and corroborate information from the broader web.

Your website is important, very important. It's usually the most important source of truth you control. It's where you control your message, explain your offer, publish your best resources, and convert visitors.

But in AI SEO, treating your website as the only thing that matters can limit your visibility.

AI systems often pull confidence from a broader web of signals. That includes third-party mentions, review platforms, industry directories, local citations, social profiles, podcasts, press coverage, community conversations, and knowledge-graph-style references.

You may have the best service page on earth, but if no one else on the web seems to know you exist, trust can be harder to build. On the other hand, a strong offsite footprint can reinforce your legitimacy everywhere.

For a deeper walkthrough of auditing and fixing third-party profiles, see Chapter 17.

Backlinks Don't Matter

The myth: Backlinks no longer matter because AI SEO is about answers, not blue links.

The reality: Links still matter, but authority now includes more than links.

You may notice that AI answers don't always show traditional blue links (the webpage results you can click in traditional search) front and center. That doesn't mean links stopped mattering. It means the way authority shows up is changing.

A good backlink isn't merely a ranking trick. It can be a trust signal, a discovery path, a brand mention, a citation source, and a clue that credible sites consider your content worth referencing.

To avoid confusion, separate these three ideas:

- **Backlink:** A clickable link from another website to yours.
- **Mention:** A reference to your brand, product, person, or website, with or without a link.
- **Citation:** A source used or shown by an AI system to support an answer.

AI SEO may involve all three.

A respected industry article that links to your guide can help traditional rankings, brand trust, and AI discoverability. A review site that mentions your product may influence which brands get surfaced even if the link isn't perfect. A cited source in an AI answer may drive visibility even if the user doesn't click.

For more on links, mentions, reviews, and authority signals, see Chapter 16.

One Universal AI SEO Strategy Works on All Platforms

The myth: One AI SEO playbook works the same way everywhere.

The reality: You need a shared foundation and platform-specific adjustments.

Different platforms behave differently. They pull from different sources, show different interfaces, handle citations differently, and serve different user expectations.

A strategy that improves visibility in Google's AI experiences may not work the same way in ChatGPT, Perplexity, Gemini, Claude, or future AI search tools. Some platforms lean more heavily on web retrieval. Others emphasize different source sets, citations, personalization, conversation history, or product integrations.

That doesn't mean you need ten disconnected strategies. It means you need one strong foundation and several smart adaptations.

The shared foundation includes these factors:

- Strong technical SEO
- Clear topical coverage
- Better factual structure
- Offsite credibility
- Consistent entity signals
- Useful, trustworthy content
- Strong reviews and proof points
- Authority from relevant sources

The platform-specific layer comes from observing how each system behaves.

For more on tracking, competitive analysis, and experiments across platforms, see Chapters 5 through 8.

TIP

Build one core visibility strategy and many surface-level adaptations. That's far more efficient than creating ten disconnected strategies.

IN THIS CHAPTER

» Creating assets AI systems can interpret, summarize, and cite

» Publishing facts, datasets, and FAQs that strengthen visibility

» Automating updates and workflows without losing trust

» Tapping experts, trust signals, and public evidence to stand out

Chapter 23

Ten Creative AI SEO Techniques

AI SEO isn't just about fixing technical issues, adding schema markup, and hoping the rest takes care of itself.

Those basics matter. A lot. But once your site is crawlable, indexable, retrievable, and trustworthy (see Part 2 of this book), you need something to bump up your AI SEO game a bit: You need assets that AI systems can interpret, summarize, reuse, verify, and cite.

That's where creative AI SEO comes in.

In this chapter, I show you ten techniques that help your brand become easier to find, easier to quote, easier to verify, and easier to trust. These aren't tricks. They're not sneaky hacks. They're practical ways to make your best information more useful to humans and more usable by AI systems.

Think of it this way: If an AI system has to choose between a vague page, an outdated page, and a page full of clear facts, examples, data, FAQs, and expert insight, which one do you want to be?

Exactly.

Creating Citation-Worthy Assets

Citation-worthy assets aren't about tricking AI systems.

It means creating useful content elements that are easy for AI systems to retrieve, understand, summarize, and quote. You're not hiding text, stuffing keywords, or building content only for machines. You're making your best information easier to find and reuse.

REMEMBER

Think of citation-worthy content as content with handles on it.

If your strongest answer is buried in a digital lasagna of vague paragraphs, don't expect AI systems, search engines, or actual humans to dig through the noise to find the answer to their query. But if you pull that answer out, label it clearly, and support it with specific details, you make the page more useful.

Good citation-worthy assets include:

- Short definitions
- Concise answer blocks
- Bulleted takeaways
- Comparison tables
- Labeled statistics
- Quote-worthy statements
- Step-by-step instructions
- Mini glossaries
- Pros and cons lists
- "Best for" fit statements

A few simple improvements can make an existing page much more usable:

- Add a couple of summary sentences near the top.
- Break long paragraphs into labeled sections.
- Pull important numbers into stat callouts.
- Use descriptive subheads that match real questions.
- Add comparison tables for tools, services, options, or categories.
- Include a short "Who this is for" section on commercial pages.
- Add a Key Takeaways block near the top or bottom.

REMEMBER

Citation-worthy content should help people first. If the content helps a real person understand, compare, or decide, it's probably useful citation-worthy content. If it only exists because you think a machine might like it, rethink it.

Building a Fact Hub

Many businesses unintentionally scatter their basic facts across the web. A fact hub gives those facts a permanent home.

A *fact hub* is a public source-of-truth page that explains who you are, what you do, who you serve, and what people should know about your brand (see Chapter 4). It's especially useful when your brand is mentioned across many places online, including directories, review sites, podcasts, social profiles, press mentions, and old blog posts.

Your fact hub can include:

- Official company name
- Short company description
- Long company description
- Founding date
- Founder or leadership details
- Headquarters or service area
- Product or service categories

- Target audience
- Pricing basics
- Official brand spellings
- Common name variations
- Policies and standards
- Media assets
- Contact details
- Notable milestones

AI systems often assemble answers from multiple sources. If your website says one thing, your LinkedIn page says another, your old podcast bio lists outdated facts, and a directory uses the wrong category, you've created unnecessary confusion.

A fact hub gives people and AI systems one official place to confirm the basics. It also helps your team stay consistent when creating sales pages, bios, press materials, review profiles, and partner descriptions.

Utilizing Consensus Kits

Whereas a fact hub tells people what's true, a consensus kit helps the market repeat the same story about you.

A *consensus kit* contains proof assets (the evidence behind your claims, such as case studies) that support your desired positioning. It gives customers, reviewers, journalists, partners, influencers, and AI systems a consistent set of evidence to work from.

A consensus kit may include these items:

- A one-sentence positioning statement
- A longer company description
- A category definition
- Founder or expert quotes
- Customer results and testimonials
- Case studies

- Product screenshots
- Benchmark data
- Methodology notes
- Review highlights
- Media mentions
- Comparison points
- Approved statistics
- Common objections and answers

When AI systems see the same claim supported across multiple credible sources, they have more context for describing your brand accurately.

Refreshing Assets Faster

Fresh beats fancy more often than people want to admit.

Many brands don't struggle because they lack good content — they struggle because their best assets slowly go stale. Screenshots age. Pricing changes. Features improve. Competitors shift. Stats expire. Examples stop matching reality.

Yet the page still sits there, acting like everything is fine.

REMEMBER

Refreshing assets faster is a creative advantage because it lets you respond to the market before competitors do. It also sends a simple signal: This brand is active, aware, and paying attention. See Chapter 13 for details on keeping content fresh.

Start with the pages that affect trust, visibility, or revenue.

These usually include:

- Home page
- About page
- Pricing page
- Product pages
- Service pages
- Comparison pages

- Case studies
- Top-performing blog posts
- Help center articles
- Methodology pages
- Benchmark reports
- Review or reputation pages

Then look for these signs of staleness:

- Outdated screenshots
- Old dates
- Broken links
- Discontinued features
- Old pricing
- Outdated claims
- Missing recent product updates
- References to old competitors
- Stats with no year attached
- Examples that no longer fit the market

You're not just polishing words. You're keeping the asset alive.

Building Public Datasets

If you want people to cite you, give them something worth citing.

Public datasets are powerful because they create original evidence (see Chapter 15). And original evidence is hard to fake, harder to copy, and much more useful than another "ultimate guide" saying the same thing as everyone else.

A public dataset doesn't have to be enormous. It just has to be useful, clear, and trustworthy.

Here are some examples:

- Annual industry benchmarks
- Survey results
- Pricing studies
- Local market data
- Platform comparison data
- Trend reports
- Original experiments
- Anonymized customer insights
- Curated statistics pages
- Rankings based on transparent methodology

For example, an agency might publish a benchmark report showing average AI visibility across 50 local service businesses. A SaaS company might publish anonymized usage trends from its platform. A consultant might publish a study comparing how different AI platforms answer the same category of question.

Sprinkling FAQs Everywhere

One lonely FAQ page sitting in the corner of your website isn't a strategy. It's a storage closet.

FAQs work best when they appear where the question naturally comes up (see Chapter 15). That's why you should sprinkle them across your site.

These are some useful spots for FAQ placement:

- Product pages
- Service pages
- Pricing pages
- Comparison pages
- Location pages
- Category pages
- Onboarding pages

- Support articles
- Landing pages
- Case studies
- Demo pages

Write answers that are direct, clear, and specific. Don't use FAQs as a place to repeat your sales pitch with a question mark slapped on the end.

A good FAQ answer usually:

- Answers the question in the first sentence
- Adds context only if needed
- Uses plain language
- Avoids vague claims
- Links to deeper resources when helpful
- Stays short enough to scan

Maintaining a Public Change Log

A public change log is proof that your business is alive. The *change log* shows what changed, when it changed, and why it matters. For AI SEO, that matters because freshness and activity can support trust. For users, it shows that the product, service, or resource is still being cared for (see Chapter 6).

A change log is especially useful for:

- SaaS companies
- Apps
- Marketplaces
- Agencies with evolving services
- Educational platforms
- Content-heavy brands
- Research-driven websites

Each change log entry should include:

- » Date
- » Short title
- » What changed
- » Why it matters
- » Related link, when useful

Here's a simple format:

> **April 24, 2026: Added AI visibility tracking for Gemini.** We added Gemini tracking to our reporting dashboard so that users can compare visibility across Google, ChatGPT, Perplexity, and Gemini in one place.

That's enough. Keep it short, clear, and useful.

Using MCPs to Automate with Better Context

Model Context Protocol, or MCP, helps AI tools connect to approved sources, systems, and workflows. In plain English, the MCP is a way to help AI work from better context instead of guessing from whatever scraps it can find.

Think of MCP as a permissioned bridge between an AI tool and trusted information. You decide which sources the tool can reach, such as documentation, product data, or internal workflows, and the tool uses those sources instead of relying only on whatever someone pasted into a prompt.

For AI SEO, the big idea is simple:

> Your automations are only as good as the context you give them.

TECHNICAL STUFF

MCP provides a structured way for AI tools to connect with approved systems and context sources. That can include documentation, databases, content libraries, project management tools, product information, analytics sources, or other approved data repositories.

If you're running a tiny website with five pages and no automation, you probably don't need to worry about MCPs yet. Focus on the simpler techniques in this chapter first.

But if your business uses AI workflows often, MCP-style thinking becomes important.

Even if you never build a formal MCP setup, you can use the principle.

Create approved context sources such as these:

- Fact hub
- Help center
- Product documentation
- Public change log
- Internal SOPs
- Brand guidelines
- Structured datasets
- Customer success notes
- Approved company descriptions

Then instruct your AI tools and workflows to use those sources first.

For example, rather than ask an AI tool to "write a product description," you can ask it to write from your fact hub, product documentation, change log, and approved positioning statement.

Creating a Trust Network

A single page can't carry your reputation alone.

You need a *trust network*, which is the collection of pages, profiles, mentions, reviews, and references that support your credibility across the web. See Chapter 18 for more on building trust.

This network matters because AI systems don't evaluate your brand from only one page. They may encounter your website, review profiles, directory listings, author bios, news mentions, customer stories, social profiles, and third-party citations.

REMEMBER

If those sources tell a consistent story, your brand is easier to understand and trust. If they conflict, your brand looks messy.

Your trust network may include:

- About page
- Author bios
- Expert profiles
- Case studies
- Testimonials
- Review profiles
- Directory listings
- Local citations
- Press mentions
- Podcast appearances
- Partner pages
- Association memberships
- Certifications
- Awards
- Help center pages
- Public methodology pages
- Social profiles

You're not just building links. You're building corroboration.

Tapping into Subject Matter Expertise

In a world stuffed with generic AI content, expertise is one of your strongest advantages.

That's because people with hands-on experience understand the unusual scenarios, common mistakes, shortcuts, objections, exceptions, and "it depends" moments that generic AI-generated articles often leave out. Subject matter expertise can come from:

- Founders
- Consultants
- Technicians
- Product specialists
- Analysts
- Customer success teams
- Sales teams
- Experienced clients
- Industry partners
- Operators doing the work every day

Turn expert knowledge into reusable assets.

You can create:

- Expert quotes
- Expert Q&As
- Reviewer notes
- Annotated articles
- Methodology explanations
- Short videos
- Interview-based blog posts
- Opinion pieces
- Comparison commentary
- Troubleshooting guides
- Sections labeled "What most people get wrong"

Index

Numerics

4-factor triage model, score each issue with, 162–163
30 days with AI SEO, 35
30 days with AI SEO, Week 1: determining baseline and benchmarks, 36
  capture the day 0 baseline, 36
    AI search, 36–37
    documentation, 37
    traditional search, 36
  deliverables for Week 1, 38–39
  select a few practical benchmarks, 38
    AI visibility, 38
    operational progress, 38
    traditional visibility, 38
  verify and strengthen entity, 37–38
30 days with AI SEO, Week 2: setting up tracking, 39
  automate tracking routine, 41
  connect analytics for traditional search, 40–41
  deliverables for Week 2, 41
  evidence library creation, 39–40
    connect analytics for traditional search, 40–41
    tracking sheet, 40
30 days with AI SEO, Week 3: taking quick wins to ship, 41–42
  bottom-of-funnel asset, 43–44
  deliverables for Week 3, 44
  focus on facts that machines can verify, 42
  refresh passages that answer questions directly, 42–43
  strengthen offsite proof, 43
30 days with AI SEO, Week 4: building a 90-Day road map, 45
  90-day themes selection, 45–46
  compare starting point to now, 45
  deliverables for Week 4, 47
  map work to metrics, 46
  weekly schedule creation, 46–47

A

accessibility, 228, 229, 313, 314
AEO. *See* answer engine optimization (AEO)
AI answers, 13–14, 19, 22, 26, 28–30, 32, 33, 42, 43, 50, 55, 62, 69, 76, 78, 112, 115, 122, 124, 166, 194, 200
  AI-generated answers. *See* AI-generated answers
  citation in, 60
  citation position, 80–81
  citations influence, 78–79
  layers of, 57
  model level, 57
  optimize, 57
  platform level, 57
  pulling competitors from Google and, 215–216
  retrieval level, 57
  tracking, 78
  turning AI answers into competitor score, 102–103
AI-assisted drafts with a human brain, 314
AI channel
  captures, 87–88
  group in GA4, 86–87
  time to fill in, 88
AI chat, 72, 74, 82, 86, 122
AI chatbot, 2, 86–88, 93, 326
AI eligibility blockers as automatic escalators, 163–164
AI-friendly HTML creation, 172
  build-validation checklist (HTML), 175–176
  core build guidelines, 172–173
  good and bad HTML structure, 174–175
  pages load, 173–174
  retrieval-friendly passage pattern, 175
AI-generated answers, revealing, 26, 28
  cite, 28
  read, 27
  retrieve, 26–27
  synthesize, 27–28
AI-generated transcripts, exercising caution with, 226–227
AI market, 107
AI models identification, 24–26
AI picks certain sources, 106
  check entity clarity, 106–107
  compare reputation footprints, 107
  find AI-ready passages, 106
AI platform, 2, 9, 51–52, 86, 91, 93
  controls, 56–57
  identification, 24–26
  and set cadence, 113
  tracking market share across, 107–108
AI-readiness checkup, conducting, 151–152
AI-ready checklist
  producing a minimum, 166
  setting up the checklist, 166–168
  tagging the results, 168
AI-ready passages, 106
AI search
  building blocks of, 52–54
  dashboard, 85–97
  pages and passages, 58
    knowing why both levels matter, 59
    writing brand-friendly passages, 58–59
  using competitive intelligence for, 99
AI Search Check, 41
AI search experiments, 110
  design the test, 110–111
    choose AI platforms and set a cadence, 113
    control for drift, 114
    create a change log entry, 113
    freeze prompts (prompt hygiene), 112
    pick a single hypothesis, 111
    small experiment prompt set, 112
  drawing conclusions and taking action, 117
    keep outcome labels simple, 117
    turn wins into playbooks, 117–118
  reading results without getting fooled, 115
    compare test movement to control movement, 116
    evaluate using the core metrics stack, 115
    look for patterns, not single wins, 116
  run the test, 114–115
AI Search Tracking template, 92
AI SEO
  avoiding pitfalls, 18
    declaring traditional SEO dead, 19
    ignoring accuracy and consistency, 19

AI SEO *(continued)*
measuring only traffic, 19
publishing faster, 19
treating AI SEO like a magic trick, 19
benefits from, 11–12
fits with traditional SEO, 10–11
goal of, 15
AI SEO myths, 325
AI content gets penalized, 330–331
backlinks don't matter, 331–332
blocking AI Crawlers, 328
content as good for AI, 329–330
Google as dead, 325
as just SEO, 327–328
rank in ChatGPT, 328–329
traditional SEO as dead, 326–327
universal AI search strategy works, 332–333
website as asset, 331
AI SEO Pro, 49
getting up to speed on signals of credibility, 59–62
integrating structured data and schema, 62–66
LLMs and AI platforms, 55–57
sifting through AI visibility terms, 50–55
working with pages and passages, 58–59
AI SEO techniques, creative, 335–336
building fact hub, 337–338
building public datasets, 340–341
creating a trust network, 344–345
creating citation-worthy assets, 336–337
maintaining a public change log, 342–343
refreshing assets faster, 339–340
sprinkling FAQs everywhere, 341–342
tapping into subject matter expertise, 345–346
using MCPs to automate, 343–344
utilizing consensus kits, 338–339
AI signals, 238–239
avoiding outdated link habits, 250
brand accuracy and consistency, 239
core brand facts, 239–240
fixing outdated and conflicting information, 241–242
positioning, 240–241
links, mentions, and citations, 247–250
old-school prospecting, 248
prioritizing, 249–250
retrieval-driven prospecting, 248
review signals, 242
review acquisition system, 244–245
review effort, 243–244
shaping review content, 242–243
sentiment, 245–246
turning mentions into stronger signals, 246–247
AI SoV score, 78
AI system, 9
sending clear signals to crawlers and, 315
crawler policy creation, 316–317
provenance, 315
signals and intentions, 317
using robots.txt, 316
AI visibility terms, 50
entities, AI search, 52
clear entity home, 53
consistent naming and descriptions, 52–53
structured data and corroborating references, 53–54
entity clarity process, 55
roles of indexes and knowledge graphs, 54
share of voice, measures, 50–52
AI winners, 100–103
answer engine optimization (AEO), 50
architecture and internal links, working with smart, 176
build-validation checklist (architecture and links), 178–179
good and bad internal links, 177–178
hub-and-spoke pattern, 178
making internal links work, 177
setting up a good architecture, 176–177
assets
bottom-of-funnel (BoF), 43–44
simple weekly system, 303
audience ownership, 12
auditing profiles, 252
entity pages, 252
focusing on the details, 255
profile pages, 253
support entity, 253–254
running a practical profile audit, 254–255
simple scoring system, 256
spotting the usual problems, 255–256
automatic escalator, AI eligibility blockers as, 163–164

B

B2B companies (business-to-business companies), 12
backlinks, striving for, 60
benchmarking competitors, with share of voice (SoV), 100–102
bias, 313–314
blanketing answer surfaces and SERPs, 267
asset type, 268–269
avoiding content cannibalization while blanketing, 270
building a SERP blanket, 269–270
query types, 267–268
BOFU. *See* bottom of funnel (BOFU)
bottom of funnel (BOFU), 139
bottom-of-funnel (BoF) asset, 43–44
bottom-of-funnel (BOFU) pages creation, 183
answer set, 184
News and Roadmap page, 190–193
Policies and FAQs page, 185–190
Pricing page, 185, 186
quick wins, 193–194
comparison and review content creation, 194
handling competitor concerns, 196
make each page answer-ready, 195–196
satellite pages from fan-out queries, 195
start with a category listicle, 194–195
controlling the narrative, 184
depth with commercial clusters, 196
check the cluster before moving on, 198
make internal links do the work, 197
one cluster until it exhaust, 196–197
simple cluster architecture, 197–198
brand accuracy, 239
branded search, 82
with context, 82
brand facts, 239
brand visibility, 25

C

canonical hub, 204
captions creation, 224–225
category legitimacy answers, 83

change log, 66, 96–97
public, 342–343
ChatGPT
creating clusters using, 144–145
projects, 129
citation gap analysis, 103–104
collect recurring citation sources, 104
group sources by type, 104–105
turn gaps into a target list, 105–106
who's-featured-where matrix, 105
citation growth and traditional rankings, 78–81
citations, 100
avoiding the wrong kinds of, 302–303
influence, AI answers, 78–79
send referral traffic, 79
track, 79
citation coverage, 80
citation position, 80–81
citation-worthy assets creation, 336–337
ClaimReview schema, 65
client-side rendering (CSR), 173
vs SSR, 174
clustering, 144, 161
opportunity, 127, 142
clusters
building and judging, 145–146
creation using ChatGPT, 144–145
focusing on one critical cluster at a time, 146
launching a simple cluster roadmap, 148
producing a pillar asset, 146–148
commercial intent, 29, 73, 133, 180
common schema, 65, 231
communities, trust in, 275–277
competitor
compare reputation with, 107
score, turning AI answers, 102–103
competitor-branded prompts, 101
consensus kits, 338–339
content publishers and media brands, 12
content rights checking, 318
content types, 318–319
setting internal rules for AI-assisted work, 320
simple permissions log, 321–322
site terms, 321
third-party content, 319–320
content schema, 64
cost-per-click (CPC), 126, 141
coverage, metrics measurement, 75–76
CPC. *See* cost-per-click (CPC)
Crawl Findings Summary sheet, 160
crawling, 152
AI retrieval red flags, 160
create a crawl findings summary, 160
high-impact issues and how to interpret, 157–160
launch a whole-site crawl, 154–155
read crawl output, 155–157
set up crawl lenses, 153
start with the right crawl scope, 152–153
render mode choice, 154
scope and limits, 154
user-agent choice, 153–154
CSR. *See* client-side rendering (CSR)
customer awareness stages, 121
Most Aware stage, 125
Problem Aware stage, 123
Product Aware stage, 124
Solution Aware stage, 123–124
Unaware stage, 122

D

dataset, publishing a clear, 232–233
decision-support tool, 97
digital PR, using expertise to drive, 296–297
expertise from activities, 297–298
pitch angle creation, 298–299
simple PR kit, 299

E

E-commerce stores, 12
entities, 100
entity optimization, 276
evidence discipline, 33
evidence library, 88
capture answers on a regular cadence, 89–90
create a simple folder and sheet, 88–89
use logs when you ship changes, 90

F

fact-based and educational content, 65
fact hub, 61, 181–182, 337–338
FAQs
bank, 234
block, 180–182
formula into play, 234
public datasets and reusable FAQs, 231–232
Policies and FAQs page, 185–190
sprinkling FAQs everywhere, 341–342
writing strong, 233
fix first
deciding what to, 161
AI eligibility blockers as automatic escalators, 163–164
group findings into issue clusters, 161
score each issue with the 4-factor triage model, 162–163
Top 10 Fixes page creation, 164
focusing on which issues to, 170
build ticket creation, 171–172
pick the top three issues, 170–171
pick the first sprint, 165
prioritized, 164–165
tag every item to a fix-it bucket, 165

G

GA4. *See* Google Analytics 4 (GA4)
Gemini, 25
generative engine optimization (GEO), 50
GEO. *See* generative engine optimization (GEO)
goal of AI SEO, 15
Google Analytics (GA), 85
tracking AI traffic with, 86
AI channel captures, 87–88
AI channel time to fill in, 88
create an AI channel group in GA4, 86–87
log in to right Google Account, 86
Google Analytics 4 (GA4), 40
AI channel group in, 86–87
Google and AI answers, pulling competitors from, 215–216
Google rankings, 100
Google Search Console (GSC), 40, 73–74, 85, 132
Google winners, 100–103
GPT, 25
grounding process, 23
GSC. *See* Google Search Console (GSC)

H

hydration pitfall, 173

J

journey compression, 82

K

keyword research template creation, 126–127
knowledge panels, 12–13

L

large language model (LLM), 49, 53, 55, 57, 61, 63
  retrieval and LLMs work together, 56
levers
  avoiding false, 33
  offsite, 31
    mentions, citations, and links, 32
    profile hygiene, 32–33
    reviews and reputation, 31–32
    SERP domination, 31
levers, onsite, 29
  content, 29
    anti-AI content, 30
    brand and fact hubs, 29
    commercial pages, 29–30
  technical, 30
links, avoiding the wrong kinds of, 302–303
link-worthy assets creation, 299–300
  making the asset easy to cite, 301
  promoting the asset, 301–302
  right asset type selection, 300–301
LLM. *See* large language model (LLM)
local businesses, AI needs business type, 12
Looker Studio, 40, 85, 91
  add an AI platform field, 93
  connect evidence library and calculate the citation rate, 95
  connect GA4 on Page 1, 92
  connect the Search Console and create prompt buckets, 94–95
  copy the AI Search Tracking template, 92
  review AI landing pages on Page 2, 93
  run a simple weekly cadence, 96

M

markup testing, 66
MCP. *See* Model Context Protocol (MCP)
measurement stack, 39
mentions, avoiding the wrong kinds of, 302–303
middle of funnels (MOFU), 139
Model Context Protocol (MCP), 343–344
MOFU. *See* middle of funnels (MOFU)
Most Aware stage, 125

N

News and Roadmap page, 190–193
nonbranded commercial prompts, 101

O

offsite levers, 31
  mentions, citations, and links, 32
  profile hygiene, 32–33
  reviews and reputation, 31–32
  SERP domination, 31
on-page basics, 214
  improving scannability, 215
  making headings pull weight, 214–215
  placing the primary keyword in right spots, 214
onsite levers, 29
  content, 29
    anti-AI content, 30
    brand and fact hubs, 29
    commercial pages, 29–30
  technical, 30
OPAs. *See* other people's audiences (OPAs)
organic clickthrough rate (organic CTR), 141–142
organization schema, 63
other people's audiences (OPAs), 273
  choosing the right, 273–274
  supplying useful content, 274
  turning one appearance into many signals, 274–275
owned assets
  aligned, 272
  controlling the narrative with, 270
    repurposing without becoming repetitive, 271–272
    topic hub, 271

P

pages
  additional places pages break down, 217
    burying the answer too deep, 218
    failing after the click, 219
    lacking support from rest of the site, 218–219
    sending weak trust signals, 218
  comparing page to true competitors, 215
    pulling competitors from Google and AI answers, 215–216
    turning competitor coverage into a better outline, 217
  diagnosing pages before making changes, 212
    choosing pages worth fixing, 212
    clarifying the job of the page, 212–213
    evaluating intent and page type, 213
  executing the fixes, 260
    cleaning up duplicate pages, 261
    connecting profiles back to website, 262–263
    correcting review profile weaknesses, 261–262
    lightweight maintenance routine creation, 263–264
    practical workflow, 263
    rewriting weak descriptions, 260
    updating for consistency, 260–261
  fixing the page and measuring the fix, 219
    avoiding change overload, 221–222
    change sufficient time, 221
    logging the change, 220
    tracking the proper metrics, 220–221
    turning diagnosis into fixes, 219–220
    wrapping up the fix, 222
  on-page basics, 214
    improving scannability, 215
    making headings pull weight, 214–215
    placing the primary keyword in right spots, 214
  prioritizing, 256
    fixing high-impact pages, 256–257
    matching priorities to business type, 257–259
    quick priority framework, 259
People Also Ask (PAA) questions, 137–138
person schema, 63–64
pitch angle, 298–299
Policies and FAQs page, 185–190
position metrics measurement, 76–77
Pricing page, 185, 186
Problem Aware stage, 123
Product Aware stage, 124
product schema, 64–65
profile description, 260

prompt cluster, 70
prompt database, 101
prompt protocols, 70
AI search prompt database, 71–73
branded prompts, 71
developing helpful prompts for tracking, 70
nonbranded commercial prompts, 71
synthetic prompts creation, 74–75
using Google Search Console, 73–74
working with prompts and intent, 70
prompt seed, 72
public change log, 342–343
public datasets, 340–341
and reusable FAQs, 231–232
publishing a clear dataset, 232–233

Q

query fan-out, 26
quick-start plan creation, 15
baseline establishment, 15–16
best pages easier to retrieve, 17
build off-site consensus, 17–18
source-of-truth, 16
track, test, and adjust, 18
Quora, 134

R

RAG. *See* retrieval-augmented generation (RAG)
recency effect, factoring in, 83
Reddit, 134
render mode, 154
reputation footprints, 107
retrieval-augmented generation (RAG), 25
retrieval systems, 26
review gating, 289
review mistakes, 292
review platforms
auditing the current review footprint, 285
matching platforms to business type, 284–285
picking the right platforms, 283–284
platform choices, 284
priority list creation, 286
steady review system, 286
asking at the right time, 287
prompting for specifics without scripting, 288–289
random requests to a repeatable process, 286–287
review requests into operations, 289
simple workflow creation, 287–288
writing better review requests, 288
reviews for long-term trust, 289
dealing with fake or misleading reviews, 291
handling negative reviews professionally, 290
improving review quality over time, 291
responding to positive reviews, 290
using reviews as feedback, 291–292
review system, 286
asking at the right time, 287
prompting for specifics without scripting, 288–289
random requests to a repeatable process, 286–287
review requests into operations, 289
simple workflow creation, 287–288
writing better review requests, 288
risk avoidance, 305–306
acquiring permission for personal and company content, 307–308
avoiding defamatory opinions, 308
creating a simple review trigger, 309–310
private information off public pages, 306–307
separating fact, opinion, and allegation, 309

S

SaaS companies (Software as a Service companies), 12
sameAs system, 206–207
sanity check, 97
schema, 62, 179–180, 182
choosing the proper, 230
common, 65
content, 64
marking up media cleanly, 230–231
mistakes, avoid, 231
organization, 63
person, 63–64
product, 64–65
service, 65
sizing up media, 229
starting with page itself, 230
structured data and, 66
types, identification, 63
using claim and evidence schema patterns, 65–66
search engine optimization (SEO), 9
search engine results page (SERP)
blanketing answer surfaces and, 267
avoiding content cannibalization while blanketing, 270
building a SERP blanket, 269–270
covering the main query types, 267–268
creating more than one result type, 268–269
domination, 31
search process, simple version of
citations, links, or mentions, 14
platform, 14
reading and synthesis, 14
retrieval, 14
search works, evolution of, 12–13
AI answers as assembled, 13–14
goal of AI SEO, 15
moving beyond rankings, 13
recognizing website, 14
self-reported wins, spotting patterns via, 81
"SEO content optimization software", 71
"SEO content optimization tool", 71
SERP. *See* search engine results page (SERP)
server-side rendering (SSR), 173
vs CSR, 174
service schema, 65
share of voice (SoV), 99
by AI platform, 102
benchmarking competitors with, 100
extend existing prompt database, 101
by intent stage, 102
measurement, 49–52
metrics measurement, 77–78
pick a realistic competitor set, 100–101
by prompt cluster, 102
record competitor, 101–102
turn presence into, 102
signals of credibility, speed on, 59
earning consensus across the web, 61–62
fact hub, 61
garnering citations and mentions, 60
signal impact measurement, 62
striving for backlinks, 60
snippets, 12
soft signals, spotting patterns via, 81
Solution Aware stage, 123–124
SoV. *See* share of voice (SoV)

SSR. *See* server-side rendering (SSR)
structured data, 62
checks, 66
focused with checks and balances, 66
and schema, 66

T

targeting decision-making pages, 294
easy to include, 295–296
finding the right opportunities, 294–295
prioritizing pages, 295
tracking the target pages, 296
technical SEO, 30
topical authority, 199–200
aligning the entities, 203–204
home and linking everything, 204–205
sameAs, 206–207
authority needs an update log, 210
consolidation matters, 209
consolidation playbook, 209–210
consolidation triggers, 209
coverage, gap analysis and depth planning, 200
mapping the topic universe, 201
running a gap analysis and adding depth, 201–203
entity alignment checklist, 205
internal linking, 206
naming consistency, 205
same claim and same wording, 205
entity alignment sheet creation, 207
freshness as authority signal, 207–209
topic game plan, 121
customer awareness stages, 121
Most Aware stage, 125
Problem Aware stage, 123
Product Aware stage, 124
Solution Aware stage, 123–124
Unaware stage, 122
topic ownership
exploring the true meaning of, 266–267
measurement, 279
mistakes, 280
practical plan, 280–282
via consistent signals, 277
owning a topic, 277–278
repeating the right content, 278
topic plan creation, 125
client knowledge base, 128–129
keyword research template creation, 126–127
knowledge base development, 127–128
topics, 130
prioritizing topics based on current rankings, 142
setting up a simple scoring system, 143
topics, finding, 130
competitor keyword gaps, 133–134
examining visibility and opportunity signals, 132
keyword gap analysis, 133–134
keywords generation from scratch, 135–136
People Also Ask (PAA), 137–138
probing for prompts, 130
Churn: Reasons to cancel, 130–131
content from competitor comparisons, 131–132
onboarding friction, 131
output format prompt, 132
sales call questions, 130
query fan-out, 136–137
user-generated content (UGC), 134–135
topics, qualifying, 138–139
qualifying with primary filters, 139
competition, 140–141
intent, 140
keyword value, 141
organic CTR potential, 141–142
relevance to offer, 139
top of funnel (TOFU), 139
track citations, 79
citation coverage, 80
citation position, 80–81
tracking AI answers, 78
tracking market share across, AI platforms, 107–108
traditional rankings, citation growth and, 78–81
traditional search works
crawling: search engines find the pages, 22
indexing: search engines organize information, 22–23
ranking: choose the best results, 23
ranking: personalization and context reshape results, 24
reranking, 24
traditional SEO, 33, 69, 199, 204
AI SEO fits with, 10–11
AI systems determination, 11
answer visibility, 10
entity clarity, 10
off-site consensus, 10
responsible publishing, 11
retrieval readiness, 10
working with pages and passages, 58–59
transcripts, 225
exercising caution with AI-generated, 226–227
format, 226
unlocking video value with, 225–226
of uploaded video, 225
trust network creation, 344–345
turning AI answers into a competitor score, 102–103

U

Unaware stage, 122
user agent, 153

V

version control, 66
visual content, using words to explain, 224
captions creation, 224–225
exercising caution with AI-generated transcripts, 226–227
running a quick media check, 229
turning one video into multiple assets, 227–228
unlocking video value with transcripts, 225–226
writing alt text to add meaning, 228–229

W

website recognizing, 14

Y

Your Money Your Life (YMYL), 311
raising the evidence bar, 311–312
removing false certainty, 312

About the Author

Nathan Gotch is an SEO entrepreneur, an author, and the cofounder of Rankability, an AI SEO platform built to help agencies plan, optimize, track, and improve search visibility for their clients. He has spent more than 15 years working in SEO, digital marketing, training, and software, helping businesses turn search visibility into measurable growth.

Nathan is also the founder of Rankability Academy and has trained thousands of marketers, consultants, and agency owners through his content, coaching, and education programs. His work has been cited by major marketing publications and SEO software companies, and he is known for making complex SEO systems practical, repeatable, and easier to execute.

In *AI SEO For Dummies*, Nathan brings together traditional SEO, AI SEO, entity optimization, content systems, technical SEO, and measurement into a beginner-friendly framework for marketers, business owners, and SEO professionals who want to stay visible as search evolves.

Dedication

To Kimmie and our children. You are the reason the work matters, and you make every chapter of life better than the last.

Author's Acknowledgments

Writing a book like this one takes far more than subject matter knowledge. It takes patience, editing, support, encouragement, and the willingness of many people to help shape a messy idea into something useful for readers.

First, thank you to my wife, Kimmie, for supporting me throughout the long writing process and for giving me the space, encouragement, and honest perspective I needed to finish. Thank you to our children for reminding me that the best work should make complicated things feel simple, clear, and worth doing.

Thank you to the Wiley and For Dummies teams for helping turn this book into a stronger, clearer, more useful resource. I am especially grateful for the editorial guidance that kept the book focused on the reader and true to the *For Dummies* style.

Thank you to the Rankability team, our customers, and the many SEO professionals, agency owners, marketers, and business owners whose questions helped shape this book. Your real-world challenges made the ideas sharper and more practical.

Finally, thank you to every reader who picks up this book to make sense of a fast-changing search world. My hope is that it helps you feel less overwhelmed, more confident, and better prepared to earn visibility wherever your customers search next.

Publisher's Acknowledgments

Acquisitions Editor: Jennifer Yee

Project and Development Editor: Linda Brandon

Copy Editor: Becky Whitney

Technical Editor: Paul Chaney

Managing Editor: Prathyusha P V

Production Editor: Tamilmani Varadharaj

Cover Image: KT Stock photos/Shutterstock